Action Planning for Cities

Action Planning for Cities

A Guide to Community Practice

Nabeel Hamdi

*Centre for Development and Emergency Planning,
Oxford Brookes University, UK*

and

Reinhard Goethert

*Special Interest Group in Urban Settlements (SIGUS),
Massachusetts Institute of Technology, USA*

JOHN WILEY & SONS
Chichester • New York • Weinheim • Brisbane • Toronto • Singapore

Copyright © 1997 by Nabeel Hamdi and Reinhard Goethert

Published 1997 by John Wiley & Sons Ltd,
Baffins Lane, Chichester,
West Sussex PO19 1UD, England

National   01243 779777
International (+44) 1243 779777

e-mail (for orders and customer service enquiries): cs-books@wiley.co.uk.
Visit our Home Page on http://www.wiley.co.uk
or http://www.wiley.com

All Rights Reserved. No part of this publication may be reproduced, stored in a retrieval system, or transmitted, in any form or by any means, electronic, mechanical, photocopying, recording, scanning or otherwise, except under the terms of the Copyright, Designs and Patents Act 1988 or under the terms of a licence issued by the Copyright Licensing Agency, 90 Tottenham Court Road, London, UK W1P 9HE, without the permission in writing of the Publisher and the copyright owner.

Other Wiley Editorial Offices

John Wiley & Sons, Inc., 605 Third Avenue,
New York, NY 10158-0012, USA

VCH Verlagsgesellschaft mbH, Pappelallee 3,
D-69469 Weinheim, Germany

Jacaranda Wiley Ltd, 33 Park Road, Milton,
Queensland 4064, Australia

John Wiley & Sons (Canada) Ltd, 22 Worcester Road,
Rexdale, Ontario M9W 1L1, Canada

John Wiley & Sons (Asia) Pte Ltd, 2 Clementi Loop #02-01,
Jin Xing Distripark, Singapore 129809

Library of Congress Cataloging-in-Publication Data

Hamdi, Nabeel.
    Action planning for cities : a guide to community practice /
  Nabeel Hamdi and Reinhard Goethert.
      p.   cm.
    Includes bibliographical references and index.
    ISBN 0-471-96928-1 (cloth)
    1. Community development, Urban—Planning. I. Goethert,
  Reinhard, 1944– . II. Title.
  HN49.C6H36   1996
  307.1'216—dc20   96-25545
                                                          CIP

British Library Cataloguing in Publication Data

A catalogue record for this book is available from the British Library

ISBN 0-471-96928-1

Typeset in 10/12pt Palatino by Mayhew Typesetting, Rhayader, Powys
Printed and bound in Great Britain by Bookcraft (Bath) Ltd.
This book is printed on acid-free paper responsibly manufactured from sustainable forestation, for which at least two trees are planted for each one used for paper production.

To: Karl, Happy, Rachel, Nadia, Oliver

What Is Action Planning?
A Guide to Finding Out

DEVELOPMENT IDEOLOGY
Page 24

CORE CHARACTERISTICS
Page 29

WORKSHOP MODALITY

PROCESS
Page 43
- *Problems and Opportunities*
- *Goals and Priorities*
- *Options and Tradeoffs*
- *Resources and Constraints*
- *Project Teams and Tasks*
- *Implementation and Monitoring*

TECHNIQUES
Page 34
- *Observation*
- *Interview*
- *Measure*
- *Resource Survey*
- *Prioritise*
- *Brainstorm*
- *Diagram*
- *Mapping and Modelling*
- *Gaming and Role Playing*
- *Group Work*

COMMUNITY PROJECTS

MONITORING
Indicators of Achievement
Page 51

COMPETENCY AND SKILLS
Page 122
- *Wisdom*
- *Communication*
- *Judgement*
- *Negotiation*
- *Optimal Ignorance*
- *Trouble-shooting*
- *Reflective Practice*
- *Improvisation*
- *Surveying*
- *Intuition*
- *Mapping*
- *Advocacy*

CITY/NATIONAL PLANS

MONITORING
Reconnaissance and Analysis
Page 54

TOOLS
Page 81
- *Community Action Planning*
- *Planning for Real*
- *ZOPP*
- *UCAT*

APPLICATIONS : CASE FILES
Page 185
- *Site Planning for New Communities*
- *Building Capacity*
- *Urban Upgrading*

Contents

Preface ix

SECTION 1	THEORIES IN PRACTICE	1
Chapter 1	Challenging the Orthodoxy of Development Practice	3
Chapter 2	Action Planning in Theory	23

SECTION 2	TOOLS FOR PRACTICE	61
Chapter 3	Deciding on Tools: Community Projects and City Plans	63
Chapter 4	Tools in Operation	81

SECTION 3	TRAINING AND EDUCATION	119
Chapter 5	Designing a Programme	121
Chapter 6	Learning in Practice: Field-Based Project Development Workshops	145

CASE FILES 185

Site Planning for New Communities: Colombo, Sri Lanka 191

Building Capacity: Boston, USA 207

Urban Upgrading: Schweizer-Reneke, South Africa 223

Index 247

Preface

This book offers theories, methods and techniques for the practice and teaching of community-level action planning. It starts with an assumption now generally accepted: the complex nature of fast-changing cities and the problems faced by their low-income majority have not been well served by the planning elite, nor by their prescriptive blueprints of some imagined future developed at the top.

Orthodox planning, whatever its rhetoric, may be proficient at making plans (city beautiful plans, land use plans, strategic plans, development plans) and devising development or regulatory controls, but is much less proficient at delivering benefits on the ground. It suffers a crisis of confidence, reflected in the growing consensus of concern about its place and value in managing cities effectively, and about its means and its ends. Its "data hungry" methods of study and analysis, its desire to maximise information, co-ordination, integration, participation, rather than "optimise resources in relation to prevailing realities", its attempts at coherence, its desire to predict and control, its inflexibility to respond to change and uncertainty, its reliance on outsiders in the form of a planning elite, and its dependence on development aid, set it apart from the pluralistic, spontaneous, market-driven, entrepreneurial and serendipitous dynamics which shape cities in practice. The result is that few of the acclaimed benefits of planning reach the poor. And even when they do, it is at a cost in management, administration and other scarce resources which cannot be long sustained.

In this book we consider an alternative: a planning process serving to ensure a stake in planning and urban governance for communities and community-based organisations in the face of progressive globalisation. It is a process where the sacred routine of planning first and acting later is displaced in favour of acting and planning iteratively, adaptively and simultaneously. Plans and planning tools emerge in action without a preponderance of study and survey. Careful consideration is given to stakeholder interest and to processes which are problem driven, community based, participatory, small in scale, fast and incremental, with results which are tangible, immediate and sustainable. It is designed to exploit all the spontaneity and inventive surprises inherent in community-level urban development. This kind of practice, whose purpose is to inform policy from the grass-roots, whose goals emerge in action and whose implementation relies on strategic, progressive interventions from government and planners, we call *Community Action Planning*. It is a term which has featured in learned journals and books for many years, but is only now finding currency in the vocabulary of planning jargon. In this sense, we should be cautious in its usage. The term "action" lends itself to the same variable definitions accorded to sustainability, participation or community. It has become a convenient prefix to much development activity, adding immediacy and practicality to processes which we have otherwise come to mistrust as cumbersome, overtheoretical and time consuming. It would seem timely, therefore, to give definition to this powerful term, which this book attempts to do, and to compile some of the theory, experience and technique which has gained it currency in the annals of practice.

In so doing, we have organised this book into three sections plus case files from practice, moving cyclically from the general to the specific, from theories to practices, from paradigms to methods, from methods to applications.

The first section introduces a revised theoretical agenda for planning based on a critical review of the orthodoxy of development practice and of planning. It traces the origins of action planning and sets out a number of working assumptions based on a new realism for planners and an alternative paradigm for practice. It defines action planning, describes its characteristics, techniques and methods, and discusses its implications for new professional skills and responsibilities. Importantly, it takes on board the critique advanced by some, that action planning often leads to city plans which are fragmented and to projects which are difficult to co-ordinate at city level. It offers a means by which community-level action plans can be effectively linked to city-level strategic plans and, more, challenges conventional wisdom by demonstrating how action plans can inform policy development as much as vice versa.

Section 2 reviews examples of participatory planning in operation, bringing together the disparate methods and plethora of acronyms and techniques into "families" of approaches in currency. It offers a range of tools for practice and provides a comparative evaluation of their participatory methods for the various phases of planning and monitoring. Further, it offers a basis for deciding where and when they are most usefully employed.

In Section 3 – Training and Education – we link the practice of action planning with its integral agenda of learning. We advance a variety of pedagogic forms and learning settings designed to nurture wisdom and good judgement as much as to instruct in skills and know-how. We make clear distinctions between the objectives of training and education and then look to their synergy in building competencies and skills for development practitioners in general and action planners in particular. We offer structures with which to plan training programmes and decide appropriate settings and training modalities. We conclude with case examples of training programmes under the theme topic "Rebuilding Communities" conducted with students and practitioners, each with clear differences in focus, in Kingston (Jamaica), Delhi, Belfast, Lima and Lublin.

In the book's final part, we present a series of case files from practice and demonstrate how action planning can usefully serve three important components of development planning. The first example is targeted to planning for a *new settlement* in Colombo, Sri Lanka, adopting principles of sites and services for new housing. The second, in Boston, USA, aims to *build the capacity* of community development corporations (CDCs) to develop vacant sites made available to communities by the local authority. The third, illustrated through our action planning programme in the township of Schweizer-Reneke, South Africa, concentrates on the *improvement of an existing settlement* and looking to ways to improve housing, health facilities, employment, infrastructure and educational opportunities. In all cases, training was integral to project development. In all cases, the underlying structure and methods are consistent, but adapted to very different settings and objectives. In presenting these cases, we have avoided extensive narratives, preferring to focus on the tools and methods employed and their underlying principles. The formats and charts which we illustrate are taken from guidebooks and manuals developed in the field and with local planners and community leaders. Pages from those manuals have been annotated by us with principles, issues and hints, which we hope will be useful for readers when preparing their own responses. They can be adapted or copied, or may spark new formats and ideas. They are not intended to be prescriptive, although each project does have its own sequence of steps and stages. For those who do prefer to follow the generic sequence adopted in the case files, a project planner is available from the authors, and this can be hung on walls or copied and can usefully track the various phases of action planning workshops. In addition, for teachers, the charts and tables are arranged in sequence and can be combined separately as a guide to designing and conducting action planning courses.

In content, the book avoids conventional First World/Third World demarcations. Indeed, it draws on examples worldwide, from First, Second and Third World countries. In style we avoid adopting a manual format, to be prescriptively followed. We recognise that most practitioners will need to invent their own tools and techniques and to make their own manuals, given that all situations are different. We ourselves have never followed the same sequence twice. Instead, we offer a menu of principles, ideas, techniques, formats, procedures for practitioners and a sourcebook which may be useful for training and education. We make no pretence to in-depth analysis of planning theory nor of international aid policy. These things are already dealt with in depth in the numerous texts we cite, and others. Our emphasis is *practice* and teaching practice, at the community level, albeit underpinned with a good theoretical understanding of the issues. The case studies we select and the accounts we offer are self-consciously anecdotal, drawing on our own work in practice and in education, and based on reflection rather than on scholarly analysis. The conclusions we draw are based on our own experience and convictions rather than empirical study.

Colleagues who have read early chapters steered us from the inevitable tendency in practice-type books to be overly instructive or linear, particularly given that this is a book produced by "outsiders". We hope we have avoided the "tell them what to do and how to do it" trap. Our own experience and much of the material which illustrates this book has been derived locally working with communities, local practitioners, local government and students, helping induce ideas and responses to problems generated from "inside" not "outside". This, after all, is the premise of Community Action Planning. Our encounters with NGOs, practitioners, governments and academics confirm the value of international experience when formulating regionally and site-specific responses. That is what this book is about.

Finally, we would like to acknowledge the many who have helped through their participation in projects and field-based training programmes and in producing material and commentary which we have used to illustrate our text – our students, in-country workshop participants, our host universities, and the many sponsors of action planning workshops and field-based training. All are individually acknowledged throughout the book. In particular, we would like to thank Vivien Walker for her assistance in typing draft chapters and for her occasional cryptic commentary, and our editors for their patience, support, ideas and editorial help.

Note

Various chapters in this book include text adapted from the following sources:

Goethert, R. & Hamdi, N. 1988. *Making MicroPlans: A Community Based Process in Programming and Development*. London: Intermediate Technology Publications.

Hamdi, N. 1986. Training and education. Inventing a programme and getting it to work. *Habitat International* 10 (3): 131–140.

Hamdi, N. 1991/1995. *Housing Without Houses: Participation, Flexibility, Enablement*. New York: Van Nostrand Reinhold; London: Intermediate Technology Publications.

Hamdi, N. (ed.) 1996. *Educating for Real: The Training of Professionals for Development Practice*. London: Intermediate Technology Publications.

Hamdi, N. & Goethert, R. 1989. The support paradigm for housing and its impact on practice. *Habitat International* 13 (4): 19–28.

We wish to acknowledge Eric Mar who helped compile the picture essay of Chapter 6.

SECTION 1
Theories in Practice

CHAPTER 1
Challenging the Orthodoxy of Development Practice

Planning in developing countries, linked, as it usually is, to development aid, conventionally serves the needs of governments and the vested interests of powerful individuals, development experts and large commercial enterprises. The instruments of orthodox planning (master plans, structure plans, sectoral investment plans, spatial development strategies, development controls – governed as they are by orthodox development theory) take too long to develop, demand substantial resources to implement and are unrelated to the realities and pace of city life. They transfer little or no immediate benefit to the poor majority of urban populations. To the contrary, these systems, fuelled as they are by the transfer of aid in the form of money, technology and know-how, cause considerable environmental damage and social injury and, all in all, further the development of underdevelopment.

The counterclaims are equally plausible, depending on political viewpoint and on what one counts and how, and who is doing the counting. Planning and development aid, coupled typically with material assistance and technical co-operation, have delivered measurable gains to all levels of urban community. With planning comes today more employment opportunity, the legitimisation of illegal settlements, and improved access to land for housing, clean water, transportation, power, better sanitation, improved health and safety. Cities are made safer, more habitable, more efficient, more profitable, not equally to all, maybe, but with significant gains to the poor and most vulnerable. And urban institutions acquire the capacity to be more efficient at delivering and managing urban services, utilities, land and money through a variety of technical assistance programmes. Planning, as a form of public control over private greed and market forces, delivers social and economic equity not otherwise available. People, after all, like planning and aid because with it they get more than they had before, despite the sacrifices.

These claims and counterclaims are well reasoned and well debated in the plethora of easily available development literature. In this introductory chapter, we summarise the orthodoxy of current development theory and planning practice and review the essence of the growing dissent which challenges its claims. We demonstrate that, whilst the language of an alternative paradigm (enablement, sustainability, empowerment, capacity building) has impressively colonised development literature, its impact on practice has yet to be felt in any significant way. Finally, we propose a number of working assumptions as a basis to exploring the way ahead.

The orthodoxy of development theory

Think of a country in the developing world – one of those which regularly feature in UN ledgers, with alarming statistics on urban poverty, urban growth rates, mortality rates, urban services indicators, population projections and the like. It is a country which typically will have the following characteristics:

- It will be making a net transfer of cash to Western banks equivalent to £9 for every £1 it has borrowed in repayments and debt servicing and which amounts to around 26% of its gross national product (GNP).

- Its major cities which exploded between 1970 and 1985 at around 135% and which are still growing at around 6% each year.

- Over 80% of its urban population living below the poverty line however it is defined (higher than the average of 28% estimated by the World Bank), most of whom will live in slums and informal settlements.

- Mortality rates, attributed one way or another to poverty or to the poverty of its government, of between 95 and 150 infant deaths before the age of 12 per 1000 births amongst the poor majority and with child malnutrition standing at 40% of its child population.

- 30% of its urban population lacking in safe water and with the quality of supply deteriorating rather than improving despite official reports, and whose municipal authorities are strained in administrative and other resources and manage to pick up between 25 and 50% of its solid waste at best.

Its government knows that collecting taxes or recovering costs from poor people is unpopular and costs more than it can ever collect (Koenigsberger 1983) – one reason for the failure of its welfare policies, which in any case it has been advised to abandon as part of its commitment to structural adjustment. It also knows that some $1.4 billion (or a fifth of its development budget which it will negotiate with a variety of international donors) will need to be spent per year up to the year 2000 in order to meet its targets for improved basic services; and that between 25% and 50% of its GNP will have to be spent on housing to provide 30 square metres of finished house for every poor family – a standard it has promoted as a minimum in its election pledges, but which it knows it cannot possibly achieve. Its current proportions of GNP expenditure on all forms of housing stands at 0.5%.

Typical of most countries, the government depends heavily on foreign financial aid for its development budget, securing funds from a variety of bilateral and multilateral donor agencies. These agencies, who will often compete for development projects, will want to invest in richer rather than poorer countries (69% of aid goes to low-income countries) and in easily manageable projects (roads, bridges, power stations, irrigation schemes) with clear targets, verifiable indicators of achievement and exit strategies. They will often tie their aid to goods and services equivalent to some $15 billion each year and will bring with them their theories, expert systems and logical frameworks which will tell how to do it best and where, when and why, and how to measure if progress is being made, and if not why not and then what to do about it. This tied aid

> *results in developing countries paying prices above the market rate. Estimates vary between 10% and 20% and recent research suggests an average 15%. This excess price is a direct subsidy to exporters in OECD[1] countries amounting to more than $2 billion a year – nearly 4% of DAC[2] aid. Not only does this represent a huge cost for developing countries and bad value for the OECD tax payer, tied aid also results in the purchase of inappropriate goods based on availability in the donor country rather than what is needed for sustainable development.*
> (Randel & German 1994, 25)

Furthermore, donors will prefer to invest in programmes which offer least risk, therefore denying essential innovations which may be needed to reach those with least resources. All aid will inevitably come with policies reflecting the national political agendas of donors and those agreed with their international partners: economic liberalisation, market enablement, government reform, private sector investment for example. These agendas will often jibe with those of the recipient government, struggling to maintain the *status quo* or to meet its targets for housing, health or education before the next round of political elections.

Now imagine that a new five-year development plan is being considered, for which the government will apply for a new round of grants and loans. In negotiating its development budget, the government will face hard choices. On the one hand, to accept the dominant or orthodox model of development aid which will be implicit in the terms of reference and conditions attached to the disbursement of money – for example, removal of subsidies, cost recovery, privatisation, alleviation of poverty. These conditions may not fit their own national needs or priorities, one reason for the failure of projects. And experience tells that some projects may be more harmful than good. People will recall, for example, the flood prevention programme of some 10 years previously when whole communities were forcibly removed and which caused serious environmental damage to an already fragile ecology.

On the other hand, the government can reject the orthodox model and align itself with those who promote endogenous development, arguing for non-hierarchical human relations, for people-driven processes, for the empowerment of communities, especially women, for self-reliance and self-fulfilment and for the "release of peoples' creativity". Under this model, they argue, there are no "front runners" to be followed – people are not the *objects* but the *subjects* of development. In this case the recipient government risks relegation to that list of politically unreliable partners who will be seen with their radical if not impractical ideas, to threaten international efforts to further economic growth and international prosperity.

How then to decide? What is the orthodox model and why the dissent? Whilst definitions vary according to political bias, in principle the orthodox model remains consistent with the Truman design of 1949 (Rahman 1991, 18–26) and closely

---

[1] Organization for Economic Co-operation and Development.
[2] Development Assistance Committee of OECD.

aligned to definitions of development provided to us by development economists during the 1950s. In simple terms, the definitions favour the market and "market-friendly" approaches which are centred around money and international trade (trade liberalisation, deregulation of agricultural markets, etc). Success is measured principally in terms of growth in GNP (Dube 1988) and in levels of consumption of goods and services. This, we are told, fuels the economy and creates benefits which then filter from the centre to the periphery and down to the poorest in the form of jobs, improved services, utilities, housing and the like. The dominant development model is, therefore, both centralist and hierarchical. That is, all major decisions are made at national or international levels in centres of power and money, in development banks, central government departments and capital cities. Under this model the poor are sometimes targeted directly by necessity – for example in more recent programmes advocating redistribution with growth – because it is they who in history as now are seen to spread disease and civil strife, drain the economy and threaten political stability and economic growth. Most orthodox development projects and their associated policies, whatever their rhetoric, "include people only as an awkward afterthought. The dominant development discourse is largely distrustful of normal human beings . . ." (Schrijvers 1993).

The rhetoric, so called, claims that "Investing in people is one of five challenges which will dominate the development agenda and shape its (the World Bank) work" in the decades to come. Investment in human resource development is on the increase, from 5% of the total lending during the 1980s to about 17% in fiscal year 1994. "We are giving much greater priority to the role of women in development" claims the World Bank, "and we will give intensified emphasis to early childhood development, including immunisation, provision of vitamins, nutritional supplements and pre-school education". (Tran 1994).

The dominant model with its global institutions and its globalisation of knowledge and resources, offers significant, contestable gains. "The reduction of spacial barriers and the formation of the world market not only allows a generalised access to the diversified products of different regions and climates, but also puts us into direct contact with all the peoples of the earth. Above all, revolutions in productive force, in technology and science, offer up new vistas for human development and self-realisation." (Harvey 1990, 109–110). In addition the changed circumstances due to climate, the depletion of natural resources, rapid urbanisation, as well as the experience of how best to mitigate against natural disasters, better utilise simple technologies for building more safely, more quickly, more cheaply, and demand habits, sources of knowledge and techniques which may be unfamiliar or unavailable to local communities and national governments. International aid and co-operation, including the transfer of know-how through technical assistance programmes, can be a catalyst to inducing required local changes in response to changing circumstances and improved knowledge. Aid can influence governments to pursue policies which would not otherwise be pursued – to reform institutions, democratise government or empower minorities. Moreover, if the circumstances are right, it will contribute to economic growth. People forget, for example, that "Korea's steady and spectacular growth was aid-based." (Hewitt 1994, 90). And, even if "poverty persists despite the achievements of aid, it would have been worse without it" (Cassen & Associates 1994, 39).

In real terms, the benefits of aid are impressive and measurable. Income per person in the developing world has doubled over the last generation. As put by Cassen & Associates (1994, 40):

> *many governments have made substantial progress in tackling poverty. Between 1965 and 1989, 14 years were added to life expectancy in India, and 12 in China; infant mortality fell by two-thirds in China and by nearly 40% in India. In other low-income countries, average life expectancy rose by 11 years over the same period and infant mortality fell by about one-third; primary school enrolment rose from an average 49% of the age group in 1965 to 75% in 1988, secondary enrolment from 9% to 25%. Most of these achievements owe a significant debt to aid.*

Overall life expectancy has increased on average by 50%; infant mortality has been halved (Tran 1994); many more people have access to utilities, services and housing. All this fuelled by some $1.4 trillion transferred in aid from rich countries to poor ones.[3]

Challenging the orthodoxy of development

Challenges to the orthodoxy of development, its claims and methods, come from a growing body of critical literature, some of them from the same sources that argue its benefits, all of which would be easy to write off as radical. This literature adamantly supports planning and notions of economic growth as fundamental for development, but much less so the orthodox means by which it is attained. In the extreme, dissenters argue that governments and international agencies are in a conspiracy against the public, and that the only going thing amongst development professionals is to keep the professions going. Critics say that all the experts and administrators who devise development programmes do so principally to safeguard the vested interests of their national and international clients as well as for their own financial self-preservation. For example:

> *The major portion of the aid money that is spent in Bangladesh flows to support specific local groups. Local consultants, managers and technicians may receive higher incomes/fees and have access to foreign travel. Indentors receive commissions from importing commodities. Contractors make huge profits from aid-sponsored construction projects. Well-placed members of the state bureaucracy may receive unofficial compensation for their services in the disbursement of foreign aid.*
>
> (Randel & German 1994, 29)

The principle objective of the dominant development model is to incorporate as much as possible all nations, economically and culturally, into one global community. What is needed, they argue, are significant and structural changes to the disbursement of development aid, to technical assistance and to the responsibilities, practices and education of development experts. Critics argue for an alternative paradigm – a

---

[3] In the 1980s the OECD's (21 countries plus the European Community) DAC increased its aid by about a quarter in real terms; but between 1991 and 1992 the DAC's disbursements rose by just 0.5%. Indications suggest that aid benefits are diminishing, except for Japan which provides one-fifth of DAC aid and plans significant increases in the next five years (*Economist* 1994).

radical shift in thinking which turns the orthodox model on its head and which would improve aid effectiveness. Critics see a crisis of purpose in development aid and call for a broad range of reforms – "adopting longer term, process oriented approaches . . . strengthening indigenous institutions, . . . increasing local participation . . . minimising aid dependency, . . . improving donor policy coherence and . . . reducing transaction costs of assistance delivery." (Hewitt 1994, 94).

The dissenting arguments are contained in a variety of past and present texts (Hayter 1981 and 1989, Clark 1986, Dube 1988, Rahman 1991 and 1995, Schrijvers 1993, Seabrook 1993, Sachs 1995) and conclude the following. The orthodox model on which planning, education, aid and technology development are based, has failed to alleviate poverty, and promotes dependency, not self-sufficiency. Its benefits simply do not reach the poorest. That linked to the orthodox model is a growing "spiral of violence" toward people and the environment, which is an outcome of development projects. That the orthodox model perpetuates educational methods and curricula, and professional values and attitudes out of pace with, and wholly inappropriate to, the needs and conditions of developing countries, in particular the poorest.

In the first place, the counterclaims suggest that development, driven by international development aid, *creates* rather than alleviates poverty and perpetuates underdevelopment. The very notion of poverty alleviation looks at poverty ". . . in terms of meeting a social *liability* rather than nourishing a social *asset*; it looks at people as objects of sympathy and invites some sacrifice from the rest of society to mitigate their suffering . . ." Instead, ". . . society has to find a strategy of economic growth which has poverty alleviation built into it, rather than pursue a growth strategy which augments poverty and then look for special poverty alleviation programmes as a palliative or 'safety net'." (Rahman 1995, 28, 30). Even the most moderate admit: "Poverty is not going down much in the Third World. Progress was being made in the 1970s, but today the proportion of people in poverty is stagnating, possibly rising in some countries; the numbers in poverty are certainly rising." (Cassen & Associates 1994, 228). The latest development in this cycle of poverty creation is economic structural adjustment[4] imposed on countries by the International Monetary Fund (IMF), which has raised prices of food and basic goods and reduced spending on education, health and other welfare programmes which benefit the poor most. Development benefits do not naturally filter from the centre to the periphery, they never have.[5] "The more common picture is of commercial considerations leapfrogging over sustainable development in decisions on aid, leaving the poor to wait for ripples of economic growth to extend to them." (Randel & German 1994, 24). Similarly, *well-being* is not an inevitable result of economic growth. "On the contrary, underdevelopment of the periphery ['the periphery' includes some 50% of most urban areas] is the result of the development of the centre. . . . development and underdevelopment are two sides of the same coin." (Dube 1988, 43).

---

[4] A review by the IMF of 19 low-income countries which had undergone structural adjustment found that their current account deficits average 12.3% of GDP before adjustment, and 16.8% in the most recent year, and that their external debt had grown from 451% to 482% (*Economist* 1994).
[5] "The World Bank figures suggest that some 2% only of all aid targeted to low-income countries in 1988 went on primary health care, and 1% on population programmes." (*Economist* 1994).

Moreover, the gap, whether measured in money, jobs, education or well-being between the centre and the periphery (or, the haves and have-nots) is widening. This is one reason why, in recent years, a growing body of non-government organisations (NGOs) have stepped in. Their task: to mediate between the demands and activities of government agencies and the needs of communities at the periphery and to channel resources to those who need it most. In their excellent book, *Making a Difference: NGOs and Development in a Changing World*, Edwards & Hulme (1992) expound the virtues of NGOs – and indicate how to work better with governments, how to scale up and become better advocates. From the host of lessons which they draw from a variety of casework, they comment: "Extensively pursuing donor preferences for service delivery is likely to convert NGOs from agencies with a mission into public services contractors." Recent critique of NGOs has focused this issue. Many NGOs have found it difficult to operate outside of the dominant model and find themselves increasingly co-opted by it.

Nor is development aid designed to promote self-sufficiency. To the contrary, its principle purpose "is that you give away a little to make sure you can keep a lot. . . . The main purpose of American aid" said Nixon in 1968 "is not to help other nations but to help ourselves" (Hayter 1981, 83). The radical view, therefore, is that "International aid is eye-wash. It feeds the Third World with false paradigms . . . The exploitive politics of the developed countries – inappropriate transfers of technology, unequal terms of trade and misdirected assistance – lead to the continued existence of underdevelopment. In the final analysis, so-called aid only strengthens dependency relationships." (Dube 1988, 43–44). These dependency relationships are reiterated by Ovitt (1989) in his condemnation of technology transfer, which remains today one of the "flagships" of development aid:

The perpetuation of dependency inherent in technology transfer allows bankers, engineers, and business people – the modern conquistadors – to ensure continued control of developing nations while at the same time presenting themselves as altruists. Their assistance is usually channelled through elite institutions in the underdeveloped countries, thereby creating a development bureaucracy that is narrowly controlled, urban based and dependent.

In the second place, development projects promote a spiral of violence. This is measured in a variety of ways: notably in man-made famines (which killed some 100 000 Bangladeshies in 1974) which result from the power of food politics; in agricultural programmes and irrigation schemes where mechanised farming displaces subsistence farming which, in turn, can cut women off from their traditional rights to land (Schrijvers 1993); and in projects which favour industrial growth, with their associated projects for new roads, dams, power stations. These projects degrade the environment and forcibly displace millions of people from homes and jobs ("In myriad cases, bank projects, supposedly targeted on the poorest of Africa's poor, not only increased inequality and hunger, but exacerbated ethnic conflicts." – Brittain & Watkins 1994); and result in forced population control ("A study in Bangladesh noted that after the serious flooding in 1984, food aid was denied women until they agreed to be sterilised . . . [In India, sterilisation] operations are carried out on a mass scale in sterilisation camps, in which in one day a record number of 1,225 sterilised women was recorded." – Gupta 1991, in Schrijvers 1993, 46).

In the third place, critique is levelled firmly at the inappropriateness of education and at the decline in morality, creativity and self-respect amongst intellectuals. This is inspired by "the overwhelming number of academics and the *bureaucratization* of academia" (Schrijvers 1993, 34), and is reflected in two dominant trends: first, in the content and organisation of academic programmes; second, in the nature of academic enquiry itself. How can these trends be explained?

First, as the competition for students and research funds intensifies, so too does the demand for schools to distinguish their merits and expertise. This search for distinction, geared as it must be to winning students, attracting research funds and influencing academic bureaucrats is, therefore, driven by market or "client"-specific rather than subject-specific need. The result is for academia increasingly to adopt the institutional values and ambitions of government grant authorities, industry and funding agencies, which it then subsumes in its research and transfers to students in the content and practice of teaching. Most students are, therefore, still taught in a climate dominated by the values and aspirations of these single or corporate clients, and by celebrity professionals and opinionated critics. The crises of vast movements of population, of protracted natural and man-made disasters, of endemic poverty, of environmental degradation or political instability, and of global realignments amongst nations, economies or development agencies, feature only peripherally in the education of architects, planners or engineers, all of whom still dominate development work (Hamdi 1996).

When there is innovation, it is driven by a management ethic, not an intellectual one, with indicators of performance designed to ensure good ratings for the next round of grant awards and to impress visiting evaluation committees. The emphasis in this respect is with performance-related targets – with staff:student ratios, accountability to central administration and improved means of staff productivity. These bureaucratic pursuits bring with them a demand for entrepreneurship amongst staff. Those who before had maintained the high ground of academic debate have voluntarily or otherwise stepped down into the swamp of commercial enterprise and competition. It is here, increasingly, and in student popularity where academic careers will be decided.

The result is that even the most conscientious find themselves paralysed by guilt or ambition, or simply "by the amount of energy it takes to keep the system going" (Lodge 1994). Those who pursue subject-specific interests – whose concerns are to improve the lot of the poor majority living in slums and shanties, and to contribute something tangible and immediately useful – find themselves discarding much of their disciplinary or intellectual rigour and, therefore, their conventional career opportunities; and most of those who chase careers, working mostly where international or corporate interests are at stake, find themselves without political reason or social relevance. These issues are reflected in the nature of academic enquiry itself, which is the second dominant characteristic of current academic trends.

Schrijvers (1993) suggests that academics can choose one of three options currently available to them in research. First is the dominant *positivist* (or reductionist) approach, based on a clear separation between the observer (subject) and observed (object). Here, observation is strictly objective and its methods are largely normative and hegemonic. That is, conclusions, models and laws are drawn up which assume universal value and relevance; and the observer assumes that he or she becomes the prime repository of that knowledge which is then passed down from those who have it to those who don't. Dependency and intellectual colonisation are inevitable outcomes.

Second is the critical approach in which political and moral values are central to research methods and teaching. Ideology and culture rather than neutrality direct the acquisition and interpretation of knowledge. Thinking, however, remains strictly separate from doing.

Third is the transformative approach, which builds on the former but whose academics do not assume that their experience or knowledge is necessarily paramount. Mediation between organisations and enablement in the process of change, are its themes, as are getting involved, learning by doing and empowerment of the grassroots. We will return to these themes in Chapter 2. Suffice it to say here, that schools find this approach troublesome because it involves work in settings which cannot easily be measured against strictly formal criteria. It doesn't fit timetables, involves activities on the doubtful side of rigorous academic enquiry, and for teachers seems to undermine their authority (Lloyd 1985, 80–83). When students step out from the idealised world of academia into the diverse, untidy, inconsistent, uncertain and competing world of practice, they therefore face more hard choices: between the idealised goals of their disciplines and the desired goals and needs of their public, between the certainty and consistency of their academic teachings and the change and uncertainty of practice, between the strict timetables to which they were taught to adhere, and the open-ended programmes of development projects, between the high ground of intellectual self-fulfilment and the "swamp" of practice.

The orthodoxy of development planning practice

The "swamp" is most pervasive in the unregulated informal settlements and slums which make up some 40% of Mexico City, 60% of Bogota, 85% of Addis Ababa and 70% of Dar es Salaam (Global Report 1987). Typically, these settlements are spontaneous and incremental in their growth. They are characterised by innumerable groups of clients with competing vested interests, conflicting values and priorities, and by fragile and "hidden" networks of organisation, high densities, petty economies – all technically difficult to service, and statistically impossible to model.

Now assume that a new development plan will be prepared for government, which will include integrating the kind of settlement referred to above into an overall metropolitan structure plan. In step the planners, architects and engineers, part of a consultant "task force" sent in to sort things out. The uninitiated quickly find themselves encumbered with conditions and processes which do not fit their general schemes, or any general theory of planning which they were taught in school. They will distrust what they see because they see it as disorganised, ugly, irrational, unauthorised, dangerous, and "unfair competition to legitimate business" (Devas 1993, 78). They will be distrustful of the very processes which Jane Jacobs described as being "of the essence to city organisation and life . . ." (Jacobs 1961).

In cities in developing countries, she could have been referring to all the entrepreneurs who speculate with land, provide services, work as money lenders and manufacturers, and as water vendors, garbage collectors and builders. Intricate and complex formal/informal partnerships develop for recycling garbage, purchasing and exchanging commodities, exerting political influence, pirating services and securing employment. In time, people build a substantial body of experience and knowledge which is rarely tapped when formulating plans, about how best to build, to profit, or dodge the authorities. When things go wrong, no one needs step in with elaborate explanations. People will usually know and will have the know-how, if not the means, to put it right. Knowing they cannot rely on official help, they will invent ways of working, as they go, tailor-made to needs, aspirations, income and profit. The market place, both formal and informal, will have much to say about what happens, as will respected elders, tradition and local know-how (Hamdi 1991/1995).

These processes we now consider both resourceful and in many ways problematic. They are resourceful because they are fast, ingenious, made up of *"organised rather than disorganised complexity, a vitality and energy of social interaction that depend crucially upon diversity, intricacy and the capacity to handle the unexpected in controlled but creative ways"* (Harvey 1990, 73). They are full of inventive surprises and highly productive. In contrast to conventional planning wisdom, at least until recently, these settlements are evidence of cities which are working. But they are also problematic, because cities develop unpredictably and are therefore strained in terms of services, utilities and government, and because these same settlements are "fragile" organisationally, and often suffer acute poverty, disease and political unrest. These processes are the essence to city organisation. "Once one thinks about city process, it follows that one must think of catalysts of these processes . . ." (Jacobs 1961).

As catalyst, orthodox planning is cumbersome, if not ineffectual. This is explainable in two ways: first by the procedures and methods it adopts; second by enquiry into the reasons it persists and the development paradigm it adopts.

Procedurally, the orthodox planning process will start with extensive "data hungry" studies the results of which will be combined into project documents, which could take some two or three years to develop and negotiate. The final document (typically 250–300 pages long) with its 10 annexes will include project justification and development objectives, project inputs and outputs, risk considerations, and exit strategies, deadlines and reporting schedules. It will be primarily concerned with ensuring proper accountability amongst the consultants, and with the production of reports, plans, and other instruments of planning – all neatly phased over a five-year project period.

The project document will predict in prescriptive detail all the activities that each subcontractor will need to undertake as part of preparing its outputs: plan documents, multisectoral investment programmes, pre-investment feasibility studies, and a variety of reports dealing with infrastructure design, improved management systems, computerised database and mapping facilities, regulatory systems, metropolitan-level integrated development processes and staff development plans. There will also be a written commitment to human resource development and institutional capacity building in the form of overseas training programmes, on-the-job training, foundation workshops, production workshops and community-based training.

As the planning process itself gets under way, it will follow, still today, the orthodox cycle of procedures promoted by Geddes – survey, analyse, plan. It will begin with the demand for a comprehensive understanding of people and places, which it will then attempt to model statistically in order to forecast future urban trends and decide the best government interventions. It will be full of good intentions.

During the course of planning, the expatriate consultant team will confront the hordes of clients whom they will have to involve and pacify if their plans are to succeed. There will be housers with their interest to build cheap houses, to upgrade slums using self-help and appropriate technologies; municipal engineers with their concern for public health and safety; community builders whose prime interest is in community organising; politicians who want to extend and consolidate their ability to govern; and international funders, who will be primarily concerned with disbursing and managing money. There will also be the port authority which owns large parcels of land in and around the city, and the military whose officers own significant tracts of land adjoining the target area and who will want to safeguard and enhance property values. There will be the housing bank through which funds for housing will be channelled, and which will depend on a good record of cost recovery in order to secure more aid money next time; and the planning authority whose chairman is slated to be the next national president. He will want quick, visible and politically safe projects which will gain him votes and which will gain his authority more political clout.

And, of course, there will be the community. They, too, will not be homogenous in their interests and demands. There will be ethnic and religious groups, local political organisations, special interest groups (women, landowners, youth organisations), abutters to any proposed new water line or road improvement or well or dump site. There will be the business community, the unemployed, the latest arrivals who have been displaced from nearby villages because of the government's latest irrigation project. Very little will be known about their commitment to all this planning and urban improvement: will they be hostile, indifferent, tolerant, sponsors, or active promoters of the government's initiatives? (Salas 1988).

Once all the data and findings are collected (assuming they are available) they will be extensively analysed before various options are then confronted. Each option itself will be subject to a thorough review based on acceptability to all the local and international "clients" and based on economic and administrative feasibility. Data collection and analysis as well as devising alternative strategies will have taken between two and three years to prepare. At this stage, spacial plans will be prepared, together with all the other instruments of planning which will have been considered as a part of the "options available" exercise.

They might include regulatory mechanisms (e.g. for building, for the private provision of public services, or legal controls for development of land), fiscal mechanisms (taxation, subsidies, recovery of costs) and direct public provision or ownership (infrastructure, public resources, powers to control private use) (Devas 1993, 46–47). With all this, there will be the demand for effective urban management, to ensure that the whole can be properly managed and that development controls can be effectively enforced. In practice, however, the more astute will have realised, after all these comings and goings, that "In many cases, tools may exist on paper, but there is insufficient administrative or legal resources or insufficient political will to enforce the instruments effectively. . . . there is no clear locus of management authority." (Devas & Rakodi 1993).

During the course of planning only "elected representatives" will have been consulted. Communities are unlikely to have been involved. They will have been "targeted" for improvement according to government priorities. They will not have initiated the project, nor helped to identify priorities, nor invited the consultants who are working on the project. In the orthodox planning model, community participation will be at best consultative, and conducted well after the major decisions have been taken. In the orthodox model it will be the planners who are the "objective experts, who will offer advice to elected politicians on the technical merits of professionally determined solutions" (Rakodi 1993). Nor will national technical counterparts have played much of a role, despite claims for human resource development. The international consultants will have been largely intolerant of "delays" to their report production schedules, despite the stipulation in their terms of reference for on-the-job training. They will see most local consultation and on-the-job training as time consuming, disruptive to their report production schedule (on the basis of which they will be paid) and interfering with their "getting on with the job" according to scheduled deadlines – one reason why capacity building and project development cannot be mixed. As one United Nations Development Programme (UNDP) evaluation report recommended: "The two activities of institutional capacity building and direct support for planning and project design do not mix well. Capacity building is a time-consuming process, dependent on the vagaries of the collaborating institution, while the production of plans and investment proposals is bound by time constraints and deadlines, and tends to take precedence over intentions to use the exercise as a means for capacity building. Projects for technical assistance where the primary objective is institutional strengthening should not therefore be burdened with tasks for preparing specific investment proposals for client institutions." (UNDP Pakistan 1993).

Once complete, and five years into the project, the whole will be neatly put on to the shelves of the planning office, until the time comes to revive the plans. Some projects will be built – the ring-road, the odd housing project, some slum upgrading. History tells that few if any development plans devised according to the orthodox model have ever been comprehensively implemented, except by "colonial style minority governments" (Rakodi 1993) and in exceptional cities like Hong Kong or Singapore.

One needs only the powers of observation to see why the huge gulf exists between the reality of the majority of fast changing Third World cities and the activity of orthodox planning, caricatured above.

For a quick test of a developing country's urban performance, do not ride from the airport by the motorway to the Central Planning Office to inspect the Regional Structure plan or the metropolitan strategy plan. Instead, find the newest shanty town outside the capital and see what, if anything, is keeping the sewage away from the drinking water. See if the layout of the shanty town would allow power and deep drainage, bus routes, local schools and services and solid housing and small workshops to be developed without bulldozing anyone. Then start walking towards whichever government office in the city centre should know whether sites and services and housing construction are getting two per cent of the nation's recorded economic activity, or ten, or what figure in between. By the time you get there you should know the answer well enough from what you have seen along the way.

(Stretton 1978, 116)

Back inside the planning offices, we will probably have found out from looking, listening and measuring that, for example, low-income groups do pay for land and services – anything between 10% and 30% of their income – especially when they have had a voice in decisions affecting the design of services, costs, repayments and tenure status. We will have come to understand that housing programmes have to be designed according to effective user demand and not according to preconceived notions of adequate housing; that most self-built housing costs some 30% less than that built by private developers and some 60% less than that built by the government; that the rate of cost recovery has been of the order of 58% for those projects with no community involvement and up to 95% where there was community involvement and where affordability and willingness to pay have featured prominently in government calculations; and that the government spends somewhere between 2% and 7% of its budget on housing and urban services, well below what would be required to build completed houses or to provide infrastructure according to standards usually demanded by the engineering department in other parts of the city (Hamdi 1991/1995).

We will have noted that a preponderance of land in public ownership – anything, say, over 30% of the total site – is difficult and expensive to maintain and usually, if designated as open space, winds up as a depository for garbage. It undermines the tax base of a neighbourhood and ends up burdening everyone.

We will have seen a significant relationship between the location of residential lots and their potential for commercial use, sometimes reflected in the size of the lot itself and sometimes in the far quicker time it takes for these lots to be built up.

We will have confirmed John Turner's principle that what housing does is as important, if not more so, than what housing is, recognizing that houses improve health, generate money for their occupants, place them close to their source of employment, and can help develop building skills, which people can then market both formally and informally.

We will have come to understand that standards must be flexibly applied, that plans must be resilient to "free or variable or unpredictable behaviour", that both physical and non-physical components of planning are intrinsically related, that people build at different rates, and that settlements take years to consolidate. We will have learned something of the resourcefulness of these settlements and will use these as starting points for planning.

But we will know that all this knowledge and all these data and most of what we have observed will give us only a partial understanding of questions that will need answers, problems that will need definition, and conflict that will need to be resolved in answer to questions once planning begins. How will land be allocated among families? What level of utilities will be provided and where will they run? How many houses or schools or clinics should be built? What kind of transportation will be provided, and where will it run? For all of these questions, we can foresee conflicts of interest, conflicts of priority and taste, and conflicts among technical alternatives. "Inventive design can reconcile some of the conflicts, but never all of them. Good neighbourhood plans have elements of exact surveying, engineering, forecasting and cost, but they are also works of art, and politics – or at their best, perhaps, works of love and justice" (Stretton 1978).

In the final phases, conclusions will be presented to the national planning authority. The national planning team will be muddled by the plethora of reports produced by international consultants which nationals will find difficult to understand. Neither the jargon, nor the technical language, are familiar to them. Few of the reports are translated into their national language.

Up on the office wall of the planning authority are remnants of the previous master plan, prepared some 10 years ago, yellowing with age and little of which had been implemented. The plans are based on unattainable standards and ideals borrowed from the new towns and garden cities of countries like Britain. They are reminiscent of the ideals expounded by 19th-century reformers like Robert Owen and Charles Fourier.

In the office where the international consultants sit, one sees colourful, digitised maps of circles and arrows with patterns of green, grey and red (all produced on the latest electronic plotter whose ink cartridge could only be bought abroad), painting a world utterly in contrast to what was observed outside. This kind of planning organises cities into discrete functional parts, separated into tidy, manageable zones. It still uses as a reference Chandigar, Brasilia and Milton Keynes, posters and photos of which drape the walls of the planning office, development controls borrowed from the land use ordinance for the city and county of Honolulu and zoning codes modelled on those in the city of Raleigh, North Carolina. The terms used to describe the plan are abstractions of reality, picked up no doubt in planning school: "magnets" to attract circulation, "communication nodes" instead of bus depots or train stations, "lines of pedestrian communication" instead of walkways. These plans are difficult to modify without sophisticated equipment, and given the limited resources which are usually available (Hamdi 1991/1995).

In the adjoining room one finds the array of imported sophisticated electronic equipment, housed in a clinical air-conditioned environment (power outputs in the city now extend to two or three hours per day), whose function is to generate a computerised database. It will no doubt incorporate geographic information systems, plotters, digitisers, printers, electricity stabilisers and variety of IBM compatible computers all worth some $250 000. The equipment will record every piece of cadastral and other information which will help model population and urban growth characteristics and predict the outcomes of interventions – assuming, that is, enough local personnel can be trained to use it – and even then assuming the personnel stay in government service once trained, given the salary attraction of the private sector in-country and abroad.

Challenging the orthodoxy of planning

Critiques of this orthodoxy in planning are contained in a variety of texts (Jacobs 1961, Stretton 1978, Sarin 1982, Koenigsberger 1983, Gilbert & Gorgler 1992, Devas

& Rakodi 1993). In summary, dissenters agree that today orthodox practices, with their inherent and implicit desire to control, model, predict and make certain, inhibit where they should promote, and weaken where they should give support to the pluralistic, spontaneous, market-driven and entrepreneural dynamics which shape cities in practice. The failings of orthodox planning across all sectors stem from "... its historical origins, its colonial history, its professional concerns with order and standards, its association with government and its domination by men." (Rakodi 1993, 219). In one example, in a memorandum dated July 1940, a British consultant was recommending for housing the separation of sexes over 10 years old, ventilated cupboards for storing food, piped water supply, and a lavatory for each house. He wrote that each house should be "kept in a proper sanitary condition and in a good state of repair and decorative condition". In the same memo, he offered recommendations to build satellite towns to provide new housing modelled on his success in such towns as Aberdeen, Manchester and Liverpool (Holliday 1940).

Planning's historical origins are, of course, also predicated on "subconscious" assumptions made in Northern Europe and the United States during the 1930s and war years, which were, and still are, irrelevant to the developing countries. These were that urban growth and social change would be slow and continuous; that the major initiative would come from the private sector which would grow in prosperity; and that the prime role of planning, given the destruction of the war years and the concern for heritage and "city beautiful", would be to preserve what was left, and reconstruct what was destroyed (Koenigsberger 1964).

These assumptions are implicitly reflected in the methods and procedures of orthodox planning, whose failings are well summarised by Devas (1993, 72–73): their concern with making plans rather than achieving any real, practical effect on the ground; their attempt to be too comprehensive; their lack of practical concern for social, economic and environmental issues; their unrealistic projections of population growth and public investment requirements; the segregation between plan making and decision making (consultants who plan, politicians who decide, people who receive); their inability to control land development, even where it is desirable; and the disparity between all their land use and zoning, which are unrelated to the forces which really shape cities. To this list can be added their inflexibility to respond to uncertainties and change, the time they take to develop, their failed attempt to identify and predict optimum patterns of development, and their adherence to standards which are unrealistic and impractical, socially and economically. In addition much planning offers up solutions, without any clear delineation of how they will be achieved – plans which may be desirable but which turn out to be unfeasible. As Edward Banfield once wrote: "When solutions are offered without specification of the means by which they are to be reached, it must be presumed that the means – if any exist – have yet to be discovered and that the 'solution' is therefore infeasible." (Banfield 1968, 262).

Why then, does orthodox planning continue to dominate planning today?

First, planners and planning practices bid for projects designed by other planners (and economists) for aid agencies who are the principal clients. These projects therefore fit the criteria and paradigms of orthodox development aid programmes discussed earlier. They are driven by the demand to promote productivity through increased mechanisation and transfer of technology (whether in health, housing, energy, agricultural output, etc.) rather than by a concern with encouraging local resourcefulness. That is, they are primarily concerned with instant, easily measurable outputs rather than *outcomes* (trained people, better managed institutions) which are less easily measurable in the short term because their impacts are usually felt progressively, and their benefits develop incrementally.

Second, planning continues to be dominated by a professional elite – engineers, economists, planners and architects – trained in universities whose teachings subscribe dominantly to the positivist (reductionist) or critical (post-reductionist) models of enquiry. Many of the elite who now head planning authorities in developing countries were trained during the 1950s in schools in Britain and elsewhere. "The influence of British and colonial planning ideas, legislation and training models was strong. Purveying a concept of planning as the control of land use and urban development as the means of achieving a healthy and attractive urban environment . . ." (Rakodi 1996, 47). It is no wonder that they view slums and informal settlements as a national failure, a threat to political and social stability, something to be eradicated. Their approach to planning is grounded in the high ground of monumental civic design, borrowed from colonial planners and modernists alike, with their rewards measured in civic design awards, and more jobs, and their prestige in the acclamations of fellow professionals, public lectures and professional journals. For international consultants, the business is also financially lucrative and dependent on a "problems industry" which many will want to sustain. "Of the $12 billion or so which goes each year to buy advice, training and project design, over 90% is spent on foreign consultants" (*Economist* 1994). The approach to problem solving is benevolent pragmatism – "bring in the consultants, (establish goals), sort out priorities, put a figure and time limit to the job and then throw in the task force". "Their mode of working is single disciplinary, they tend not to trust people who they see simply as the object (rather than the subject) of enquiry" and consumers of projects (Chambers 1993). They prefer single-function projects coupled with, preferably, lots of technology transfer, which stimulate private sector investment, visibly raise public expectation of a better future, and transfer significant benefit back to the donor countries. Their spacial plans are behaviourably deterministic and, in compliance with the orthodox development paradigms, represent end states. In other words they are determined by pre-set *goals* with targets and deadlines rather than by development *processes*. Community means corner shops and public squares, good behaviour means good housing and clean neighbourhoods, and good work habits mean office parks, business centres and industrial complexes. They will argue that better education means building universities, better health still means building more hospitals, healthy play means playgrounds and recreation centres, healthy housing proper houses and so on.[6] These projects, it is argued, are more efficiently designed and produced by professionalising decision making and centralising resources and

---

[6] In 1988–89, for example, 33% of Japanese aid went on building hospitals (*Economist* 1994). In sub-Saharan Africa in the 1980s, only $1 of aid went on each primary pupil; $11 on each secondary pupil, $75 on each university student.

production capabilities. Only then can resources and capital be properly managed; quality, cost, demand and supply can then be more efficiently controlled and the benefits more equitably distributed. As their careers develop, the planners, engineers and architects are promoted increasingly into management and policy-making roles, detached from the grassroots (Chambers 1993), thus ensuring the continued separation of thinkers from doers.

Third, the political and sometimes professional *will* to see projects through is simply not there. Governments are willing to go along with planning in the knowledge that it generates residual money for its own local staff and its own projects, without any risk that much of the planning itself will be implemented. Disentangling plan making from plan implementation is therefore expedient for governments and sometimes also for international development agencies. Both can be seen to be doing something without the entanglements and risks of actually seeing it all through to implementation (Devas 1993). In addition, it offers the opportunity, without much risk, to express through planning the expectations and good intentions of government, to secure public sympathy and international good standing.

These issues have led some to conclude that planning and planning professionals are today "troubled by chronic disagreement about its [planning's] ends and means, its theories and methods, and even about the need for it to exist at all." (Stretton 1978, 4).

Working assumptions

First, the complex nature of fast-changing cities and the problems faced by their low-income majority cannot be successfully managed by reductionist, professionally dominated, top-down planning, nor can city plans be easily rationalised deductively according to prescriptive blueprints or master plans. Planning based on these means is mechanistic and often makes things worse. It demands sources of information, accuracy of data, surveys and site plans, as well as comprehensive understanding, political goodwill, economic stability and institutional capabilities – all of which are in short supply.

Practices based on prescriptive, reductionist thinking and management displace ordinary people including marginal entrepreneurs, the poor and most vulnerable, in favour of project officials, businessmen, contractors and development workers, drawn usually from a professional elite and sometimes from foreign countries. And, rational management displaces the very processes which are vital to the health and survival of low-income communities – the opportunity to be *spontaneous*, to *improvise* and to build *incrementally*. These processes require "flexible and changing definitions of roles, obligations, procedures and methods, collegial authority and free lateral communications." (Chambers 1993, 12–13). Instead, reductionist planning with its models of rational management seeks predictable "end states" which impose restrictions (rather than cultivate conditions), whose processes are normative, inflexible, and based on "sacred prototypes" and pre-ordained rules. These processes are based on fixed roles, objectives, obligations, procedures and methods.

Second, the sacred routine in development practice of planning first and acting later – of building programmes and projects only after deciding policy – is counterproductive and wrong headed. Good practices do not necessarily derive from good policy, because what is desirable as policy to national and international experts and bureaucrats is not always in the interests of ordinary people and therefore is often unmanageable in practice.

Good practice derives from good practice. It derives from the experience of those who do it and think about it, monitored, evaluated and then passed *down* from generation to generation, passed *across* from one project or community to another, and passed *up* to government and government institutions so that they can devise what we have become accustomed to call "support policies".

What we see, instead and despite the rhetoric, is a wide gap between policy makers and field staff, government institutions and community organisations, expert knowledge and local knowledge, and between development objectives and development realities. This is partly inspired by recent trends amongst the international elite, to drop "projects" in favour of what most ordinary people see as abstractions: policy development, institutional capacity building, government reforms and the like, put together by people who sit in development banks, city offices and ivory towers. This is partly also because policy makers (never the same people as project makers) fail to recognise that there is as much knowledge of what works best, and what does not, built into the experience and actions of ordinary people.

Third, and as a corollary, little or no institutional learning, when it does occur, finds its way back into everyday practice. Despite the importance placed on project monitoring and evaluation, not enough learning takes place. And even if it does, it usually winds up documented in extensive reports which no one knows quite how to use. While these reports represent a substantial accumulation of data and sometimes analysis, they have little impact on practice. There are, of course, all kinds of people who make evaluations, numerous reasons why they do so, and various methods which are used. There will have been municipal authorities, political groups, international funding agencies, central government housing authorities, church groups, user groups, architects, planners and engineers, all of whom will have had some say – some more than others – in programming and implementation. Most likely, each will have been looking to judge outcomes based on its own history of success or failure, to validate its approach, invalidate its competitors' approaches, safeguard the status quo or get more work. Each party will be selective about what it measures and how it measures what it sees. Unfortunately, most monitoring ends up as bookkeeping and most evaluations are self-serving. Neither has much to do with learning, nor with institutionalising lessons learnt – one reason why policy remains uninformed about practice.

How then could these assumptions shape new practices? The current and growing disappointment with orthodox planning methods, and the educational systems which underpin them, has led to new paradigms which an increasing number of academics and practitioners now advocate, and which form the basis to new methods now filtering into planning practice. It is these alternatives to which we will now turn.

References

Banfield, E.C. 1968. *The Unheavenly City Revisited*. Boston: Little, Brown & Co.
Brittain, V. & Watkins, K. 1994. A continent driven to economic suicide. *The Guardian*, 20 July 1994.
Cassen, R. & Associates 1994. *Does Aid Work?* Oxford: Clarendon Press.
Chambers, R. 1993. *Challenging the Professions*. London: Intermediate Technology Publications.
Clark, J. 1986. *For Richer For Poorer*. Oxford: Oxfam.
Devas, N. 1993. Evolving approaches. In Devas, N. & Rakodi, C. (eds), *Managing Fast Growing Cities*. Harlow: Longman Scientific & Technical.
Devas, N. & Rakodi, C. (eds) 1993. Planning and managing urban development. *Managing Fast Growing Cities*. Harlow: Longman Scientific & Technical.
Dube, S.C. 1988. *Modernization and Development: The Search for Alternative Paradigms*. London: ZED Books.
Economist 1994. Foriegn aid: the kindness of strangers. *The Economist*, 7 May 1994, 21–26.
Edwards, M. & Hulme, D. (eds) 1992. *Making a Difference: NGOs and Development in a Changing World*. London: Earthscan Publications.
Gilbert, A. & Gorgler, J. 1992. *Cities, Poverty and Development*. Oxford: Oxford University Press.
Global Report on the Human Settlements, 1987. Oxford: Oxford University Press for the United Nations Centre for Human Settlements (HABITAT).
Hamdi, N. 1991/1995. *Housing Without Houses: Participation, Flexibility, Enablement*. New York: Van Nostrand Reinhold; London: Intermediate Technology Publications.
Hamdi, N. (ed.) 1996. *Educating for Real: The Training of Professionals for Development Practice*. London: Intermediate Technology Publications.
Harvey, D. 1990. *The Condition of Postmodernity*. Oxford: Basil Blackwell.
Hayter, T. 1981. *The Creation of World Poverty: An Alternative View to the Brandt Report*. London: Pluto Press, in association with Third World First.
Hayter, T. 1989. *Exploited Earth: Britain's Aid and the Environment*. London: Earthscan Publications.
Hewitt, A. (ed.) 1994. *Crisis of Transition in Foreign Aid*. London: Overseas Development Institute.
Holliday, C. 1940. *City of Colombo Memorandum on Town Planning*. Colombo: Department of Town and Country Planning, July. In Hamdi, N. 1991/1995. *Housing Without Houses: Participation, Flexibility, Enablement*. New York: Van Nostrand Reinhold; London Intermediate Technology Publications.
Jacobs, J. 1961. *The Death and Life of Great American Cities*. New York: Random House.
Koenigsberger, O. 1964. Action planning. *Architectural Association Quarterly*, May 1964.
Koenigsberger, O. 1983. The role of the planner in a poor (and in a not quite so poor) country. *Habitat International* 7 (1/2): 49–55.
Lloyd, M. 1985. Schools: the challenge of change. In *The Architect as Enabler*, special issue of *Architecture and Competitions*, pp. 80–83.
Lodge, D. 1994. *The Guardian*, 29 October 1994.
Ovitt, G. 1989. Appropriate technology: development and social change. *Monthly Review* 40 (9): 22–32.
Rahman, M.A. 1991. *Towards an Alternative Development Paradigm*. IFDA Dossier 81. Nyon Switzerland: International Foundation for Development Alternatives.
Rahman, M.A. 1995. Participatory development: toward liberation or co-operation? In Craig, G. and Mayo, M. (eds), 1995. *Community Empowerment*. London: ZED Books.
Rakodi, C. 1993. Planning for whom? In Devas, N. and Rakodi, C. (eds), *Managing Fast Growing Cities*. Harlow: Longman Scientific & Technical.
Rakodi, C. 1996. Educating urban planners. In Hamdi, N. (ed.), *Educating for Real: The Training of Professionals for Development Practice*. London: Intermediate Technology Publications.
Randel, J. & German, T. (eds) 1994. *The Reality of Aid 1994*. London: ActionAid.

Sachs, W. (ed.) 1995. *The Development Dictionary: A Guide to Knowledge and Power*. London: ZED Books.

Salas, J. 1988. An analysis of Latin American autoconstruction: a plural and mass phenomenon. *Open House International* 13 (4): 2–11.

Sarin, M. 1982. *Urban Planning in the Third World. The Chandigar Experience*. London: Mansell Publishing.

Schrijvers, J. 1993. *The Violence of "Development"*. Utrecht: International Books.

Seabrook, J. 1993. *Victims of Development*. London: Verso.

Stretton, H. 1978. *Urban Planning in Rich and Poor Countries*. Oxford: Oxford University Press.

Tran, M. 1994. Learner lender pledges to be more responsive. *The Guardian*, 20 July 1994.

UNDP Pakistan. 1993. *Sindh Secondary Cities. Development Planning*. Report of the terminal evaluation mission. February 1993.

CHAPTER 2
Action Planning in Theory

The life of a modern nation or city is very complicated. The citizens have intricate patterns of common and conflicting interests and tastes and beliefs, and individually and collectively they have very unequal capacities to get what they want for themselves or for one another. From that tangle of powers and purposes comes a social life so complicated and partly unpredictable that any understanding of it has to be incomplete. Investigations therefore have to put up with knowing less than everything. They have to choose what questions to ask and what general types of answers to accept. They have to select and simplify.

Stretton (1978)

In 1964, Otto Koenigsberger set out an alternative approach to conventional planning, consisting of "a series of *action plans* controlled by a set of *performance standards* and forming part of a *guiding concept* for the whole urban region". It was in response to his frustrations, and those of his practising colleagues, to an orthodoxy in planning which they saw as unresponsive to the needs of fast-changing cities and the failure amongst planners and city officials to recognise the urgencies of the tasks involved in solving its problems and controlling its development.

Building on those early beginnings, advocates of action planning (as well as action science and action research) have assumed objectives, which have been constantly rediscovered and modified over the years, which would turn the tide in favour of more responsive planning, less regulated by officialdom, and more by the inevitabilities and resourcefulness of everyday life. First, they sought to equip planners with an improved means with which to guide (rather than control) city development, and to map its spatial, social and economic process; second, they sought to match the needs of people more closely to the goals of planning. This they would do through radical revisions to the orthodox paradigm of development and through continuous monitoring of urban systems, so that investment could be targeted according to need. Feedback of information would encourage more learning and would in turn enable progressive revision to city plans. Third, they proposed improvements to the efficiency of planning by speeding up planning operations. They would employ rapid and selective techniques with which to identify "the dominant features of the city and the character and aspirations of its major social groups" (Safier 1974). More fundamentally, they would measure successes in tangible results on the ground, accepting limited resources and, when possible, working closely with communities and other local organisations.

These worthy objectives are today finding expression in planning practices which share common themes: their methods are less normative, less standardised in their procedures, less dependent on comprehensiveness and not so much dominated by the "old style British school which produced master plans nor by American schools which wallowed in statistics" (Cook 1979). Instead, what has emerged in practice is a *planning framework*, flexible, simply structured, untied to any specific sequence of operations, guided by informed improvisation, reiterative and adaptive in its processes, and based on action and experience rather than lengthy surveys or study. Within this framework, practitioners are "free to start, to make mistakes and to learn on the run" (Chambers 1992). It is a framework guided by the imperatives that "poor people are creative and capable, and can and should do much of their own investigation, analysis and planning"; that outsiders (funders, experts, public officials) have a strategic role to play as convenors, disseminators, catalysts, facilitators and policy formulators creating opportunities for discovery and a context for work which can be understood by all.

Planning and planners would assume a new purpose: to help remove barriers to learning opportunities, improve access to public services and create a climate of opportunity for people to help themselves (Cook 1979). The new task would be to create conditions in which members of a community can engage in "public reflection on substantive matters of concern to them, and also on the rules and norms of inquiry they customarily enact . . ." (Lewin 1947, in McGill & Horton 1973, 13–14). Planners would also assume a new professionalism. This would be based on new assumptions about reality and on revisions to their methods, their responsibilities and their mode of working. The challenge would be: "how best to proceed in a context of uncertainty, indeterminacy, diversity, mutual causality, increasing complexity and often accelerating change" (Pretty & Chambers 1993, 2).

In this second chapter, we expand on these themes, and advance principles for practice based on a new realism about planning and its capacity to guide and manage cities. We review the new realism and an alternative paradigm which underpins the methods and ideas of action planning, and identify its essential characteristics and its menu of operations and techniques. Finally, we discuss the processes of action planning and illustrate a means by which community action planning can inform city-level strategic plans through progressive monitoring.

The new realism and the alternative paradigm

Early definitions of action planning fell far short of radical reform. For Koenigsberger (1964, 7)

> *planning the speed and sequence of operations would form an essential part of each action plan. Timing was to be such that the planner would always be one jump ahead of the official dealing with land acquisition, who in turn would be expected to be always one jump ahead of those who were to plan and build roads and public utilities. These, in their turn, would always have to be one jump ahead of the public and private investors, and the agencies concerned with the distribution of already developed plots. The conveyance of land would have to be at least one jump ahead of construction, and the operations of the buildings would have to be synchronized in such a manner that houses, blocks of flats, schools, dispensaries, markets, shops, community services, public transport and recreation facilities would grow up in the right order. This*

emphasis on timing of the operations in the action programmes had two objectives. One was to shorten the period of time between investment and return. The use of the term "market research" and the emphasis on timing were both intended to induce public authorities to plan their operations similar to those of large financial or commercial undertakings . . . The second objective of the emphasis on timing was the use of action programmes as tools of employment planning . . . Action programmes could be stepped up to achieve conditions of full employment when these were wanted and slowed down to provide working power for other purposes should this be required.

Whilst Koenigsberger's new order was clear in its demand for reforms, it held on to assumptions borrowed from the very orthodoxy which he claimed to challenge as both time consuming and ineffectual.

In it he assumed that public authorities could improve their status as providers of housing, services and utilities by adopting the values and operations of their formal private-sector counterparts (and yet, few public authorities have met their housing targets); that planners could continue to act as principals in city processes, if only they could keep one step ahead of everyone else (which they found they could not); and that investment back into public administrations as principal planning institutions would strengthen their capabilities to deliver benefits which would find their way back to those in most need in the form of housing, education, health and utilities. In practice, this has rarely been achievable. He also assumed that careful "synchronisation" would improve planning efficiency, which is precisely what cannot be relied upon; and that, all in all, his process would deliver rewards to professionals through enhanced opportunities for "conscious shaping of the urban environment and for the realisation of urban design".

Later, Koenigsberger (1987) was to revise his ideas. He was to conclude that most development in Third World cities followed lines of least resistance, not plans drawn up by architects and planners, and that most major cities were planned according to self-help principles. More importantly, what emerged was a willingness to accept that the vast majority of slums, squatter settlements and land invasions were a sign of healthy cities which were working and which were, in any case, unstoppable. They offered principles which planning was bound to take on board as part of a new realism in city planning, which Devas (1993, 100) summarised as follows:

- That urban population growth was inevitable.

- That the form of cities would continue to be determined largely by the decisions of individuals and organisations rather than governments.

- That there were limitations on the abilities of governments to intervene effectively in the urban system.

- That governments, particularly those that were debt-laden and undergoing structural adjustment, would continue to face resource constraints.

- That the poor have a limited capacity to pay for services, utilities and housing and that standards of services currently provided are, therefore, rarely affordable by the urban majority.

In addition, planning processes could not be tidy or linear following the survey–plan–action sequence; most urban institutions had limited capacities to implement plans; and most planning authorities had an equivalent limited capacity to enforce regulatory systems of development control. Incrementalism is the way most programmes and projects will continue to develop whether in housing construction in urban projects or in institution building. And finally realism about the nature of political agendas and political processes, recognising why plans are so often not implemented and seeing politics not as an obstacle to the implementation of a plan, or a programme, but as a framework within which an implementable plan or programme must be developed. This new realism about city development has dislodged old ideals, reflected today in four dominant trends.

First, in changes in development policy promoted by donors, with the emphasis today on market enablement, and on urban management. However one chooses to rationalise its origins, this trend demands of planning an expanded agenda of new initiatives which *de facto* links planners to the *real politik* of city governance and to the current and progressive trend toward globalisation. Plan making and regulatory controls are minimised in favour of the new agenda whose emphasis is managerial. It includes fiscal and land market management, institutional co-ordination and capacity building, market supply of housing, services and utilities, and environmental regulations. Assumptions about public responsibility have given way to public/private partnerships. And it is recognised that non-government and community-based organisations have an increasing role to play in the supply and management of facilities at the local level. All these are amongst the management tools which are necessary to good governance, seen as fundamental to sustaining progressive improvements to city systems, attracting private-sector investment and promoting greater efficiency.

Second, we see a new definition of public responsibility and a new role for development practitioners. This is inspired by the trend toward "enabling" and away from "providing" and is based on a new pragmatism. This revised role is illustrated in Figure 2.1. It accepts mutuality between local demands and city-level strategic needs, between government interventions and community action, between large-scale producers and small enterprises, between project development and resource management, between some providing and a lot more enabling. And yet, it recognises the limitations on both sides of the paradigmatic fence.

As we have noted, the orthodox paradigm suffers failings in practice due to its principal concern with economic growth measured in GNP, its professional dominance and its top-down government control. Conversely, critique of the alternative paradigm is levelled at its populist idealisms, its *ad hoc* nature geared to solving problems where and when they arise; and, therefore, its ineptitude (and seeming lack of concern) at building broader and strategic urban policy. Promoters argue precisely what has yet to be proven: that people always know better than experts, best solutions always derive from the grassroots, power is always more equitably exercised by communities, and projects are always more efficient if they are designed, implemented and managed by community-based organisations (CBOs) and NGOs. Moreover, it assumes "relationships of trust and accountability between politicians and officials and a willingness on the part of

ORTHODOX PARADIGM	THE ALTERNATIVE PARADIGM
"Providing"	"Enabling"
• Increase productivity-growth in GNP as a goal	• Encourage resourcefulness/well-being as a goal
• People as objects of development	• People are subjects of development
• Professionals as benevolent pragmatists	• Professionals as populist idealists
• Promotes dependency	• Promotes self-sufficiency/empowers
• Professionals/governments as prime actors	• CBOs/NGOs as prime actors – professionals as catalysts, governments as enablers
• Promotes technology transfer (products)	• Promotes appropriate technologies (processes)
• Produces projects/concerned with outputs	• Management of resources/concerned with outcomes
• Information as data (things/surveys)	• Information as knowledge (systems/oral testimonies)
• Centralises production and decision making	• Decentralises production/devolves decision making
• Prefers standardisation	• Promotes variety/flexibility
• Instant projects, prescriptive plans	• Incremental projects/progressive programmes, adaptive planning
• Consolidated (formal) industry, preferring large organisations	• Fragmented (informal) industry based on small enterprises

Figure 2.1 Comparative characteristics of the orthodox (providing) and alternative (enabling) paradigms.

the powerful to share power . . . which are precisely what cannot be assumed." (Devas 1993).

A similar blinding idealism pervades the search for appropriate technologies (ATs) – a key tenet of the alternative paradigm. AT's emphasis on low capital costs, local materials, grassroots decision making, collective rather than individual efforts, user control, community empowerment and economic self-sufficiency contrast sharply with the big business and large capital which fuel the transfer of technology (Hamdi 1991). AT, to many, is the alternative paradigm in practice.

And yet, appropriate technology is limited by its own claims to self-sufficiency, and demonstrates precisely the shortcomings of the alternative paradigm which it embodies. These shortcomings are not easily accepted by its practitioners.

> *It is fine to prescribe windmills as an energy resource to poor people as long as it is clear that by doing so the AT expert is imposing a limit on the degree to which the windmill-powered economy can grow, on the types of products it can produce, and on the extent to which its people will emerge from poverty . . . AT cannot, by definition, solve national economic problems except in so far as these problems are the sum of local needs.*
>
> (Ovitt 1989, 26, 27)

This new realism about appropriate technology suggests that governments were not so much interested in technologies that were appropriate, as those which contributed to their national economies and earned foreign exchange, which locally sustainable technologies did not do well.

From a political and mostly Marxist standpoint, AT is seen as old forms of intervention, but dressed up to look new:

> *In advanced capitalist and Third World countries alike intermediate technology and self-help philosophies are put forward as a solution: build your own house, grow your own food, bicycle to work, become an artisan and so on. To those in the Third World who have done all these things and who are still rarely far from starvation, such appeals to be more self-reliant must strike them as being a rather curious form of radicalism.*
>
> (Burgess 1982)

Most ordinary people see AT as a "poor man's technology" – something you do because there are no other alternatives. Whilst small may be beautiful, it is also, in practice, very difficult.

Third, this thinking about new paradigms, about market enablement, and the imperatives of city development referred to by Koenigsberger coincided with revisions to development ideology articulated by many including Schumacher in 1973 and by Dag Hammerschold in 1975. New definitions emerged designed to promote "a minimum of organisation that would serve the benefits of planning while leaving individuals the greatest possible control over their own lives."

Schumacher (1973, 53–54) put it this way:

> *In the affairs of men, there always appears to be a need for at least two things simultaneously, which, on the face of it, seem to be incompatible and to exclude one another. We always need both freedom and order. We need the freedom of lots and lots of small, autonomous units, and, at the same time, the orderliness of large-scale, possibly global, unity and co-ordination. . . . What I wish to emphasise is the duality of the human requirement when it comes to the question of size: there is no single answer. For his different purposes man needs [requires] many different structures. . . . For constructive work, the principal task is always the restoration of some kind of balance.*

Schumacher and others have been consistent in their demand for processes which are fast, practical, resource efficient, culture specific and people driven, and whose benefits reach the poorest. Many have conceptualised blueprints for a preferred future – none less compelling than that offered by Dag Hammerschold in his 1975 report – "What Now: Another development" (in Dube 1988, 46). In it he suggests:

> *a course of development that is need-oriented, endogenous, self-reliant, ecologically sound and based on structural transformation. It is aimed at meeting human needs, endogenously defined and with primary focus on those who have been deprived and exploited. It recognizes the importance of equality, freedom of expression, conviviality and creativity. Each society is left free to operate according to its values and cultures and articulate its own vision of the future. No universal model is to be imposed; each society can build its own. For development a society has to rely essentially on its inherent strength, although collective self-reliance is not ruled out. Rational utilization of the biosphere is built into the model: outer limits have to be respected and local ecosystems handled sensitively. From the little community to the global human community structural transformations will be needed to evolve participative decision-making mechanisms. Capacity for self-governance will have to be strengthened.*

These powerful ideals have been difficult in practice. They would polarise a new breed of academics and practitioners around themes which would threaten the political interests and livelihoods of development "conquistadors" as well as the orthodox routines of planning authorities: self-sufficiency, well-being, empowerment, decentralisation, enablement, community participation and appropriate technologies were until recently unfamiliar terms in the jargon of public administrations.

Finally, new methods and approaches have emerged which challenge the old-style determinism in planning and urban design, and which will demand reskilling development professionals. Approximation and serendipity are today more the norm – the quest for scientific precision is displaced in favour of getting things roughly right, or right enough to proceed confidently. Rapid and participatory methods of appraisal and reconnaissance have displaced market research and lengthy analytical study. Furthermore, planning would incorporate into its processes those who were best at getting things done and mostly without concern for a balanced or "synchronised" programme, who typically include private and public-sector entrepreneurs, landowners, squatters, private developers, civil servants and public officials (Cook 1979).

Pretty & Chambers (1993, 2) proposed several themes that lie at the core of the new approach:

The affirmation of individuals and their differences . . . ; a pluralist stance giving voice to individuals and groups so as to participate in decision making; knowledge and associated technology are seen as contextual in time and space, and so limited in their transferability . . . ; the future is recognised as uncertain and indeterminate with a sensitive dependence on current and contextual conditions.

How then are these trends incorporated into the operations and procedures of action planning? What important characteristics do they imply for practice, and what menu of operations and technique can be usefully employed?

Characteristics

Many of the characteristics of action planning are similar to those of Participatory Rapid Appraisal (PRA) (Chambers 1992). Action planning differs, however, in three significant ways.

First, its origins derive from physical, social and economic planning rather than applied anthropology or farming systems research. Its preoccupations, we have seen, are with improving the efficiency of planning processes and in response to finding new roles, responsibilities and relationships for planning institutions and planners. Unlike PRA it is, in the first place, less directed at community development or community empowerment, although it recognises both as important tenets of an improved planning process.

Second, the preoccupations of action planning are traditionally and intrinsically urban rather than rural. Much of what is therefore assumed in rural communities cannot be assumed in cities. In urban communities, people are often engaged in a wide variety of economic activities, formal and informal, and do not share common economic dependencies. There are fewer natural resources at hand with which to gain employment, become self-sufficient, or minimise dependence on state institutions. To the contrary, in cities, communities are often heavily reliant on local authorities for land, housing, services and utilities. Communities are often more heterogeneous, where the origins and interests of people are diverse. Many in urban settlements are transient, lack security of tenure and, therefore, commitment to their "host" community (Mitlin & Thompson 1994).

Third, action planning serves both local-level problem solving and city-level strategic planning. In addition to serving the needs of the community, its objectives are also strategic, building broader policy-level planning which is essential to managing urban growth, housing, services and utilities in ways which are equitable and cost effective.

Finally, action planning is usefully applied to four areas of activity: to urban improvement, capacity building, new development planning, and for planning under crisis, i.e. rebuilding communities which have suffered political or natural disaster.

With these differences in mind, action planning does share a number of operational characteristics with PRA, based substantially on the enabler paradigm illustrated in Figure 2.1. These are:

- problem based and opportunity driven
- based on achievable actions
- participatory, encouraging rapport and partnerships
- reliant on local knowledge and skills and traditional wisdom
- non-reliant on complete information
- small in scale, community based
- incremental rather than comprehensive plans
- starting points rather than end states
- fast, not rushed
- visible, tangible outputs

It will be seen in later examples (see "Case Files") that action planning is problem driven and exploits opportunities which present themselves before work starts and as work proceeds. Dealing with problems which stakeholders will prioritise and building on opportunities such as existing organisational structures, employment potentials or available skills, ensures that programmes at the outset will be recognisable as needed and tangible. New goals are set on the basis of what is achievable, which will be discovered as work proceeds. As such, action planning avoids *maximising* information, co-ordination, integration and participation and instead works to optimise resource uses in relation to actual conditions and existing constraints. The methods are pragmatic – the beginnings less than best, whether for engineers, government officials or communities. Local knowledge and skills are given dominance "with preference for activities which are administration sparing rather than administration intensive" (Chambers 1993). Whilst actual programmes may be broad in scope, their beginnings are small in scale and community based. Broader programmes are worked toward incrementally through a series of small-scale "additive" projects coupled with strategic policy-level interventions. Appropriate technologies and local enterprises are promoted – enterprises which will not only get their materials, services and utilities from formal outlets, but will also supply them. Linkages are therefore established between formal and informal systems of production, between large producers and small manufacturers and between different kinds of technology. Systems of production, purchasing and supply emerge that link local markets with urban ones. The multiplicity of large outlets, small manufacturers and even pavement sellers, offers variety in quality and price of goods and services, and therefore much-needed flexibility to local entrepreneurs and families. All these activities "stimulate productivity and employment in exactly the sector where they are most needed" (Peattie 1982). Improvements to housing and small enterprises are helped by selective government interventions offering access to resources, cheap credit, variable servicing and training.

"Starting points" rather than "end states" become key. In this respect, experts act as catalysts, introducing the necessary methods and techniques, bringing ideas and experience from elsewhere, identifying further opportunities and possible courses of action, disseminating principles, helping to remove legal, legislative and other barriers which get in the way of getting things done, and often providing political legitimacy to local inhabitants.

At the core of action planning and underpinning its characteristics is *stakeholder participation,* yet such planning recognises severe constraints to consensus amongst stakeholders because "the influence of power, authority and gender inequality are likely to be great" (Moss 1993). In this sense, action planning is heavily biased toward building coalitions and fostering co-operation between government and non-government groups, between often competing government departments, between expatriate or outside experts and their local professional counterparts, and between community groups with sometimes differing vested interests, particularly early in programme preparation. Partnerships do not happen, however, just because they are a good idea. Nor is it useful to talk in abstract ways about partnerships between sectors, such as private and public or formal and informal. Usually, participatory programmes happen if and when people and organisations are convinced that their interests will be better served in partnerships rather than without them.

Effective partnerships begin with a discovery of common interest and subsequently with inducing a convergence of interests as a prelude to planning. Informally, these are processes that occur everyday: "Individuals seeking information and action on their own problems, converge with other individuals with similar needs for research and action . . . The convergence of interest . . . establishes a special phase of participant commitment and involvement which is continuously drawn upon and further developed as the process proceeds" (McGill & Horton 1973, 22). In considering these issues, it may be relatively easy to mobilise interest, secure commitments, reach consensus and involve people in neighbourhoods that are *integrated* or *parochial*. In these places, people already share a common view, there is social homogeneity, they speak a common language, or they may be ethnically related. Whilst this level of homogeneity may be a good basis to participatory planning, it can also present severe limitations, particularly where the participatory process is introduced from outside. "Participation in an ethnically or traditionally based neighbourhood which is dominated by a paternalistic–hierarchical social order is likely to reinforce existing inequalities and result in growing contradictions." (Lewin 1991, 20). Interventions in these kinds of neighbourhoods, with the potential to organise, may need to break down traditional barriers and will be in stark contrast to those that are diffuse, stepping-stones, transitory, or non-neighbourhoods.[1]

Many new settlements, for example, are *diffuse* in the sense that they may start with little or no community structure. Homogeneity, in other words, cannot be assumed. Interventions are difficult here because of lack of community organisations and because initially it is not clear whose interests will, therefore, be served. In *stepping-stone communities*, planners face a different set of issues. In these places, people are transient, have no long-term commitment locally, and, if dissatisfied, will probably move rather than get involved. *Transitory neighbourhoods* may be going through a class or ethnic turnover – from middle income to upper income, for example. There will be old-timers and newcomers, and their differences will be acute. In this context, how can differences be reconciled? Who is it one plans for? The *non-neighbourhood* is most difficult for participatory planning and yet often in most need of collaborative action. Such settlements are often highly deprived socially, physically and economically, devastated by new highways or other development, with abandoned buildings and derelict sites, and with communication which is weak and loyalty which is highly fragmented. Each of these differences in social and physical configurations demands methods and techniques tailored specifically to the circumstances. Each will place limits on the degree of collaboration possible and, therefore, on the extent of outside intervention which may be necessary to get things going.

Community action planning methods advocate a participatory process for reaching decisions. If they are conducted in a climate of protest or activism, they will be viewed with suspicion by local leaders, who will suspect them as set up to expose local activists and co-opt protest. "While building a wider process of consultation under the guise of participation, vociferous or ambitious members of the community may also become clients of an agency." (Nelson & Wright 1995, 16). Where project objectives do not match political ones, those who count will not get involved. This lack of proper representation can be a serious limitation to the planning process.

Whatever the conditions and circumstances, sometimes action planning workshops can inadvertently raise expectations. Local participants may come up with "wish lists" that local government officials might want to see implemented to appease their public, and so the officials will make promises that are ill-considered technically, financially and administratively, and that later they cannot meet. Most

---

[1] From notes based on a lecture delivered by Phillip Clay, Department of Urban Studies and Planning, MIT, Cambridge, MA., autumn 1981.

who come to planning workshop sessions have a large measure of scepticism about official intentions given their past experience with government. Probably most of their contacts in the past with public authorities have been confrontational, and so many people may be bewildered by the new gestures. They will come to the workshops, if they come at all, ready to get what they can out of government. Under these circumstances, the question "What do you need?" can often draw the response "What can we have?". Robbins (1988) describes this as the manipulative posture in participatory planning.

Sometimes the presence of high-ranking officials inhibits the participation of members who see themselves as subordinates and may therefore offer what Robbins (1988, 171) calls "the subordinate view". In this instance, people "will try to frame answers in ways which they feel will give [officials] what they want or that will carry favour or approval." They will be reluctant to voice opinions that may be seen to be in stark conflict with official policy. In the same way, local people in the presence of outsiders may tell experts what they think experts want to hear by way of courtesy and thus "conceal aspects of social life, or needs may be expressed in terms of things which the project is perceived as being able to deliver." (Moss 1993).

At other times, and for similar reasons, minority ethnic groups will be reluctant to express their concerns for fear of reprisals or harassment and will fall in line with the majority point of view. In these respects the choice of appropriate technique and level of interventions is paramount.

Most times, it is likely that those who will be most reluctant to get involved will be local professionals. To many, this kind of work will lack the prestige and the rewards they had come to expect through their education as architects, engineers or planners. They will view this work as largely unglamourous, inglorious and unlikely to earn them a place in the annals of planning history. They think they will spend endless hours, evenings and weekends in meetings troubleshooting problems and negotiating alternative courses of action. Remuneration is likely to be small, much smaller than that of their international counterparts, their working environment is far worse than those working in offices, and some even feel threatened if meetings get out of hand. Few projects will have conventional "completion" dates, and they will therefore be unhelpful to conventional careers; it is not easy to compile a portfolio of projects or point to success. On top of it all, they will be under considerable peer pressure to demonstrate their creative individuality and to make good in a world that measures success in terms of professional status and prestige, usually counted in the amount of money earned, the size and location of their practice, the number of buildings built and the kind of people they know. It is unlikely that there will be much status earned, or "worthwhile" contacts made, or buildings of architectural significance built while working within the slums of Bombay, Cairo or Lima.

Some say that participatory processes of action planning take too long, that people do not know what they really want even if asked, and even when they do know, they are not properly equipped to get it.

Continuous and prolonged participation such as in the planning and implementation of integrated projects, the management of community facilities and services or loan and revolving funds requires an institutional framework, voluntary and time consuming engagement and

> *solidarity or social consensus which contradict or which are alien to the experience horizon and informal mode of communication of the residents of squatter and other low income settlements.*
>
> (Lewin 1991, 12)

Others say that the rapid techniques employed will be too rushed in the face of the time it takes to design proper projects, to ensure they are properly resourced, to get the political commitment, and so on. This "rush" toward implementation is bound to lead to mistakes which will be costly to resolve later. Yet others hold that these participatory processes increase the burden of management on already overburdened administrators, which results in delays and let-downs.

> *Participation usually failed to achieve its goals where it has reinforced the traditional existing leadership structure and dominance, where it has overburdened the neighbourhood or where residents' priorities and felt needs were not taken into account. Delays, bureaucratic constraints and attitudes as well as lack of co-ordination among the related agencies or departments or with the neighbourhood have contributed to demotivate the residents and diminish the expected impact of mobilisation and participation.*
>
> (Lewin 1991, 12)

There are, of course, truisms in all these criticisms. Do people want to get involved? Not always and certainly not unless their energies and time can result in tangible improvements to their quality of life, unless the benefits are greater than the costs (Eyben & Ladbury 1995). Do these programmes always serve the interest of poor or minority people? Not always. In cities worldwide, public participation has served in many instances to empower local communities who are organised to resist developments that may be of direct benefit to the poor who may not be so well organised. At other times, "empowered local groups could be seen as a threat to state institutions, or themselves want to threaten them" (Pretty & Chambers 1993, 24). Finally, participatory programmes are often an excuse for professional incompetence, or offered to communities by way of appeasement, by government. Participatory planning, they charge, is a measure imposed by those agencies and by poverty; most people do not want to get involved unless they have to.

Action planning menu

At the root of all action planning processes is a menu of operations and techniques for practitioners designed to incorporate the characteristics of action planning reviewed above. These include:

- direct observation (looking)
- semi-structured interviews (listening)
- measuring, learning from precedents
- resource surveys
- prioritising

Action Planning in Theory 35

Figure 2.2 Water lines can tell about water supply, water pressure, accessibility of standpipes or maintenance. Photo taken in Northern Sudan.

- brainstorming
- diagramming
- mapping and modelling
- gaming and role play
- group work and intermixing

Direct observation enables the planning team to see for themselves the conditions of the urban setting under consideration. It enables them to check information on maps and plans, which may already be out of date, with circumstances as they are. It enables them to form a preliminary opinion about how things work, based on a variety of indicators: long lines at standpipes might tell about catchment areas, inadequate water pressure, poor maintenance, or unanticipated densities, for example. Puddles will tell about poor drainage, accumulated garbage about the efficiency or appropriateness of solid waste collection (Figures 2.2 and 2.3). Planners will observe the kind of small manufacturing enterprises in existence, who plays where, who shops where. As with PRA techniques, transect walks are useful when organising observation. Similarly, groups can be organised to observe neighbourhood issues while others observe plot and house-level issues.

36 Action Planning for Cities

Figure 2.3 Informal collection of waste can tell about existing enterprises, recycling, market and production opportunities. Photo taken in Alexandria, Egypt.

Direct observation closely parallels *semi-structured interviews* – listening to the needs, problems and aspirations of local inhabitants, shopkeepers, women, children, respected elders and other key informants. Stories and oral testimonies tell how and why things work or do not work and who suffers or benefits. Individual interviews, community or group interviews and focus group discussions, and field diaries are all useful techniques. Whilst direct observation reveals information about the visible structure of settlements, interviews tell about the hidden social and economic structure of the community and can be formal or informal. Formal interviews, guided usually by questionnaires, have specific issues to which interviewers may need answers. Informal interviews are usually conversational and conducted in familiar settings, involving open questions, where one advances gradually, takes one's time and uses the vernacular in language and style (Beaudoux et al 1992).

Looking, listening and talking are usefully supplemented with *measuring* and counting – a process more quantitative than qualitative, and which offers an additional set of precedents for the sizing of roads, walkways and plots and for deciding acceptable distances to standpipes, the nearest clinic or school. We may count the number of manholes and service connections, establish where the highest land values might be and then look at where the greatest commercial activity occurs. We attempt to correlate the relative percentages of public and private land to the likely burden this implies on maintenance and administration. We might measure land utilisation percentages, circulation length area ratios and densities, all indicators of the wealth and proper functioning of urban areas.

Resource surveying, mostly conducted by communities, offers an overview of local resources which may be mobilised in any important programme proposed. Talent surveys establish who can do what, whether there are teachers, carpenters, plumbers, builders, car mechanics and the rest. Such surveying also identifies whether someone owns a truck or car which may be rented to transport materials, whether others own tools they may be prepared to loan or rent, whether there is existing space in schools or houses for the new nursery school or community centre and whether empty lots owned by the church or local authority can be used for community benefit – for play areas, new clinics or new housing. In addition, natural resources can be noted, so that later with maps and diagrams their uses and abuses can be evaluated.

Prioritising or ranking involves all stakeholders who, in view of the problems they face, decide their priorities on the basis of needs and feasibility. Prioritisation is a continuous process beginning with problems and ending with possible projects. Communities decide what they want according to now, soon and later, and continuously modify their priorities according to projects or programmes which *can start* now and those that must wait until soon or later, while, for example, money is raised, approvals sought or materials accumulated. Assessments of what communities can do themselves, versus what they may need some help with, may help reshuffle the early ranking order, as may the apportionment of budgets for each project area.

Brainstorming in mixed groups or focus groups in either open discussion or via maps and models is the principal means for exploring alternative ways to solve problems. During brainstorming, individuals or groups are not necessarily required to express commitment to the proposal nor to defend their position, nor should ideas be "evaluated" during brainstorming as this may inhibit creativity. People should not worry about right or wrong, feasible or unfeasible, but concentrate on generating ideas, discovering alternatives and soliciting responses from others.

Common to all action plans, whether for information gathering or proposal making, is *diagramming*. At the early stages in the planning process, seasonal calendars, time lines, daily routines and pie charts can tell much about population structure, the effect of seasonal climatic variation on work habits, or distances to work. Many of these diagrams can be generated by community groups and need little graphic sophistication. Later, diagrams may be useful for representing organisational structure and work schedules. Household diagrams can document household

Saturday, 3 August AM
We begin to take a visual survey of the village to discover boundaries. We make conversation with a man on his way to the village Doolgolla. He invites us to go and see his houses as well as the adjacent houses owned by his brothers. The village has about 400 houses; apparently a number of carpenters and masons live here. Although the village shares an edge with Sevanagama, it is in a different Gramodaya Mandala.

Later we talked to a builder from Doolgolla. He normally contracts to build an entire house with a labor-only estimate. The owner is liable to supply materials. When a price is agreed, he is normally paid daily, from which he pays his help. He has built a house in Sevanagama. This was built in 21 days. He guesses that the labor bill for his house was from Rs.10–14,000. It is a very big and elegant house for Sevanagama.

He also has a preferred technique for the roof. He uses cement/asbestos sheets, because he feels they are less expensive and last longer. Although the material itself is more costly, the framing required is substantially cheaper. He says a tile roof may leak after 15 years, whereas the corrugated asbestos will last for 100 years. He also points out that the sheets are perhaps better for this cool climate because they are less drafty.

One of the family members living in this group also has a house being expanded by the builder. He showed us a drawing done by Builder A that shows the finished floor plan. He has also laid out the foundation for this house and is apparently the best qualified in the Doolgolla area. These men are all impressed with his ability.

Sunday, 4 August AM
We spoke to Builder A again about the village. A little history was mentioned – first Cadjun roofs, then round tiles and finally the present rectangular tiles. He also mentioned the change from small windows to big ones. He feels that tiles are the best thing to use now, although corrugated cement/asbestos sheets are also very good. Tiles are easy to transport on the hill paths and individual breakage is less of a concern. There is also the danger of wind blowing the sheets off. Tiles are cooler. He does not like metal roofs because they are very noisy in the rain. The local name, appropriately enough, was 'takaran'.

He offered to take us to his parents house where he lived before moving to Sevanagama. Their village is called Galkanda, and is on a hill above Sevanagama. His parents house was built about 20–22 years ago, when he was doing his training (age 17).

Tuesday, 6 August AM
We went off in search of the two remaining master builders on our list. We found out that Builder B lives in Kandearawa, a village just downstream from Sevanagama. He got involved when the owner of the Shrama Nivasa, a relation of his, got in touch with him. He did all the planning, lay-out, masonry, etc. A friend helped with the roof carpentry. He has built seven additional houses there, and also the community center. His brother built the temple. The GM chairman paid for the temple and center. The owners paid for work on the houses.

There are two ways the owners will pay: Either by contract or daily pay. Generally, those with lesser resources pay daily and act as laborers when possible. At Sevanagama, this was only possible in the evenings, mornings, or on days off from work. A mason is paid Rs.60/day and laborer Rs.30/day, plus their meals. Those that contracted to have the work done did not help and usually had permanent jobs. Of the eight houses he built, five were for contract, three for daily pay. Owners are responsible to furnish/pay for all materials.

He had straight-forward advice on the costs of doing a roof as well. Because the timber for tiles is much greater than for asbestos sheets, he felt the decision should be made on the basis of timber availability. If it is locally found and used un-surfaced the tiles make more sense. But if only surfaced lumber is available (and is much more expensive), he thinks the sheets are better.

Wednesday, 7 August AM
We went to see Builder B while he was working building . . .

Figure 2.4 Looking, Listening and Measuring. From the diary of Andrew Sletterback (1986) in *Learning from Sevangama – Insights into Aspects of Support-Based Rural Housing in Sri Lanka*. (Internal MIT/NHDA report)

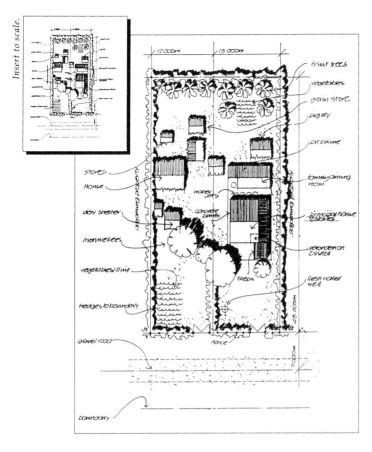

Figure 2.5 Measuring plot plans in Battambang, Cambodia, in order to predict potential for densification – a basis to providing adequate water supply. (Source: Parker et al 1994)

routines and lot usages – which later form the basis for further analysis of space needs and the sizing of lots or houses.

Mapping and modelling are useful participatory ways of documenting information and of expressing views and opinions about a neighbourhood in a non-confrontational setting. The focus for all is the maps and not the individual offering opinion or concerns. Cognitive or social maps, for example, map events in peoples' past and present experience and can reveal social and political relationships which will need to be considered when preparing proposals. They can link resource distribution with ownership and caste or population patterns, and later will help in analysing proposals in terms of their impact on social groups. Cognitive and social maps are large-scale maps on which all stakeholders record their perceptions, feelings, sentiments, prejudices, wants, needs and suggestions. Information is layered progressively using paper and glue, and equally progressively information is revealed about physical problems and needs, about people with influence, who owns what, how territorial claims work among different age groups, different religious orders, who goes where and when, who uses what and so on. Other kinds of maps may

Figure 2.6 Resource surveys in La Pintana, Santiago, Chile, to determine the community's capacity to undertake its own housing improvements.

include urban-level typography maps, identifying differences in pattern and density between one area and another, on the basis of which infrastructure and other services and utility deficiencies can be recorded. Simple models of parts of neighbourhoods made from scrap material can detail problems and issues for specific corners of a site at a large scale. Planning for Real models enable people to evaluate conditions in their neighbourhood and then to place proposals for improvement, which can then be prioritised according to now, soon or later. The making of maps and models by communities and other action planning participants helps break down barriers between "them" and "us" and builds a sense of co-operation among participants.

Games and role playing are sometimes strategically employed in action planning processes to build awareness and sensitise planners to key issues. Some games are designed to simulate potential outcomes (if you do this, then this is likely to happen). Others are used to teach skills or build awareness of planning procedures and potential hurdles in the planning process, or to familiarise people with planning jargon. "Serious games combine the analytic and questioning concentration of the scientific viewpoint with the initiative freedom and rewards of imaginative, artistic acts" (Abt 1970, 11–12). Sometimes within the context of gaming, role play can be used to build awareness of the needs and desires of groups of people who may not be well represented during the planning phases. Participants may be

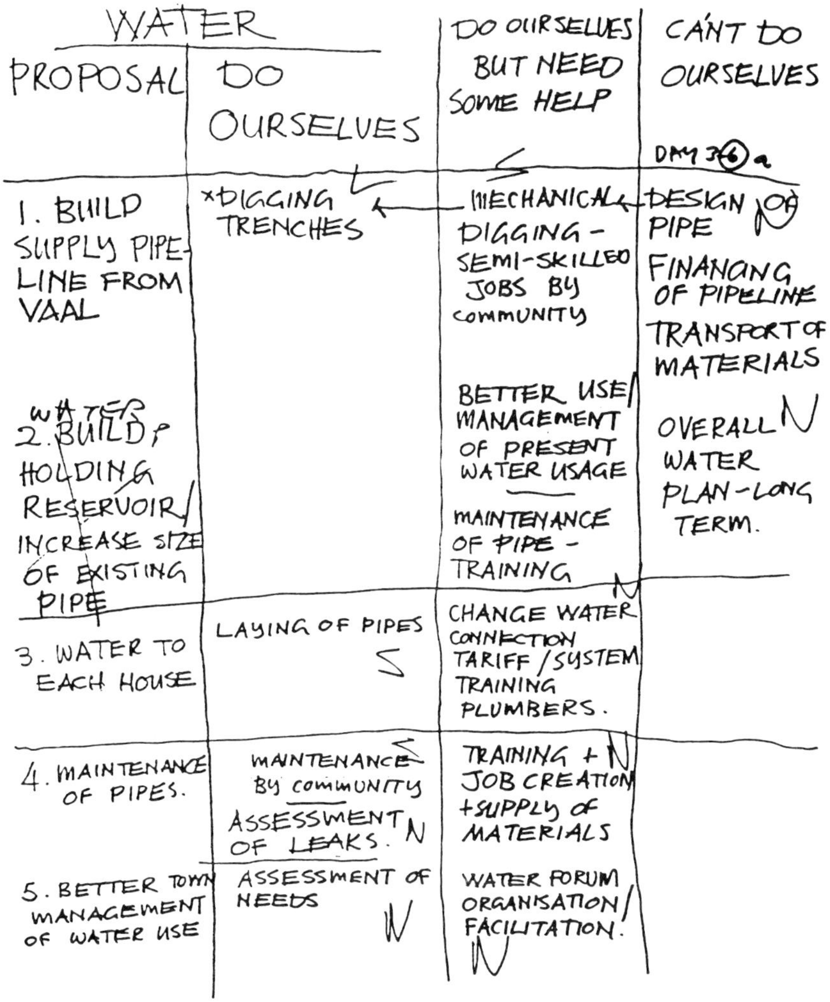

WATER PROPOSAL	DO OURSELVES	DO OURSELVES BUT NEED SOME HELP	CAN'T DO OURSELVES
1. BUILD SUPPLY PIPE-LINE FROM VAAL	×DIGGING TRENCHES	MECHANICAL DIGGING – SEMI-SKILLED JOBS BY COMMUNITY	DAY 3 6 a DESIGN OF PIPE N FINANCING OF PIPELINE TRANSPORT OF MATERIALS
2. BUILD HOLDING RESERVOIR / INCREASE SIZE OF EXISTING PIPE	WATER	BETTER USE / MANAGEMENT OF PRESENT WATER USAGE MAINTENANCE OF PIPE - TRAINING	OVERALL N WATER PLAN – LONG TERM.
3. WATER TO EACH HOUSE	LAYING OF PIPES S	CHANGE WATER CONNECTION TARIFF / SYSTEM TRAINING PLUMBERS.	
4. MAINTENANCE OF PIPES.	MAINTENANCE BY COMMUNITY ASSESSMENT OF LEAKS. N	TRAINING + N JOB CREATION + SUPPLY OF MATERIALS	
5. BETTER TOWN MANAGEMENT OF WATER USE	ASSESSMENT OF NEEDS N	WATER FORUM ORGANISATION / FACILITATION. N	

Figure 2.7 Prioritising procedures for water supply in Schweizer-Reneke, South Africa. N denotes "now" and S denotes "soon".

asked, for example, to role play or diagram their experiences in childhood, in order to expose the importance of considering children's needs in development. At other times, men can role play the role of women to highlight the burden on women in development settings. Picture analysis can be used to highlight differences in perception and values held by participants. People are asked to describe what they see in any one photograph or drawing and to discuss how conflict may develop from different understandings of the visual image. They are reminded that any one group's understanding is as good or correct as that of any other group. The purpose is to build appreciation that differences will not necessarily be threatening. Building trust is equally important to project planning. Trust walks, where one person leads

Figure 2.8 Children diagramming their needs for a community centre in Southside, Kingston, Jamaica.

another in blindfold with verbal instruction, can be useful in this respect, and these games have been applied in developing community relations in children's play (see Playboard 1990).

Finally, *group work and intermixing* of disciplines, of gender, of age groups, of experts with community people, of managers with technical staff, is fundamental to the process of action planning. Forming and reforming groups during information gathering, mapping or modelling, and proposal development, and later forming project teams around specific topics of shared concern – housing, water, employment – or shared aspirations, expose participants to the widest possible range of interests and demands, and builds co-operation amongst constituencies.

Action planning and process

Conventional analytical planning has tended to follow a linear routine of survey–analyse–plan. As illustrated in Chapter 1, procedures typically begin with extensive data collection, followed by lengthy data analysis. Options emerge for encouraging growth lines, locating industrial development, targeting infrastructure, improving transportation and so on. Each option will undergo a thorough review, involving the respective authorities, before a plan is prepared. The plan will usually form the basis to a variety of development controls which will be difficult to enforce. These development controls are then linked to policies which are designed to encourage

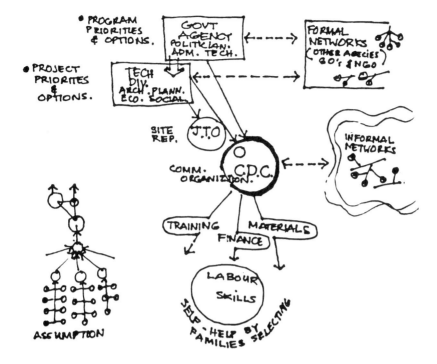

Figure 2.9 Diagramming organisational structures in the Navagamgoda projects, Sri Lanka. (Source: Solomon J. Benjamin)

more private-sector investment, for example in housing, service provision, infrastructure development. It is a lengthy process, culminating in inflexible plans which often run into difficulty during implementation, because they assume institutional and administrative resources which are rarely available. Once complete, and at best, other consultants are often hired to work on its implementation. At worst, the whole sits on some planning authority's shelf until the next round of planning. Today, this "arthritis of orthodox planning still paralyses urban management practices in developing countries" (Baross 1991, 4).

In contrast, action planning typically includes the following phases whose final objective is *implementation*, whatever the sequence of work:

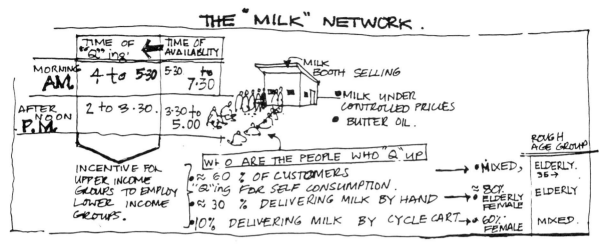

Figure 2.10 Diagramming the milk run in Bhogal, India, in order to understand networks and relationships. (Source: Solomon J. Benjamin)

- problems and opportunities
- goals and priorities
- options and tradeoffs
- resources and constraints
- project teams and tasks
- implementation and monitoring

The process begins with identifying problems – in a manner which avoids apportioning blame – and with identifying opportunities. It will begin on site, in a workshop setting, the site having been selected for improvement from the many others with equal need probably because the community had successfully negotiated "votes for improvement" – promising local party members a block vote in the next round of elections in return for better housing and utilities and more investment in jobs and health services.

Problem solving will depend on problem finding and should be "focused on well-defined spatial units whose boundaries usually do not coincide with the routine

Figure 2.11 Communities in Topeka, Kansas, working with maps.

operational boundaries of the intervening agencies. It is through repeated social articulation of the "problem", usually incubated through a long history of political pressure, which defines its spatial location and extent, rather than arrived at through a series of analytical planning studies." (Baross 1991, 4). The initial list of wants might be "favorite laments of individuals ('we must stop squatters') or slogans of politicians ('provide water for all'). It is also likely that problems which may be high on the planners' agenda have no resonance at the institutional or political level (increased co-ordination, lower standards, preservation of aquifers). Yet sieving out individual or clusters of problems which are widely held and strongly believed to be solvable within a foreseeable future . . . is the crucial starting point for action planning, establishing the initial condition for pursuing legitimate objectives for planning." (Baross 1991, 15).

Analysis at this stage will focus on clarity with four objectives in mind: to avoid preconceptions about solutions which will come to mind as problems are discussed (e.g. our children need more facilities for play, why can't we have a new playground); to observe where there is already consensus about issues; to flag potentially

Figure 2.12 Programme development through cognitive mapping. (Source: W. Mike Martin)

conflicting demands; and to read what seem to be differences but are in fact similarities expressed or interpreted in different ways. In all, the need is to position problems well enough in order to induce appropriate solutions. An example will illustrate.

There was, on one site, an agreed demand to improve health services in the area. The community representative had asked for a new clinic to be built, assuming this to be the obvious route to improvement. After more analysis, local officials argued that a clinic existed within a short bus ride for most families and that investment in building was neither justified nor necessary. Official standards suggested a perfectly adequate match between the existing facility and its catchment, its size, location, and the services it offered. More analysis, however, revealed that the real issue of concern was not the availability of a clinic but accessibility to it. People were intimidated by the formal procedures for making appointments (which in the absence of telephones usually required at least two trips), by the long wait once there (for which many people would lose a full day's income), by the preference given to those of higher income or class, and by the expense of the bus ride. Thus, a very different set of issues was revealed.

The first options considered included a mobile service facility, converting an existing unused building into a medical centre, and creating a special unit within the existing clinic to expedite diagnosis and treatment. In practice, however, the medical team argued that the most common cause of complaint was diarrhoea (something which will have been confirmed after a short visit to the clinic) and its associated symptoms of dehydration. If this were so, they argued, then local community-based paramedics might be trained to identify symptoms

Figure 2.13 Working with models in Cambridge, Massachusetts, using scrap material.

and to train families in the use of oral rehydration, a simple self-administered procedure that would relieve the burden on central medical facilities, speed the process, cut costs, generate income locally, and save lives. They might need to train people in personal hygiene and food preparation, storage and feeding, and therefore correct the conditions that caused the problem. When symptoms are not diagnosable locally, families would continue to be referred to the existing nearby clinic, where paramedics might mediate between families and doctors and so facilitate access.

In this example, community members expressed a desire for a particular facility. The planners then identified the legitimacy of their demand and the source or cause of their complaint. What might have been a simplistic, inaccurate and wasteful response became a package of responses: training paramedics, training families, a well-tried process of self-help treatment, facilitating access to existing services and locally staffed informal clinics serviced periodically by a mobile unit. A "system"

48 Action Planning for Cities

MENU OF OPERATIONS	PHASES OF WORK					
	Problems Opportunities	Goals Priorities	Options Tradeoffs	Resources Constraints	Projects Tasks	Implementation Monitoring
Direct Observation	×			×		×
Interviews	×			×		×
Measuring	×			×		×
Resource Surveying				×		
Prioritising	×	×	×		×	×
Brainstorming		×	×			
Diagramming	×		×	×	×	
Mapping/Modelling	×		×			
Gaming/Role Play	×		×			
Group Work	×	×	×	×	×	×

Figure 2.14 For each phase of action planning a menu of operations and techniques are usefully employed.

emerged more suited to the complexity of conditions actually encountered, and substantially cheaper than a fully staffed new building.

The progressive definition of problems, prioritised, interpreted and positioned according to cause and effect (why is it a problem and to whom), is a basis to goal setting – what do we need, what resources do we have, what can we build on, what can we realistically expect to achieve? Goals are prioritised according to need and then ranked according to feasibility. Alternative strategies are worked out for how to get what is needed, and again prioritised according to urgency, desirability and feasibility. For each option we devise, we give some consideration to the risks involved, the investment entailed, the commitment demanded, and the likely constraints to be encountered. How likely is it that we will we get what we want if we ask for a new school building and what or who is likely to get in our way? Should we modify this demand? How much money will it entail and what investment of time and energy? To what extent will it tie us down over the longer term in repayments, tasks, time, and so on? Constraints are analysed in terms of what or who will get in the way of getting projects going, which will typically include institutional, financial, technical, environmental or political hurdles which have to be overcome. Once identified, ideas and procedures for overcoming hurdles are brainstormed – who can help, how and when. Doable projects are identified – those that can start sooner rather than later – and then analysed in terms of their resource demands and their relative dependencies and interdependency.

We want to judge how some of the objectives, strategies and the solutions are interconnected – how dependent or independent they are of each other.

Action Planning in Theory 49

Figure 2.15 The start to a field-based action planning workshop in Sri Lanka.

Within each functioning system, some parts are more crucial than others. Components that handle the planning or steering for the whole system are more critical than those that take care of some small aspect of a technical routine. One may ask: on what does everyone and everything depend? On what do many things depend? Relatively few things depend? Rather than a condition of equality or a classless state, we find arrangements of subordinate and superordinate units.

(Winner 1977, 184–185)

We consider which components or clusters of components will have greatest bearing on the proper functioning of the whole. A hierarchical order will appear and will need to be understood to avoid delay in project development. We may want to review each of the strategies devised in the early phases of programming in view of these linkages – not to change ideas or reshuffle priorities, but perhaps to rearrange our approach, introduce components of design that may not have featured, or devise alternatives that are more likely to succeed. This is an evaluative and reformative process, based often on experience and reflection rather than on a discrete phase of work. It might suggest more appropriate phasing of work or additional interventions that may be demanded from government and professionals.

Linkage analysis involves two related processes. The first involves ranking the hierarchical order of importance of project parts and phases. The second deals with types or categories of linkages.

The first is best illustrated by example. It is common practice for public utility lines to be installed along public thoroughfares. The water line is installed in the road rather than through houses, with spurs feeding individual houses. It is done this way so that if there is a breakage in any one house, the entire system is not disrupted.

The laying of pipes assumes a hierarchical order. Even decisions on whether households should receive individual supplies or whether to charge for their utilities does not delay the installation of the mains. This hierarchy of pipes sets up hierarchies of organisation. The main supply is managed and controlled by a collective body – a community group, a local authority, a co-operative. It need not interfere with details of house design and construction, which it would do if the pipes ran through the houses. The public authority can install its utilities before, during or after house construction. It is independent of house connection and even independent of deciding how many households there will be, precisely where they will go, and how tall buildings will be, except in the most general way. The household manages and controls its own installation. It can even choose to ignore the main supply if, for example, it does not want to pay for it, and continue to fetch water from the nearby standpipe or pay for it through local vendors. Simple as it is, the arrangement provides substantial flexibility, achieved largely through commonsense design.

The second thing to think about in linkage analysis is the nature of the linkages themselves. We go about this task by considering three categories, which we will call *consequential*, *complementary* and *conflict*. In the first case (consequential), there will be things we *need* to do to ensure the success of what we *want* do. We need to supply clean water to improve health; we need training if clean water is to remain clean until the time it is consumed. Providing direct water supply to each household, with all good intentions to control the quality of water and prevent disease, could result in much poorer sanitation and an increase in health risks, unless better systems of wastewater removal are also installed. "There is no point in designing a scheme which is dependent on daily solid waste collection, or monthly emptying of septic tanks, if the only services available are weekly or annually." (Kirke 1984, 237). In the second case (complementary), the things which we need can be used to greater advantage when linked to other things which we want in the interests of broader community, urban, or national gain.

Let us first illustrate how consequential and complementary linkages can work. Let us assume that a water-borne sewage system is proposed as one component among others for improving conditions in a settlement. Two consequential links are immediately identified to ensure the success of this proposal and to validate the decision in the first place. The first is an adequate supply of water; the second is an effective system for controlling garbage disposal. In different ways, both ensure that the system will remain free of garbage, although each may be independent so far as installation and timing of installation are concerned. In this case, decision-making responsibilities are clearly defined and independent, other than the usual task of co-ordinating the work of contractors, sewage, garbage, and water.

In the second case, links may need to be made so that initial interventions can contribute to broader developmental gains. In the previous example, we may want to link the control and disposal of garbage to an equivalent programme of health education, and connect garbage directly in people's minds to the health hazards facing every family. Garbage collection may also be linked with employment generation. Here it could be handled by local enterprises, releasing the burden on local administrations and generating income in the process. Depending on the scale and organisation of this enterprise, garbage can be recycled, generating small-scale commerce and industry, and so more money. Government may even contemplate two further interventions to support these activities. First, they could create a market for these goods. Second, they may issue small business loans and even tools to encourage the enterprises.

One further point is worth making here: most problems of high priority usually take the longest to implement, and their success and impact are usually measured and felt over relatively long periods of time (examples are employment generation, health improvement and better education). Effective services, such as garbage collection, cannot be delivered without access to settlements. And access cannot be secured unless there is some measure of land regularisation. Communities with garbage collection at the top of their priority list will need to know why work starts by regulating land. And having discovered this, community members may decide that regulating land will be too disruptive because people will have to move, houses will have to be removed, some will lose land for road widening, others will quibble over the precise boundary to their site, and people will appear on the tax register. For all these reasons, residents may seek alternative ways to dispose of garbage, not necessarily based on access for the municipality's trucks. An important distinction has to be made between priorities and starting points; the two are often muddled.

The third kind of linkage, which completes the analysis, is to expose connections that could lead to conflict. Even when all parties have agreed, for example, on solution A, conflicts may arise because in doing A we find we will also have to live with B. If B outweighs the advantages gained by A, then clearly A is the wrong course of action, whatever its merits. In this case, we may either change or modify A or, more likely, work toward A over a longer time frame whilst first ameliorating B. The situation is made more complex if A is something demanded by one party and yet the impact to B will largely be felt by another. In this case, the second party will have to convince the first that what is likely to be bad for them will also be bad for the public at large. In other words, their interest in dealing first with B will have to converge to avoid delay and prevent raising expectations.

During the final phase of planning, project teams are formed and a plan of action is devised and phased with timetables, costs, commitments and responsibilities. "Whilst these projects may be ill-conceived, uncoordinated, technically naive, fragmented, socially unproductive (just to list a few of the common criticisms advanced from the armchair of analytical planning), they represent developmental avenues behind which the desire (and a degree of competence) to implement is manifested." (Baross 1991, 19).

Project monitoring and urban reconnaissance

For city-level planning, community action plans serve to offer an early insight into the organisational capabilities of communities, the responsiveness of planners and government authorities, the appropriateness of standards and city-level planning procedures, the potential for partnership, and the resistance of those in charge to change or adapt. They are vehicles for learning and for identifying institutional capabilities and training needs, as much as for solving local problems. They offer a basis with which to organise communities in ways to lobby city authorities for strategic city-level change. In this way, action planning serves important strategic functions which can influence policy and ensure local-level participation in the governance of cities. Neighbourhood organisations and community groups can "carry their development beyond the bridges, schools, cottage industries or day-care centres" (O'Gorman 1995, 213) through a variety of mediums (newspapers and television, popular movements, political negotiations) and so influence or help formulate public policy.

The rationality of action planning lies in the proposition that once sufficient work is done at the neighbourhood level pressure begins to build up to act at city level. This philosophy of "acting to induce others to act" starts, in contrast to the orthodoxy of analytical planning, with project planning not with data studies. The objective is to channel lessons from the local level to city or strategic-level institutions. Thus, as illustrated in Figure 2.16, monitoring and learning from the local level enables structure plans to be formed, modified or validated, and policies to be influenced.

Local plans are monitored and evaluated in terms of city needs and resources – for health, transportation, water and housing, for example. On the basis of these assessments, city-level investment options can be decided and policy implementation considered. Through time, data will be gathered and progressively updated in order to monitor performance and judge the impact of policy – and be fed back to (as it was derived from) local-level problems and opportunities. It is here that planners or NGOs play a new and facilitator role: "to carry the community struggle to other levels of society – especially to project funders – consistently and constantly, without losing touch with the base community, in order to influence the transformation of society." (O'Gorman 1995, 213).

Monitoring (learning), therefore, plays a key role in action planning, more so perhaps than otherwise. Project leaders and managers will want to know the impact of their work at two levels. First they will consider whether it meets the objectives of the programme at the *local level* as well as assessing the value of methods employed. They will want to ask: how is it working and what can we learn? Second, what impact is the programme likely to have at *city level*?

At the project level, indicators of achievement will be developed. Many of these will be strictly quantitative and can be measured – the amount of water delivered, the reduction in diarrhoeal diseases, the number of houses built. Others will be less easy to measure and will be more qualitative or judgemental in character, assessed in terms of good, adequate, fair or bad. Qualitative assessments are, therefore, best done with beneficiaries and project operatives – women whose participation was to be encouraged, managers whose efficiency was to be improved, children whose access to play facilities or schools were to be facilitated, small entrepreneurs who were to benefit from new lines of credit or from business starters.

A monitoring team of informants is established who may meet in "workshop" settings and report back periodically over an agreed period of time. This method of participatory monitoring and appraisal helps link project criteria directly to the failures, successes or benefits as felt by beneficiaries, and, furthermore, ensures that local and project-level people will have a voice at the "high table" of policy makers, or at least will have channels to it.

Action Planning in Theory

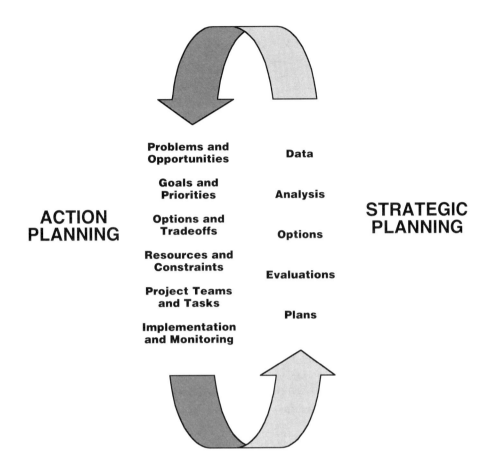

Figure 2.16 From action plans to strategic plans.

Beaudoux et al (1992, 124–128) suggest a number of indicators for monitoring which, when compared together, serve to cross check the benefits and anomolies of projects.

- *Technical indicators*, as with others, can be assessed both quantitatively and qualitatively. Quantitatively, road improvements may have reduced flooding and improved access for vehicles. Qualitatively, for pedestrians, access remains poor. Quantitatively, new standpipes may have reduced walking distances. Qualitatively, the supply of water remains inadequate. Quantitatively, new housing will have increased the stock of houses. Qualitatively, the houses may be too small or of the wrong kind.

- *Economic indicators* will, for example, judge the cost-effectiveness of programmes, or the increased level of earnings due to employment programmes, or the effect of starter loans for small businesses. Comparing these to the technical indicators can identify anomolies. For example, in South Africa housing subsidies have been reasonably successful in targeting low-income families, counted in the number of loans disbursed. However, when cross-checked against technical criteria on the ground (how many new houses), the number of new houses built was not reflected according to the loans disbursed. Further analysis indicates that of the 15 000 rand subsidy paid to families earning less than 800 rand per month, some 10 000 rand went in fees and charges, leaving little to invest in housing.

- *Operating or organisational indicators* tell about the functioning and effectiveness of organisations during project delivery, management or maintenance. An informal organisation for solid waste collection which depends for its earnings on good quality waste is unlikely to be effective in collecting the garbage from low-income areas. In Helwan, Egypt, co-operatives were unfamiliar culturally as decision-making entities, in lieu of systems which were largely dependent on patronage. In Cambodia, participatory community organisation as promoted by outsiders was mistrusted in view of the history of community organisation under the Khmer Rouge.

- *Social indicators* inform about difficulties for one group or another (women, for example, or minority ethnic groups) to be involved in programmes, or to have taken advantage of loan schemes or enterprise development. This kind of assessment may lead to alternative programmes directed specifically at the excluded groups – such as the Grameen Bank's strategy of targeting loans to women – or to a reformulation of programmes. Access to schools, clinics or new housing are good indicators of discrimination, territorial demarcations a sign of control, and so on.

- *Environmental indicators* judge the impact of interventions on the environment. This may include assessing the impact of improved sanitation on health, or the impact of projects on the ecology of neighbourhoods. Low-resource projects for housing, for example, which promote locally available material, may result in deforestation or in soil erosion.

Whilst all the above indicators are directed at assessing the performance of projects and programmes at the local level, they can also inform urban-level interventions and the strategic needs and operations of cities.

This process from local to strategic-level planning, where interventions are decided according to the strategic needs of cities linked to the deficiencies and other demands of localities, is guided by a parallel process of urban-level monitoring, using rapid techniques of *reconnaissance and analysis*. This process might include the following operations:

- *Identify typologies*; maps, aerial photos, field observations, census, cadastral.
- *Map characteristics*; income, housing, plot sizes, density network efficiencies, growth patterns, land markets.
- *Establish deficiencies*; housing, services, utilities, employment.
- *Target sectoral investment*; deficiency analysis, urban priorities.

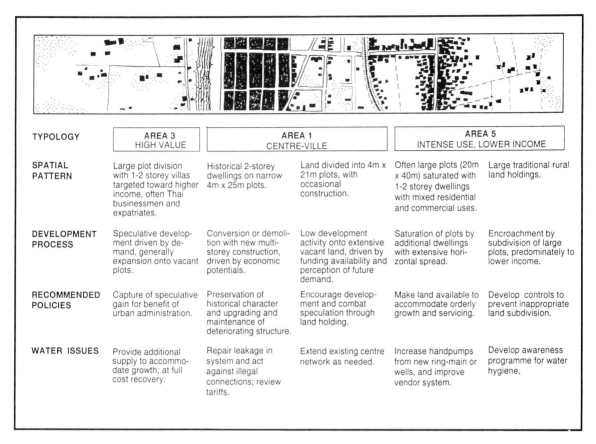

Figure 2.17 Identifying urban characteristics or typologies as a basis to deciding interventions and monitoring urban development. (Source: Parker et al 1994)

- *Decide policy interventions*; policy framework, institutional capacity, investment targeting, human resource development, legal and legislative frameworks, financing.

Urban-level reconnaissance utilises maps, aerial photos, field observations, secondary sources of data and any other census or cadastral information which may be easily available. As much, it would be based on talking to people – to community leaders, local entrepreneurs, families and public officials – and listening to stories, problems, needs, desires and the like. The emphasis is on sampling the dynamics of city systems, assessing from the grassroots the impact of interventions, and speculating on future growth and development. The information is rudimentary, sometimes out of date and always incomplete, but need only be good enough to get a sense of how things work, who is in charge and where best to intervene. It will have provided a profile or "snapshot" of city characteristics as illustrated in Figures 2.17 and 2.18 which show rapid appraisal techniques for mapping and monitoring, in Battambang, Cambodia, directed in

SUMMARY OF RECOMMENDATIONS	*To address uncertainty about the extent and direction of urban growth:*	*To address lack of institutional capacity:*
	1. DEVELOP MONITORING PROCEDURES AS A TRIGGER TO INVESTMENT PLANNING FOR INFRASTRUCTURE.	**2** PROVIDE URBAN MANAGEMENT TECHNICAL ASSISTANCE TO THOSE INSTITUTIONS RESPONSIBLE FOR PLANNING AND SUSTAINING WATER AND SANITATION EFFORTS.
IMMEDIATE ACTIONS:	■ Develop and <u>set-up monitoring</u> programme. ■ <u>Prepare basic plans</u> on a "need to know" basis (eg.: topography levels at key points on aerial photography) as required by various agencies as a base for future GIS mapping and planning systems. 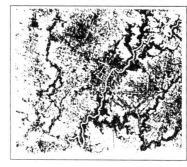	■ Provide <u>technical assistance</u> to four levels of government: *Strategic level:* Enhancement Commission (Province): Policy analysis and programme development *Programming and Implementation level:* Urban Improvement (Embellishment) Commission (Town): Programme development, management training, and technical support *Implementation level:* Village Chiefs (Town): Leadership and awareness training *Community level:* Villages: Awareness programmes. Technical assistance would include: advice on appropriate policy interventions in response to town development, assessment of programmes, coordination and supervision of mapping, short-term training needs and coordination of workshops. Expertise would include: water and sanitary engineer, urban planner, social development/training advisor. ■ Undertake <u>annual workshops</u> to coordinate policies among agencies, training centres, universities and technical colleges.
SHORT-TERM ACTIONS:		■ Organize comprehensive <u>training programmes</u> for local government staff, stressing both management and technical skills.

Figure 2.18 From action plans to strategic plans – recommendations for Battembang, Cambodia. (Source: Parker et al 1994)

this case to planning for its infrastructure development. Local university staff, NGOs, local authorities and other public officials will have taken a lead role in reconnaissance, guided by a professional team of planners, demographers and social development experts. In the example illustrated, the process took some two to three months to complete.

At the same time, the process above, and in particular the typologies identified, would provide "early warning" indicators of the magnitude, direction and form of growth and of changing land markets. Key indicators of change might include population growth, land values, densification patterns, property title transfers, and building construction activity. The process itself could be carried out in several ways: by training local communities to keep tabs on the key indicators identified above; by using spot satellite data or aerial photographs. For example, use could be made of higher resolution and cheaply available large-format satellite imagery to generate scalable photographic images and later, if needed, to build future GIS data files. Whilst actual population estimates would continue to be generated from ground surveys, spot images taken, say, every six months would provide conclusive

To address uncertainties in overcoming current deficiencies in water supply:

3. DEVELOP MEASURES WHICH CONSIDER WATER SYSTEMS CATERING TO DIFFERENCES IN DEMAND AND WHICH CAN BE EASILY EXTENDED TO MEET UNCERTAINTIES IN GROWTH.

- Develop appropriate <u>measures for both piped and vendor water systems</u> for differences in circumstances. This may include a ring main to reinforce existing networks which provides an alternative supply source for existing private vendor systems and which can be expanded in response to growth.

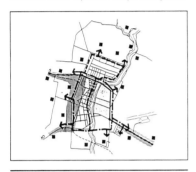

To address lack of appropriate land policies and procedures:

4. DEVELOP LAND POLICIES TO REDRESS INEQUITY IN ACCESS TO SERVICES AND LAND, AND WHICH AMELIORATE THE NEGATIVE EFFECTS OF LAND SPECULATION AND LAND HOLDINGS.

- Develop general <u>policies and regulatory framework for priority areas</u>: Informal low income (Typology Area 5), Formal speculative (Typology Areas 2 and 3), Centre-ville preservation and maintenance (Typology Area 1), and Commercial strip growth (Route 5, both east and west of town).

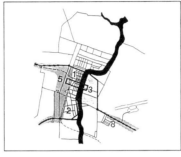

- Assist in developing <u>comprehensive policies</u> for urban area.

To address loss of institutional memory:

5. DOCUMENT METHODOLOGY FOR LOCAL USE AND POTENTIAL WIDER DISSEMINATION.

- Prepare <u>operating procedure</u> to institutionalize methodology.

- Prepare <u>documentation</u> for wider dissemination (Rapid Low-cost Monitoring System).

Figure 2.18 (continued)

evidence of the extent, direction and speed of spatial development. In all respects, some technical assistance might be desirable – to set up systems, train local staff and build the institutional capability to monitor changes effectively.

References

Abt, C.C. 1970. *Serious Games*. New York: Viking.

Baross, P. 1991. *Action Planning*. Rotterdam: Institute for Housing and Urban Development Studies, Working Papers No. 2.

Beaudoux, E., Crombrugghe, G. de, Douxchamps, F., Guenuea, M.-C. & Nieuwkert, M. 1992. *Supporting Development Action from Identification to Evaluation*. London: Macmillan Press.

Burgess, R. 1982. Self-help housing advocacy: a curious form of radicalism. A critique of the work of John F.C. Turner. In Ward, P.M. (ed.), *Self-help Housing: A Critique*, pp. 56–57. London: Mansell Publishing.

Chambers, R. 1992. *Rural Appraisal: Rapid, Relaxed and Participatory*. Brighton: Institute of Development Studies, Discussion Paper 311.

Chambers, R. 1993. *Challenging the Professions: Frontiers for Rural Development*. London: Intermediate Technology Publications.

Cook, D.B. 1979. City strategies and action planning. Paper presented at a course on "Managing Urban Growth" at the Economic Development Institute, the World Bank.

Devas, N. 1993. Evolving approaches. In Devas, N. & Rakodi, C. (eds), *Managing Fast Growing Cities*. Harlow: Longman Scientific & Technical.

Dube, S.C. 1988. *Modernisation and Development: The Search for Alternative Paradigms*. London: ZED Books.

Eyben, R. and Ladbury, S. 1995. Popular participation in aid-assisted projects: why more in theory than practice? In Nelson, N. & Wright, S. (eds), *Power and Participatory Development*. London: Intermediate Technology Publications.

Hamdi, N. 1991/1995. *Housing Without Houses: Participation, Flexibility, Enablement*. New York: Van Nostrand Reinhold; London: Intermediate Technology Publications.

Kirke, J. 1984. The Provision of Infrastructure and Utility Services. In Payne, G.K. (ed.), *Low-Income Housing in the Developing World*, pp. 233–248. New York: John Wiley & Sons.

Koenigsberger, O. 1964. Action planning. *Architectural Association Quarterly*, May 1964.

Koenigsberger, O. 1987. The intentions of housing policy alternatives, their development and impact in the third world since the 1950s. Paper presented to the "International Symposium on the Implications of a Support Policy for Housing Provision", Development Planning Unit, University College, London, 9–11 December.

Lewin, A.C. 1991. Neighbourhood participation in urban projects: The role of the donor agencies. Unpublished paper presented to the GTZ Experts' Conference, Dakar, Senegal.

McGill, M.E. & Horton, M.E. 1973. *Action Research Design: For Training and Development*. Washington, DC: National Training and Development Press.

Mitlin, D. & Thompson, J. 1994. Addressing the gaps or dispelling the myths? Participatory approaches in low-income urban communities. In RRA Notes, No. 21. November 1994. *Special Issue on Participatory Tools and Methods in Urban Areas*. London: International Institute for Environment and Development.

Moss, D. 1993. *Authority, Gender, Knowledge: Theoretical Reflection on the Practice of Participatory Rural Appraisal*. Overseas Development Institute Network Paper No. 44, December 1993.

Nelson, N. & Wright, S. 1995. Participation and power. In Nelson, N. & Wright, S. (eds), *Power and Participatory Development*. London: Intermediate Technology Publications.

O'Gorman, F. 1995. Brazilian community development: changes and challenges. In Craig, G. & Mayo, M. (eds), *Community Empowerment: A Reader in Participation and Development*. London: ZED Books.

Ovitt, G. 1989. Appropriate technology: development and social change. *Monthly Review* 40 (9): 22–32.

Parker, S., Gunne-Jones, A., Goethert, R. & Hamdi, N. 1994. *Battambang Urban Water Development Cambodia. Final Report Urban Planning and Mapping Study*, March 1994. Report prepared for the Overseas Development Administration (ODA).

Peattie, L.R. 1982. Some second thoughts on sites and services. *Habitat International* 6 (1/2): 131–138.

Playboard, September 1990. *Play Without Frontiers: A Policy Document on Community Relations in Children's Play*. Belfast: Playboard.

Pretty, J. & Chambers, R. 1993. *Towards a Learning Paradigm: New Professionalism and Institutions for Agriculture*. Brighton: Institute of Development Studies, Discussion Paper 344.

Robbins, E. 1988. Doing socio-cultural analysis: implications for practice in the field. In Goethert, R. & Hamdi, N. (eds), *Refugee Camps: A Primer for Site Planning – Land, Shelter, Infrastructure, Services*. Draft manual prepared for the United Nations High Commission for Refugees, Geneva.

Safier, M. 1974. An action planning approach to possible patterns and solutions for accelerated urbanisation. Presented at the Royal Town Planning Institute Overseas Summer School, September 1974.

Schumacher, E.F. 1973. *Small is Beautiful: A Study of Economics as if People Mattered*. London: Abacus.
Stretton, H. 1978. *Urban Planning in Rich and Poor Countries*. Oxford: Oxford University Press.
Winner, L. 1977. *Autonomous Technology: Technics-out-of-Control as a Theme in Political Thought*. Cambridge, MA: MIT Press.

SECTION 2
Tools for Practice

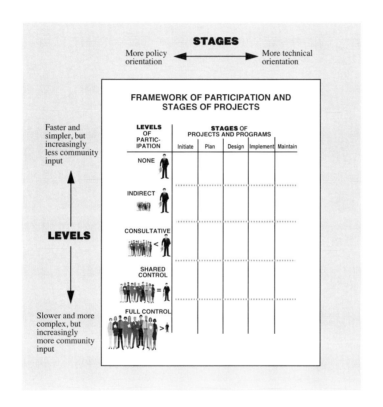

CHAPTER 3
Deciding on Tools: Community Projects and City Plans

What good is running if one is on the wrong road.
English Proverb

Tools and techniques for community-level planning have proliferated in recent years, exemplified in the plethora of handbooks and planning guides designed to maximise community participation. How does one decide the appropriate package from the many choices now available?

Tools and techniques, if they are to be practical, must be simple to use despite the complexities of the circumstances they are likely to confront. They demand flexibility in their framework which is easy to modify and which adapts to differences in specific demands from site to site and case to case. The best tools have been designed from practice and modified as a result of direct experience in field applications, rather than from theory–method–practice routines.

In this chapter, we offer a framework for thinking about tools and techniques, for deciding appropriate *levels* of community participation for the various *stages* of projects and deciding appropriate partnerships between communities and "outsiders".

In considering the framework, we propose five levels of community involvement – none, indirect, consultative, shared control and full control – for each of five strategic stages of project planning – initiation, plan making, design, implementation and maintenance. Whilst the framework helps position choices across a wide range of demands, the key to effective community action planning is *shared control in plan making*, as illustrated in Figure 3.9.

Tools and techniques

As defined in this discussion *"tools"* refers to a comprehensive approach when working with communities, starting with identifying problems on through to an action plan. Tools offer a broader development perspective for project work, rather than the more narrow perspective of technique for achieving a specific task. Tools are composed of a bundle of techniques which provide the ways for undertaking specific tasks. The "Community Action Planning/Microplanning" workshop approach used by the authors falls in this category of "tool", as does "Planning for Real" offered through the Neighbourhood Initiatives Foundation. There are a relatively limited number of comprehensive tools available for community processes which have a longer history of use. Chapter 4 will review the most prominent four used in the field.

As distinct from tools, *"techniques"* are modalities with which to perform specific tasks. For example in doing participatory workshops, various "techniques" are used at each stage: how to "break the ice", how to get people to participate, how to avoid domination by one or other person in groups. Good techniques should only mediate the process and should not predetermine or influence the outcome. There are many good handbooks and reports which cover in detail all aspects of technique and no attempt will be made to review these here. However, as a resource for the practitioner, a selection of references are included at the end of this chapter and Chapter 4.

Underlying concerns of community processes

Experience shows that there are several key issues which recur when preparing development plans with communities. These need to be considered at the start of projects. They include how to carry over the process into implementation, how to avoid excessive dependency on the outsiders, how to avoid "highjacking" by professionals, how to assure continuity and how to expand and learn from pilot efforts. One of the marks of a "good" tool is how it incorporates these considerations in the family of techniques that it uses.

Throughout the participatory process *dependency* haunts communities. It is tempting to rely on professionals to step in and quickly solve selected issues, which in the short run may be advantageous but as a precedent for the long term solves little. It is also tempting for the professionals to position themselves as the sole source of information. This unequal access to information polarises power and can lead to full control of the participatory process by outsiders. One result is that professionals often assume superiority and lose the essence of a true participatory process involving mutual interchange of knowledge. Professionals come to *dominate* the process instead of providing *assistance* to it.

Related to dependency, there is the danger of outright *"highjacking"* of community efforts by outsiders serving their own self-interest. Robert Chambers,[1] in his book *Rural Development: Putting the Last First*, expressed this well and makes an interesting comparison between the practitioner and the academic researcher. The practitioner is too often judged by his or her peers according to a professional value

---

[1] See, for example, chapters on "How Outsiders Learn" and "Whose Knowledge".

structure, rather than the success of the community effort. One result is the tendency to experiment at the expense of community needs.

Most difficult is the task of *assuring continuity* after a participatory community process has been initiated. The euphoria of the moment and the dynamics of the interaction are generally difficult to sustain, and successful processes must have a built-in vision toward the long-term goal of implementation. The moderator of the workshop can no longer call on his/her "bag of tricks" and the community must stand on its own strengths. An outcome of any community event must be the explicit recording of "next steps", which includes who does what and when. Successful participation must lead to concrete projects. The ultimate test, after all, is implementation of a plan, and not the plan itself. Communities can rapidly lose interest and become discouraged when their efforts lead nowhere.

Related to continuity is *expansion* of a successful process beyond an initial pilot effort. Pilot, or one-off projects are relatively easy to undertake. The problem is expanding any programme for wider application. Three related factors make this difficult: (1) the difficulty of assuring support beyond an initial effort, (2) the lack of political will, and (3) the lack of a conceptual underpinning. To expand implies a higher risk due to continued involvement, since the nature of the process tends to be open-ended and results unpredictable. Furthermore, programme expansion requires involvement of others outside of the community who may not share community concerns. These may be at the city level or even at the provincial or national level.

Expansion is more difficult starting from a bottom-up approach as commonly found in many NGO projects, due to their limited funds. Top-down experience is harder to find, except for the landmark Sri Lankan case with their Million Houses Programme. This deliberate, central governmental programme to improve neighbourhoods targeted both rural and urban areas and set about inventing a structure that could deliver improvements in a participatory methodology throughout the country. The Community Action Planning/Microplanning approach by the authors was developed to provide the mechanism to carry this out and an integral training-of-trainers programme was designed which provided the skills for widespread dissemination.

Technique is the key to overcome many of these difficulties. For example, one way to overcome a tendency of dominance is to limit the role of outsiders by formally structuring their involvement in ways which mitigates opportunities for dominance. This should not be left to improvisation nor given excessive flexibility. Techniques need to be mastered by participatory practitioners but should be biased toward community inputs.

Use in training, or coupling training with doing, is one way that the tool can address expansion goals and a training component should be integral to the process. Prerequisite for long-term success of projects and programmes is an effective in-place community leadership structure and closely linked is leadership strengthening and development. Failure to strengthen or develop leadership is a failure of the tool applied.

Later in this chapter a comprehensive approach is illustrated that couples the appropriate tools used for a linked city plus community framework, and provides a mechanism for tackling strategic and community concerns.

66 Action Planning for Cities

A framework for thinking about tools

As an aid for examining tools and techniques, the *stages of a project or programme* are linked in a matrix to their appropriate *levels of participation* (see Figure 3.1). The level or degree of participation, ranging from no participation to full control by a community, is on the vertical axis. On the horizontal axis are the phases, or stages of projects and programmes, starting with initiation through to maintenance. The matrix allows examination of the levels of participation and helps us to understand where community involvement would be most necessary, or where the community would be better served through other methods, albeit with limited community inputs.

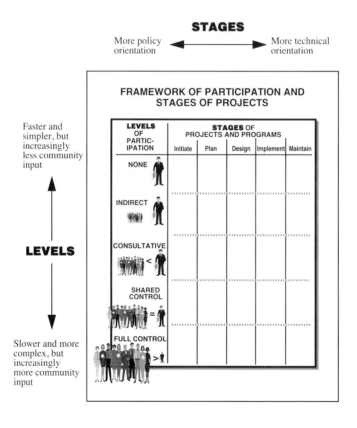

Figure 3.1 General framework for positioning participation efforts.

The matrix assumes three underlying premises: (1) Community participation is not taken as an end in itself, but more as a means toward community development. This is not to say that community participation *per se* is not desirable, but instead should be biased toward tangible outcomes. (2) Both city and community interests are equally legitimate and mutually reinforce each other. (3) Appropriate techniques vary according to the degree – or level – of participation desired or achievable and related to the stages of a project. The modality of interaction is considered the most important.

Levels and stages are linked to the tools and techniques employed. These are critical in achieving desired interaction and outcome. For each level, tools need to be identified which are appropriate to the goals. For example, at the "consultative" level techniques that bring out responses of the community are needed. At the "indirect" level ways must be found to quickly obtain information about a community.

The levels have been divided into five groups, according to the degree of community and professional interaction and involvement thought desirable in meeting the objectives of the programme. Symbols are used in the figure as metaphors to show this relationship (see Figure 3.2).

The community and the outsider

The *community* are those families who identify themselves as belonging to a specific area characterised by shared interests to get something done, whatever their differences. There is both a spatial and social dimension.

It is obvious that there are various types of communities, some highly organised and cohesive, and others with only a spatial relationship and no social identity. Three types are identified in Chapter 4 that are important when undertaking action planning workshops: the "ideal participatory", the "transitory" and the "reluctant" community. For the purposes of the matrix, "community" represents the full range of types. Part of the task of a participatory tool is the strengthening or development of a sense of community which allows it to achieve its goals, and this is an indicator of the efficacy of the method and not prerequisite for involvement in a participatory action.

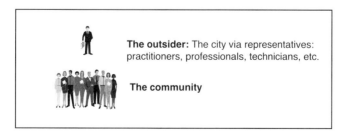

Figure 3.2 The community and the outsider.

Outsider is a metaphor for the city via its representatives, the practitioner or professional. This may include the technical staff of municipalities, hired consultants or NGO representatives. The role of the outsider varies, from active involvement as in the moderation of a workshop, to a passive role when acting as a resource. Outsiders will always be outsiders: they can never *fully* understand the situation of the community, nor speak on its behalf. However, they do have much to contribute, and the appropriate structure and format of tools and techniques is the link to allow this to occur.

The relationship between community and outsider varies according to the level or degree of participation and responsibility assumed (see Figure 3.3). The outsider assumes a "surrogate" role when the community has little or no involvement in the programme or is at best indirectly involved. The outsider becomes an "advocate" when the community acts as an "interest group". As interest groups communities have a direct claim on the outcome but the power of decision remains outside their jurisdiction. When both community and outsider share responsibility both assume a "stakeholder" role and both assume active involvement in planning. Conversely, in the "principal/resource" relationship the community has full responsibility for a project and draws on professional help as needed.

One further point to note from the figure: the type of participation involved (interest group, stakeholder, principal) needs to be agreed in order to avoid conflicts in perception between participatory partners.

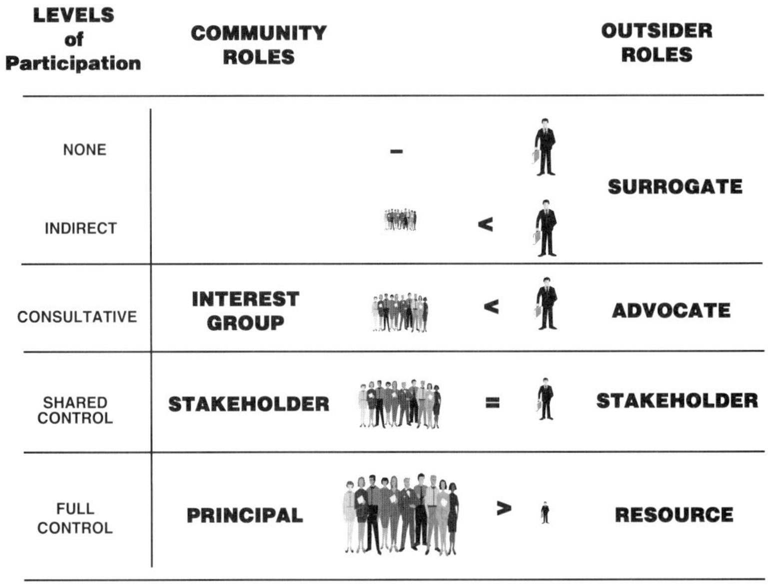

LEVELS of Participation	COMMUNITY ROLES			OUTSIDER ROLES
NONE	—			SURROGATE
INDIRECT		<		
CONSULTATIVE	INTEREST GROUP	<		ADVOCATE
SHARED CONTROL	STAKEHOLDER	=		STAKEHOLDER
FULL CONTROL	PRINCIPAL	>		RESOURCE

Figure 3.3 Roles of community and outsider related to levels of participation.

The levels of participation

Five levels of participation are used in the matrix, organised according to the degree of community involvement.[2] The relationship is as follows:

None: The outsider is solely responsible in all respects, with no involvement of the community. One commonly finds this occurring in circumstances demanding sophisticated technical know-how. Such programmes are not essentially site specific, and others are citywide. A city-based sewage treatment plant is one example.

Excluding community involvement from projects has a high element of risk in that projects may not fit the needs of the community. However, the no participation approach offers a quick response when urgent action is needed.

Indirect: This is similar to "none" but information is site specific. The outsider takes full responsibility for project work, and receives information about the local situation from secondary sources: reports, censuses, etc. It is an activity carried out remote from the area. The community is essentially treated in the abstract and does not directly feature. This is possible in areas which are politically stable and where extensive information is available. An example is determining the amount of water used per day for sizing pipes in a network when upgrading a community.

Two factors are required for successful "indirect" participation: (1) availability of sufficient reliable data, and (2) skill in collecting and analysing data. Absence of either one makes the indirect approach problematic.

Speed of delivery is again an advantage at this level. The risk of inappropriate response is lessened but for fast changing situations the indirect relationship is not appropriate.

Consultative: Outsiders build on information directly received from a community. Their role is principally to gather information and decide actions accordingly. There are several forms of consultation, from information gathering and decision making, from large group consultation to individual surveys and interviews. This level is appropriate where the community's role is an *interest group* but less where they are considered as *stakeholders*.

In one form the outsider presents ideas and solicits feedback from a large number of participants, and then bases action on interpreting the information received. This is typical of public assemblies where the intent is mostly to transmit information and little feedback is required. This is customary with large projects which affect a community but are not directly related to it, for example, in the case of a highway that will pass in the vicinity.

---

[2] The levels are quite similar throughout the literature, although there are variations according to the perspective of the various authors. The precise term sometimes varies. Arnstein, in her influential paper in 1969, developed eight levels of citizen participation based on a redistribution of power: manipulation, therapy (non-participation), informing, consultation, placation (tokenism), partnership, delegated power and citizen control. Burke (1979) considered participation as a matter of right, and identified five roles: review and comment, consultation, advisory, shared decision making and controlled decision making. Wulz (1986) described six different forms which introduced relationships between architect and residents: representation, questionnaires, regionalism, dialogue, alternative co-decision, self-decision. Burns (1979) brought in the concept of experience in classifying the relationship: awareness, perception, decision making and implementation. Masaaki (1993) used five levels when studying the degree of participation and identified the level at the various project stages: highly specified, informed, consultation, partnership and control.

The structure and techniques of consultation with larger groups become particularly important to achieve maximum participation, but the very nature often precludes effective participation. The number of participants in relation to the outsider is important: the smaller the number the more effective the feedback. The arrangement or staging of the event should also be carefully considered: positioning the outsider on a raised stage inhibits participant input, the manner of responses must be inviting rather than threatening, and so forth.

Community surveys and individual interviews are appropriate here. These are more effective in securing inputs but require more time and effort. The PRA[3] family of techniques is one of the more effective ways to involve communities as direct participants in the process of data collection because they are low cost, fast, and solicit local insights.

Consultative involvement is less effective in soliciting ideas from communities, but useful in getting a general sense of acceptance of ideas or approaches. Often consultation has been used as a device to rationalise public actions. Public presentations are so managed as to become self-serving and the event becomes strictly pro forma with feedback unwelcome. The risk of inappropriate response is related to the skill in communication and the ability to develop a plan of action as an outsider.

Shared: At this level the community and outsider interact as far as possible as equals. Each starts with the premise that the other has something to contribute and due deference is given. Both are therefore stakeholders in the project, and this is considered the most important level for effective community/city interaction. Concerns from the larger strategic level as well as concerns from the local level present valid issues for discussion. The effect of forcing the recognition of different viewpoints could lead to creative solutions which arise outside of customary practice.

Shared decision making requires a relatively small group to be effective. How small is small? Sessions need to include a core group of stakeholders who represent the variety of vested interests in the community. With large groups (more than say 25) there is the potential danger that sessions become unwieldly, less participatory and can easily shift into a "consultative" level. Dividing into smaller groups is a partial solution and works when there is originally relative harmony and agreement on goals amongst the participants. Good technique may be summarised into good communication.

Several approaches have been effective for shared participation. Community Action Planning (or Microplanning as it is also known), Planning for Real and ZOPP are all methods that have been successfully applied. The bundle of techniques in each of these methods is selected for maximum interaction amongst vested interest groups, avoiding bias. Chapter 4 will explore these in more detail.

The nature of shared responsibility is both a strength and a weakness of the process. There is a risk that neither community nor city will fully accept an agreement and embrace it as its own. Again, the technique selected is important to mitigate against this outcome to ensure a sense of "ownership".

Full control: The community dominates and the outside practitioner is a resource. The outsider observes or provides technical help when needed. Properly, this is not

---

[3] PRA: Participatory Rapid Appraisal. A family of techniques with community collection of information, developed initially for rural areas. See Chapter 2 for additional discussion of this approach.

shared participation but rather complete empowerment of the community. Empowerment is one of the often-stated goals of community participation, and this level represents the dream in practice.

Rigid control or rule by a dominating few in the community are concerns when it comes to community control. It is simplistic and naive to assume that communities are inherently benevolent in action, and problems of exclusion of minorities, favouritism and restricted representation cannot be ruled out.

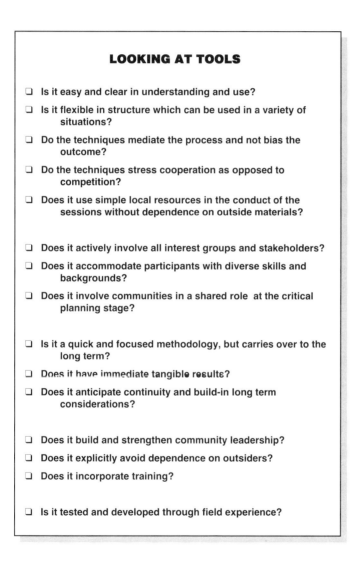

Figure 3.4 Summary checklist for assessing tools.

The stages of projects and programmes

The stages of projects and programmes provide the horizontal axis to the matrix.

- *Initiation*: This stage begins the process. Perceived problems, lack of basic needs, deficient services, and new policy initiatives are some of the ways the process begins. The basic goals and objectives are defined at this stage, and the general scope is decided. No specific skills are needed to initiate a project.
- *Planning*: Here the details are decided. The specific activities are defined, the budget is determined and agreed, and the resources needed are identified. This is the key stage in a project. Some skill is needed, but good judgement is the priority and technical expertise can be provided as a resource. Techniques of planning are necessary, although they can be quite simple and uncomplicated. The general planning of the implementation stage is also included here.
- *Design*: The details are developed at this stage. Often technical expertise is needed at this level.
- *Implementation*: The project is executed at this stage. Buildings are built, infrastructure is installed, programmes are established, and people are trained. Practical management skills are necessary for smooth and timely implementation.
- *Maintenance*: This is the long-term, on-going repair and upkeep of the agreed project.

Using the matrix to consider appropriate levels of participation

The matrix can be used to illustrate and better understand the different situations of participatory involvement. Each has its distinctive "footprint".

A typical project without emphasis on participation takes a "stair-step" form as seen in Figure 3.5. Projects are initiated at all levels and the level of participation declines as one moves on through the stages of a project or programme. There is a widespread conservative reluctance to involve communities in the design and implementation of projects. Communities are seen as a threat to professionals and/or are seen as not being useful, due, for example, to their lack of skills for proper implementation. Participation is seen as slowing the process, making implementation, budgets and timetables difficult to meet.

Other types and views of participatory involvement are illustrated in Figures 3.6 to 3.8 (together with comments).

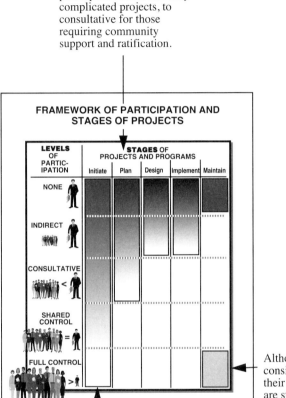

Figure 3.5 Participation in a typical project.

74 Action Planning for Cities

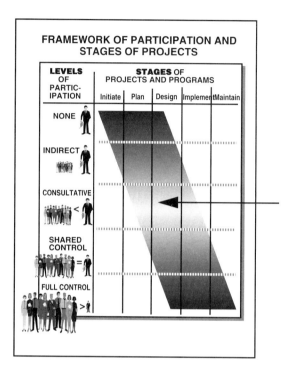

Government maintains control in key areas, and passes responsibility of implementation to communities. The notion of a means to cheap labor often prevails.

The common perception that participation offers low cost labor is shown in the matrix above. Control is maintained by the authorities, and the labor required for construction becomes the responsibility of the community. The resultant pattern is a parallelogram skewed from top left to bottom right

Many of the early site and services low income housing projects followed this model. Community groups would be designated to dig drainage ditches and trenches for water and sewage and clear site areas for schools and other facilities.

Projects of this nature were not overly successful, since "what" and "how to do" are imposed by outsiders. In the case when communities are compensated for their labor, they assume the role of "service contractor" to public authorities, rather than "partners in development".

Figure 3.6 Common perception of participatory projects.

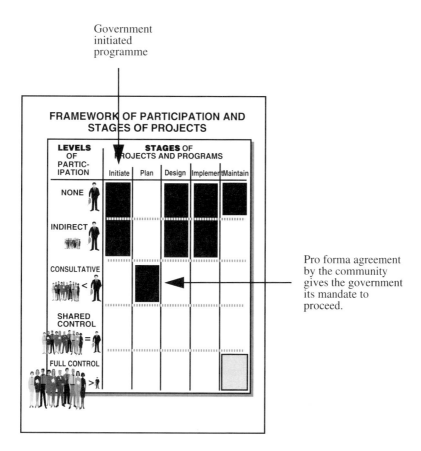

Projects that only involve communities at the Consultative level is patterned in the figure above. This pattern is common when there is reluctance to involve communities, or when the ideal of participation is at the early stage of acceptability. This pattern is also seen in projects which are outside of the community and where the purpose of the authorities is to "inform".

Consultation is often taken as the mandate to proceed with a project, and the remainder of the project is then carried out with no further involvement. This type of project is often labeled as "participatory".

Figure 3.7 Pro forma deference to participation.

76 Action Planning for Cities

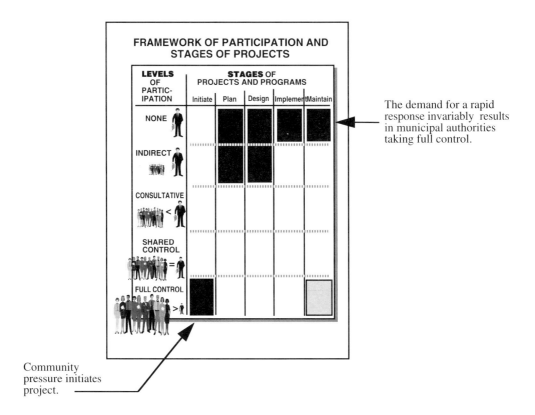

Going from "None" to "Full Control" in the Levels of participation, there is a tradeoff in speed in delivering projects and programmes and the activities become more complex. When the interest is in "getting it done" quickly, there is often hesitation with further participation, despite agreement on participatory efficacy. It is ironic that cities will exclude communities from further involvement to expedite implementation after being pressured by communities to act. The community is involved only at the initiation stage and often in confrontational settings. Further community inputs are not acknowledged as helpful in the process, which highlights the question: are the ends or the means more important?

Figure 3.8 The irony of "getting it done" quickly.

A model for participation

The key to effective Community Action Planning is shared control in plan making, as illustrated in Figure 3.9. Each stage of the project involves the community and the city in a relationship which serves their mutual interests best. The bias is on decision making and delivery of agreed outputs. Participation *per se* is not the main criteria.

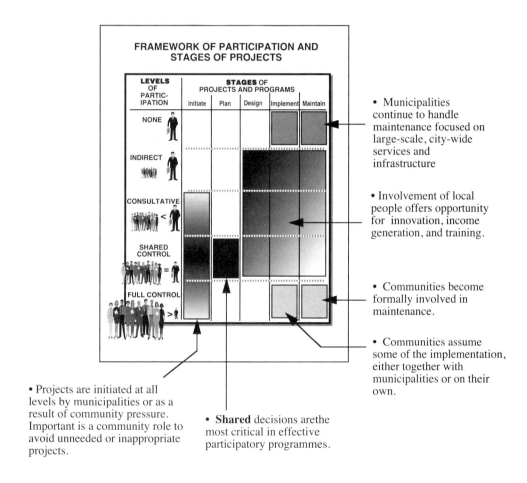

Figure 3.9 A model for participation.

- The *initiation stage* may be at the "consultative", "shared control", or "full control" level. The underlying requirement is that the community has a role in all cases, and can take the initiative *if needed*. It is bottom-up biased, since the community would be the direct initiator and recipient of the action.

- The *plan stage* is seen as the most crucial for the community and the city to be jointly involved. This is the stage at which key decisions are taken and the full project programme is defined. Communities have the choice of further active involvement, for example as in implementation to lower costs, or they may choose to share responsibilities, or even not to participate further. It is important that all vested interests have been considered.

- The *design stage* is less crucial for full community involvement. However, it offers the potential advantage of inducing innovative solutions if methods and ways can be devised to involve and work effectively with communities. The tradeoff is more time-intensive preparation. It also requires a change in customary practice and an acceptance that technical knowledge does not assure primacy.

- The *implementation stage* is also less critical, but it should not be seen as rationalising the "cheap labour" myth. In some cases implementation is better carried out by the city authorities, particularly when large machinery is necessary or because of technical complexity. The implementation of projects can often be coupled with programmes which generate income for small entrepreneurs and community-based organisations (collecting garbage, managing water supply, manufacturing building components for example) and for skills training.

- At the *maintenance stage* both city and community are involved. Each participates according to where and what it can best contribute. In some cases communities can provide labour and shift funds saved to other uses. Alternatively, hiring of local people can be a means of pumping income into a community. Garbage collection is a larger area activity but also a community activity. Day-to-day maintenance of school buildings can readily be managed by community members, while major repairs often require significant financial resources and technical skills. Clear, definite tasks must be agreed and a realistic assessment of capacity must be made for shared maintenance to be successful.

Using the matrix to design the process

The matrix can also be used in programming the complete cycle from project initiation through to maintenance. It can help identify new ways of organising projects. Given specific parameters to meet, a project can be structured utilising the tools and techniques appropriate at each stage. For example, if the goal is speed in response to a crisis, the matrix might be applied as illustrated in Figure 3.10.

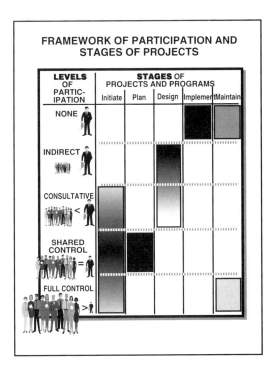

The matrix shows a project where speed is the goal. Initiation could be either in response to the demands of the community or the identified needs of the city, or jointly through "shared" decision making, developed in a workshop session. Planning would be jointly undertaken as a shared process. Design would be through consultation, with implementation through city mechanisms. The workshop would be designed to be short and focused on planning. Design responsibilities would be done at city level, with occasional consultation with the community.

Figure 3.10 The matrix as process design tool.

When is a project participatory?

Does it matter? As we have seen, the relationship between the community and the city differs for various stages and in various forms of interaction. Depending on purpose, any of the levels identified may be appropriate. But in all cases the stakeholder relationship at the planning stage is the key and this is the essence of a true participatory project. Without stakeholder participation, results have repeatedly been wasteful in resources and administration and with little benefit to a community. Participation does matter at the planning stage.

References

Arnstein, S. 1969. A ladder of citizen participation. *Journal of the American Institute of Planners* 35: 215.

Burke, E.M. 1979. *A Participatory Approach to Urban Planning*. New York: Human Science Press.

Burns, J. 1979. *Connections: Ways to Discover and Realize Community Potentials*. New York: McGraw-Hill.

Chambers, R. 1983. *Rural Development: Putting the Last First*. Harlow: Longman Scientific & Technical.

Masaaki, Y. 1993. Learning from each other: participatory community design in the US and Japan. Thesis, Master of Architectural Studies, MIT, Cambridge, USA.

Wulz, F. 1986. The concept of participation. *Design Studies* 7 (3): 153–162.

CHAPTER 4
Tools in Operation

Attendance is not participation.
　　　　Anonymous

Amongst the variety of community-level planning methods available, four families of approaches are distinguishable and reviewed in this chapter. All have been tested in a variety of countries and under widely differing circumstances. The four families are:

- *Community Action Planning* or *Microplanning*, developed by the authors.
- *Planning for Real*, developed by Tony Gibson and the Neighbourhood Initiatives Foundation.
- *ZOPP* (or GOPP in English: Goal Oriented Project Planning), championed by the German Agency for Technical Cooperation (GTZ).
- *Urban Community Assistance Team* (UCAT), developed from the American Institute of Architecture's U/DAT approach in the United States.

The four families of tools share a number of characteristics:

- They are problem driven. Their procedures are defined to respond to problems encountered on site. Actual problems as well as perceived problems are considered.
- They offer a ranked order of priority. Problems and issues are prioritised to a manageable few which can be undertaken within available resources. Innovation comes from the creative ways in which projects are designed and implemented.
- They are pluralistic. They value partnerships between community and outsider, in all stages of project development. Their interactive techniques strive to further this end and they invite differences of opinion which encourage dialogue and creative solutions.
- They strive for a process which is transparent and understandable by all.
- They stress progressive documentation of processes and results as a means with which to promote learning and encourage follow-up.

82 Action Planning for Cities

- All use an intensive workshop format as their primary modality.
- Their focus is implementation. Projects and programmes, rather than study or research, is the goal. As Chambers (1983) notes, they fit into the "positive culture of practitioners, engaged in time-bound action".

In this chapter we will examine each of the four families of participatory planning in terms of their relative effectiveness in key stages of action planning: to build community, identify problems, develop strategies, plan for implementation, get things going and prioritise projects. We will offer a comparative evaluation of the methods and techniques as well as their relative dependency on outsiders, their emphasis on implementation and their ability to be easily expanded in scale. The evaluation offers a basis for deciding where and when each may be usefully employed. Finally, we demonstrate the means by which community projects can be effectively linked to city plans and also how action plans can inform policy development.

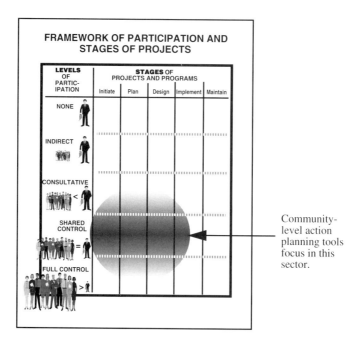

Figure 4.1 The four tools in the general framework.

Community Action Planning (Microplanning)

This approach has been developed by the authors during their collaborative work over the past 15 years. Their participatory approach catalysed in Sri Lanka as part of the Million Houses Programme, a national-scale participatory programme internationally applauded. In Sri Lanka it was applied nation-wide and has become a model emulated in programmes internationally.

The key element of Community Action Planning (CAP) is an active, intense community-based workshop, carried out over a period of two to five days, depending on the specific goals of the workshop. The output of the workshops is a development plan which includes a list of prioritised problems, strategies and options for dealing with the problems, and a rudimentary work programme describing who, when and what is to be done. Integral to the method is the *shared relation* between the professional technical inputs and the community.

The workshops are programmed over specified intervals – once each year tends to be appropriate – with the implementation of agreements during the interval.

The set-up for the workshop requires a minimum of preparation, materials and training. What is required is a motivated community and a confident moderator/facilitator/organiser who can take the lead in assuring that announcements are made, participants identified, a location selected, a few materials collected, and finally can help in running the workshop. Much of the preparation is done by the community. A designated person often takes responsibility for the logistics. Moderators need not be highly skilled and can adapt the style and content to suit their own temperament and the prevailing circumstances. Training of moderators/facilitators can be minimal, but they are strongly advised to participate in an actual workshop in order that they can capture the dynamics of the event as much as understand its procedures.

Materials required are limited to markers of some kind, large sheets of paper (any kind: wrapping paper, newsprint, cardboard, unfolded boxes), and a place for display of outputs.

The location should be in the community and accessible, rather than in government offices. Example locations have varied from formal classrooms to sitting on the ground with the back of a makeshift store as display space. This offers familiarity to participants, emphasises the bias toward the community, and allows instant corroboration of issues.

The start to the process is *problems definition*. Both perceived problems – those felt as being a problem – and "real" problems – those that are measurable – are included without initial distinctions.

The process adopts four general phases of work:[1]

- *Phase I*: PROBLEM IDENTIFICATION AND PRIORITISATION: What are the problems?

---

[1] The Case Files illustrate a variety of ways in which these basic phases may be applied. Examples are included from Sri Lanka, Boston, USA, and South Africa. Note the flexibility and freedom in adjusting the specific phases to suit the particular circumstances.

- *Phase II*: STRATEGIES, OPTIONS AND TRADEOFFS: What approaches and actions are most suitable to deal with problems?
- *Phase III*: PLANNING FOR IMPLEMENTATION: Who does what, when and how, and how to get it going?
- *Phase IV*: MONITORING: How is it working and what can we learn? (A variation of this phase is sometimes included in Phase I in identifying problems.)

At each phase *charts* structure the workshop and are completed by small, mixed-background/mixed-discipline groups during the workshop sessions. The charts are prepared on large pieces of paper for display purposes and with a minimum of formality to highlight the working nature of the sessions. They remain with the community as a record of discussions and agreements. At the conclusion, the community has a prioritised list of problems, a plan of action for implementation for key agreed options, and an appointed person to liaise with the authorities.

Participants at the workshop include a cross-section of community representatives, technical officers from the various departments (sanitation, water, housing, health, education, etc., dependent on the nature of the municipality organisation). The facilitator plays a key role as moderator and must have the confidence of all participants.

The original handbook explaining Community Action Planning (at that time called Microplanning) was prepared for the National Housing Development Authority of the Government of Sri Lanka and for its technical staff. The handbook was later expanded with the addition of an introduction on the conceptual background, a section describing the workshop dynamics in Santiago, Chile, and a section on assessing the impact one year after Microplanning workshops were held in four communities (Goethert & Hamdi 1988). A modified version was prepared as a "Training of Trainers" guide as part of the dissemination of the methodology throughout the country.

Subsequent to the development of the methodology in Sri Lanka, the approach had been used by the authors and others worldwide, in Bangladesh, South Africa, Boston (USA) and Poland. It is being used extensively in Central America by the regional version of the International Union of Local Authorities (IULA). It has not been successful in Boston because of the underlying political commitment required. There local authorities feared that the outcomes would not match official expectations, despite their funding of the preparation of a locally-oriented handbook (Hamdi et al 1988). The methodology was selected by the World Bank's Economic Development Unit for its municipal programmes throughout Latin America and translated into Spanish.

The process is flexible and variations of the approach with their explanatory handbooks have been prepared to address specific circumstances. In Bangladesh a version was prepared that linked training of local technical officers, participatory community upgrading, and the on-going strategic planning effort in Dhaka and Chittagong. In South Africa the method is being used as part of the township upgrading, and a pilot project was undertaken in Schweizer-Reneke, North-Western Province, with subsequent workshops in the planning stages. A summary of the guidebook prepared from the workshop is included in the Case Files.

Tools in Operation   85

Figure 4.2 Community Action Planning (South Africa): the workshop is located in the community to encourage participation.

Figure 4.3 Community Action Planning (Bangladesh): plans provide the base on which to collect community information.

86 Action Planning for Cities

Figure 4.4 Community Action Planning (Bangladesh): A small group discusses issues around a plan during workshop.

Figure 4.5 Community Action Planning (Bangladesh): a public "show" attracts people to workshop findings.

Figure 4.6 Community Action Planning (Chile): Community members participating in surveys to identify problems and opportunities.

In all cases where Community Action Planning was used the fundamentals were retained: rapid, intense, field-based workshops, a problem-driven agenda, equal community/technical participation and documentation.

Planning for Real

Planning for Real has been used "since the late 1970s as a means for giving local people a 'voice' and professionals a clear idea of local people's needs in order to bring about an improvement to their own neighborhood or community." (Neighbourhood Initiatives Foundation 1995). Whilst its origin is in Britain, it has become increasingly widespread throughout the world. In recent years the Planning for Real kit has become popular in some developing countries and a modified version is under development.

Planning for Real uniquely builds around a community-assembled model on which problems and improvements are identified through pictorial "option" cards. The model and the cards have several underlying purposes. They overcome the difficulties of verbal communication by providing an "alternative currency" to words as a means of exchanging views and information. The model provides a common reference point around which to structure inputs, and allows a broader perspective of issues as well as providing a physical base for placing suggestions.

Throughout the process there is considerable awareness about the shifting relationships between the various participants and their degree of commitment. This relationship drives the process by building on an informal, non-committal start which progressively strengthens the commitment around shared knowledge and an emerging common purpose.

Planning for Real is distributed in the form of a "kit", a small box which contains basic instructions on how to conduct sessions, a sample model, cutout masters for physical items (e.g. houses) and non-physical attributes (e.g. problems and opportunities: play areas, high crime areas, etc.). Instruction is provided through four "packs": publicity, suggestions menu, priorities and follow-up. Each provides props and suggestions with techniques in managing the sessions. The style of the kit is simple and deliberately crude, which makes it accessible and unforbidding to communities. Much is hand-lettered, and only in recent versions have more typewritten materials been produced.

The process has three basic stages. In the first stage the model is assembled within the community, either by volunteers, a local club, students, or others as a way to involve key people. The model is generally at a scale of 1:200 or 1:300, but models have ranged from 1:50 to 1:500. It is built in sections of lightweight material to be readily transportable by hand. This model is used to publicise public meetings to begin the process of identifying problems and opportunities. Training sessions are then held with a few local residents to familiarise them with the process. In the next stage public meetings are held where cutouts are placed on the model as a way to identify issues of concern to the community. Around these issues small *ad hoc* "working parties" are formed on specific topics, for example, traffic, shopping facilities, play areas, work opportunities, etc. These working parties then meet to work out details and to negotiate between conflicting interests and priorities, using a "now, soon, later" chart as guide. Collectively these series of activities are intended to develop a momentum that continues into specific practical proposals. The "follow-up" pack offers suggestions for keeping things going and recommends other useful publications.

Planning for Real is particularly effective in mobilising community support and interest. Specific projects are also identified and implementation is set in motion.

Materials needed are minimal. Sheets of polystyrene are suggested as the model base which are glued to cardboard or other hardboard for stability. Markers, pins, tape and glue are needed, as well as access to photocopying facilities for duplication. The workshop location can vary, but must be large enough to accommodate the model. Common community spaces are preferred.

A knowledgeable moderator is generally needed to start the process, although a community member with some background in community development could readily pick up the key concepts through the "kit". Sufficient time is needed for an effective exercise. Three months is suggested for the initial stage of mobilisation, setting up a steering group, building the model and publicising the sessions.

Participants are largely intended to be from the target community, with government officials, local councilors and professionals present to answer questions, when requested. It is acknowledged that these officials and professionals are "absolutely essential", but the style and technique seems to adopt an "us against them" stance. For example, in the public sessions the professionals and officials are

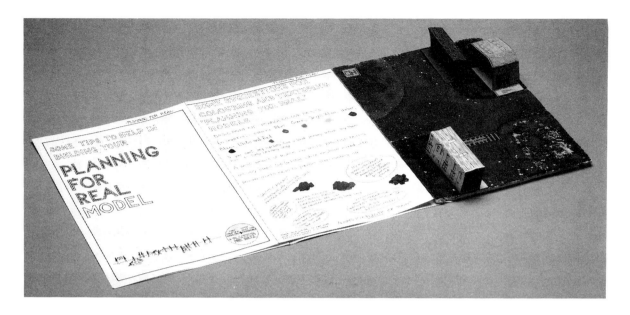

Figure 4.7 Planning for Real: the "kit" provides instruction and materials for carrying out a workshop. (Source: Tony Gibson)

Figure 4.8 Planning for Real: the "kit". (Source: Tony Gibson)

90 Action Planning for Cities

Figure 4.9 Planning for Real: a workshop in Cambridgeport, USA, with Tony Gibson and participant.

welcomed but then are admonished not to talk unless directly asked. Their role seems to be set up as "resource" and less as "stakeholder".

Planning for Real stemmed from the "Education for Neighbourhood Change" programme in Britain in the 1970s. It has been used in many communities throughout Britain and reportedly over 40 packs are in use. It has been used in several award-winning projects and is cited for bridging the language gap in minority areas of Spitalfields and East London. Currently the "kit" is promoted by the Neighbourhood Initiatives Foundation, which also offers a large selection of supplementary support material. Local language versions have been developed in Holland and Germany, as well as in Poland. A version which considers the special circumstances of developing countries is currently in the testing stage.

ZOPP: Goal Oriented Project Planning

The ZOPP[2] approach (or GOPP – Goal Oriented Project Planning – as it is sometimes presented in English) is used and promoted by the Deutsche Gesellschaft für Technische Zusammenarbeit (GTZ – the German Agency for Technical Cooperation). The approach provides a systematic structure for identification, planning and management of projects developed again in a workshop setting, with principal interest groups. The ZOPP output is a planning matrix – the *logical project framework* – which summarises and structures the main elements of a project and highlights logical linkages between intended inputs, planned activities and expected results. The ZOPP approach is used for essentially all German-funded projects and is a prerequisite for funding approval. We have adopted the label "ZOPP" to encompass all of the logical framework methodologies in deference to its principal initiators, the German development agencies and particularly the GTZ.

It was initially called the "Logical Framework Approach (LFA)" when developed for the US Agency for International Development (USAID) in the 1960s. It continued to be developed by various UN agencies, but the GTZ has strongly embraced the approach and developed it into a practical systematic tool. USAID has largely abandoned the use in its projects, due, it seems, to its complexity and inflexibility.

ZOPP enjoys widespread use by the larger donor organisations, partially because of the orderly structuring and documentation of information as well as its demand for more skill in application. ZOPP includes various subparts used to clarifying projects, and the logical project framework itself is often required by agencies in their project appraisal. The British Overseas Development Agency (ODA) requires the "Log Frame" in research project proposals. The OECD's Development Assistance Committee (DAC) is promoting its use among member countries, and the Nordic countries and Canada make use of it in development aid programmes as well as occasionally in domestic public investment. It is mandatory for DANIDA – the Danish aid agency – projects. Use at the community level is also noted, but may be the exception.

The GTZ recommends the ZOPP methodology for all stages of project preparation and implementation. Experience by the GTZ indicates five logical levels[3] of the ZOPP in a standard project cycle.

---

[2] ZOPP: The German acronym for Zielorientierte Projektplanung.
[3] Section 4211 of the GTZ "organizational manual" defines these five stages in detail, with recommendations for persons and organisations to be involved.

- *Pre-ZOPP*: an in-house exercise by agencies in preparation for deciding on a project.
- *Appraisal ZOPP*: an in-house appraisal for preparing terms of reference of a project.
- *Partner ZOPP*: prepared in-country; co-ordination of conclusions and recommendations with staff of project country
- *Take-off ZOPP*: prepared in-country; preparation of the plan of operations with in-country personnel responsible for project implementation.
- *Replanning ZOPP*: prepared in-country; adjustments during project implementation.

Other ZOPPs are recommended annually in projects to update planning as needed.

Although the GTZ outlines an elaborate systemisation of the approach, the approach is viable for community-based planning without the need for the elaborate structuring of levels. Indeed, the "take-off ZOPP" and "replanning ZOPP" are essentially community based and participatory.

ZOPP workshops last from one day to two weeks, with a typical session lasting one week. It is customary in some ZOPPs to sequester the participants in distant locales to enforce unhindered focus on the activities. To mitigate participant dissatisfaction, the locations are invariably selected for their desirable features, and a venue in distant resorts is not uncommon. Participants are selected to represent all interest groups, project technical staff as well as high-level authorities, and community leaders. A basic premise is that the main interest groups must be represented from all levels, particularly top government officials.

A ZOPP requires a moderator with a high degree of experience and skill. The GTZ often brings a highly trained and paid external consultant to moderate their ZOPPS, and to achieve moderator status a special course must be completed. An elaborate custom-built suitcase is provided to ZOPPs with markers, pins, glue-sticks, varied coloured shapes and sizes of paper strips. A smaller "refill" suitcase is available as materials are exhausted in subsequent workshops. A typical session is led by a moderator with participants sitting facing large sheets of paper fixed on panels, walls, etc. As participants go through the exercises, the results are affixed to the sheets with pins to allow adjustment, and glued permanently at the end of each day. This information is typed at the end of each day and becomes a part of the workshop record.

The ZOPP has two phases: analysis and project planning. The *analysis phase* has four substeps, with the identification of "real" problems as the driver for the exercises.

- *Participation analysis*: an overview of persons, groups and organisations connected to a project and their interests, motives, attitudes and implications for project planning. This is done in a chart form.
- *Problems analysis*: major problems grouped into a problem-tree with cause and effect and identification of the core problem. The problems are noted on cards – one to a card – and organised by smaller groups.

Tools in Operation 93

Figure 4.10 ZOPP (Kenya): cards are used to solicit inputs from participants.

Figure 4.11 ZOPP (Kenya): small groups work out "problem-trees" to focus issues.

Deutsche Gesellschaft für Technische Zusammenarbeit (GTZ) GmbH Dag-Hammarskjöld-Weg 1 D-6236 Eschborn 1	PROJECT PLANNING MATRIX (PPM)	Project Title:		PPM prepared on (date):
		Project No.:		
		Est. Project Duration:	Country:	
SUMMARY OF OBJECTIVES/ACTIVITIES	OBJECTIVELY VERIFIABLE INDICATORS	MEANS/SOURCES OF VERIFICATION		IMPORTANT ASSUMPTIONS
OVERALL GOAL to which the project contributes 1. How do we word the OG, taking into account the results of the analysis of objectives?	INDICATORS that overall goal has been achieved 9. How do we define the contents of the OG (in the various phases), i.e. the contribution to the achievement of the OG, so that they become measurable? Note: Quality, quantity, time and possibly location and target group.	12. Which database is available, or which documents have been drawn up or can be obtained elsewhere, to prove that the OG has been achieved?		for sustaining objectives in the long term 8. Which external factors will have to occur in order to assure sustained continuity of the achieved contribution to the OG in the longer term?
PROJECT PURPOSE 2. With which PP (independent of factors manageable by the project management) will we make a considerable contribution to the achievement of the OG?	INDICATORS proving that the project purpose has been achieved (end-of-project status) 10. How do we define the contents of the PP (in the various phases), i.e. the achievement of the project purpose, so that it becomes measurable? Note: Quality, quantity, time and possibly location and target group.	13. Which database is available, or which documents have been drawn up or can be obtained elsewhere, to prove that the project purpose has been achieved?		for achieving the overall goal 7. Which external factors will have to occur for the anticipated contribution to the overall goal to actually take place?
RESULTS/OUTPUTS 3. Which results/outputs (as a whole and in effective combination) will have to be obtained in order to achieve anticipated impact (the Project Purpose)?	INDICATORS proving that the results/outputs have been achieved 11. How do we define the contents of each individual result/output (in the various phases) so that they become measurable? Note: Quality, quantity, time and possibly location and target group.	14. Which database is available, or which documents have been drawn up or can be obtained elsewhere, to prove that the results/output have been achieved?		for achieving the project purpose 6. Which important assumptions in relation to the results/output 1 to . . ., that cannot be influenced by the project or have been consciously defined as external factors, must occur in order for the project purpose to be achieved?
ACTIVITIES 4. Which activities (also as complex packages of measures) will the project have to tackle and implement in order for the results/outputs 1 to . . . to be obtained?	SPECIFICATION of inputs/costs of each activity 15. What does it cost and what inputs are needed (including personnel inputs in man-months) in order to implement each individual activity?	16. What records voucher for the costs entailed, consumption of materials, use of equipment, inputs of personnel, etc.?		for achieving the results/outputs 5. Which important assumptions in relation to the activities 1 to . . . that cannot be influenced by the project or have been consciously defined as external factors, must occur in order for the results/outputs to be obtained?

DEVELOPMENT HYPOTHESIS
If the project purpose is achieved, then a contribution is made towards the overall goal

If these results/outputs are obtained, then the project purpose is achieved

MANAGEABLE FACTORS
If these activities are carried out, then results/outputs are obtained

Figure 4.12 ZOPP: the Project Planning Matrix (PPM). (Source: GTZ, 1988, p. 15)

- *Objectives analysis*: a restatement of the problems into realistically achievable goals; this is often done by rewriting the problems into outcomes, often by reversing the cards.
- *Alternatives analysis*: identification of objectives and assessment of alternatives according to resources, probability of achieving objectives, political feasibility, cost–benefit ratio, social risks, time horizon, sustainability, and others factors as decided by group. An exercise prepared on charts.

The *project planning phase* has as its outcome the Project Planning Matrix (PPM), sometimes called the project planning framework. The PPM is a one-page summary of *why* the project is carried out, *what* the project is expected to achieve, *how* the project is going to achieve these results, *which* factors are crucial for the success of the project, *how* success can be measured, *where* data is required to assess project success, and *what* the project will cost. All of this information is combined in a 4 × 4 matrix (see Figure 4.12 for an example of a matrix format).

The ZOPP has been cited for its rigidity and rigour, and the need for all participants to actively take part in order for it to succeed. Overly directive moderators and disinterested local partners are some of the reasons that the ZOPP has sometimes failed to achieve its full potential.

The Urban Community Assistance Team (UCAT)

The Urban Community Assistance Team is the name we give to the R/UDAT (Regional/Urban Design Assistance Team) family of tools. The key feature is an invited interdisciplinary team of professionals who address problems at various scales, ranging from city and regional issues down to neighbourhoods. The team, together with local supporters, then prepares recommendations and development schemes. The Urban Community Assistance Team (or UCAT) is touted as an urban management technique where all vested interest groups are invited to participate.

We have coined UCAT as the preferred name since it better expresses the spirit of the approach and distinguishes this family of tools from Otto Koenigsberger's usage of the term action planning (see Chapter 2). The title encompasses its urban focus, its notion of providing professional assistance, and its use of group or team work. Since 1992 in Britain this approach has been labelled by some as "Action Planning" and promoted by various groups including the Prince of Wales's Institute of Architecture, although there the term "Task Force" has also been used. In its one-day form it is sometimes called a "charrette", drawing on the intensity of the event and its design origins at the Paris Ecole des Beaux-Arts. Other labels abound and there is little consistency in use. Terms include Design Assistance Team, Community/Urban Design Assistance Team, Design Day, Future Workshops, Planning Weekend, and Urban Design Action Team, among others (Beaudoux et al 1994).

The UCAT originates from the R/UDAT – Regional/Urban Design Assistance Team – events pioneered by the American Institute of Architects since 1967. Hence its "design" orientation and its prevalent use by architects and physical planners. Since 1967 over 110 events have been carried out by the AIA in the United States,

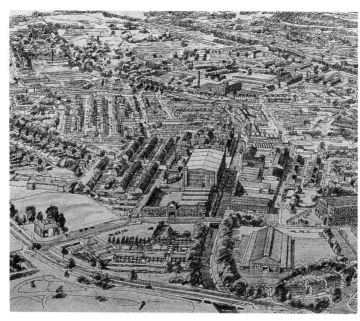

Figure 4.13 UCAT: the "vision" of the Rochdale Canalside planning weekend. (Source: John Thompson & Partners)

and the approach has been eagerly adopted in Britain where dozens of events have been held. Recent uses have been in Eastern Europe and the approach is spreading in popularity. Because of its professional origins, firms can easily adopt UCAT as a part of their services. UCAT is a voluntary activity, but is being considered as part of the statutory planning process in England and Wales. Its application in developing countries has been limited. It is included here because the approach itself incorporates useful techniques which are potentially of use in developing countries.

The planning event is generally carried out over a planning weekend, or over a several-week period – labelled as a Task Force. A four to five-day period is typical.

The process incorporates four phases (Wates 1996):

- The initial *"getting started"* phase, which can take up to three months. Here a steering committee is formed which solicits interest from local groups and prepares a budget and starts fund-raising activities.

- The *"preparation"* phase, which is approximately six months, but varies from event to event. Here momentum and enthusiasm for the event is built up, team members are identified, extensive information is gathered and the broad picture of problems is identified. The professional team typically includes between 8 to 12 people.

- The *"event"* itself, which is recommended to be over a weekend, usually four to five days total.

Figure 4.14 UCAT: children also can help. (Cecilienplatz, Berlin-Hellersdorf – Source: John Thompson & Partners)

- The *"follow-up"* phase, which includes the on-going activities stemming from the event.

The event itself has four main stages:

- The *"problems or issues"* stage, where key problems and opportunities are identified.
- The *"solutions or options"* stage, where options are brainstormed.
- The *"synthesis"* stage, where teams analyse and determine strategy, and where a report is prepared.
- The *"production"* stage, where the recommendations are presented to the community at a public meeting. This stage is seen as particularly important since it gives an opportunity for the outside and professional team to explain in detail their suggestions.

Figure 4.15 UCAT: plans provide the vehicle around which to discuss issues. (Cecilienplatz, Berlin-Hellersdorf – Source: John Thompson & Partners)

Not much information on the actual conduct of the workshops is noted in the various handbooks, which makes the process more difficult to appropriate by the untrained. Workshops settings are suggested, and small group work teams are encouraged. The techniques consist of general guidelines, for example, use flip-charts and markers to document ideas, making sure everyone's ideas are included, and so on. The domination of the process by professionals assumes, perhaps, that technique is less important than outline, although too often professionals are exactly the ones lacking in skills when working with community groups.

Materials needed are modest in smaller sessions and consist of flip-charts, markers, pins, tape and so forth. In larger events the list runs to almost 60 items and includes computers and overhead projectors. For the larger events, space becomes an issue and relatively sophisticated facilities are recommended. This is indicative of the First World context of the approach but it is presumed that more modest settings would not compromise the approach.

Figure 4.16 UCAT: a group photo at the end of the weekend builds solidarity. (Cape Hill Windmill Lane, Sandwell Metropolitan Borough Council, UK – Source: John Thompson & Partners).

Outcomes are targeted at three levels: an immediate set of proposals for action, a short-term agenda for the local steering committee to continue, and a long-term programme of activities. Proposals tend to emphasise physical planning, oriented around development plans, with less emphasis on social, economic and institutional recommendations. This is not surprising considering the architectural origins of the approach. But it also recognises the importance of a physical frame around which to focus actions, similar to the "Planning for Real" approach. Others indicate that the most viable outcomes of UCAT are its coalition-building functions and the development of co-operation amongst the various interest groups (Lampkin 1981). In all cases the published report is a key output and much effort is directed toward this end. Print runs of up to 1000 in multicolour with extensive photographs are not uncommon.

Residents are only one group participating in UCAT events, and outside and local professionals, business leaders, local authorities, volunteer agencies and neighbourhood groups seem to dominate. The professional biased team seems to assume three types of roles: as educators, as dispensers of solutions and as mediators.

Costs of running events are usually high, and funding is a big concern. Handbooks caution against underfunded events and suggest shortening the event when funds are scarce. Local authorities contribute heavily to funding which often ensures their dominance.

A comparative matrix of project goals

How do the four families of tools compare in what they deliver? Figure 4.17 shows the four families on the horizontal axis and the principal outputs of participatory programmes on the vertical scale. The six outcomes and goals listed are commonly cited in participatory projects, and are used as benchmarks for comparing the tools:

- *Building community*: Community cohesion and development of community leadership should be a clear goal and implicitly encouraged. Some tools make these goals explicit and are structured accordingly.

- *Identifying problems*: Priorities must be set and problems focused around a few key issues. The explicit determination and ranking of problems is the driver of most tools.

- *Developing strategies*: Options must be identified and selected, and specific actions determined.

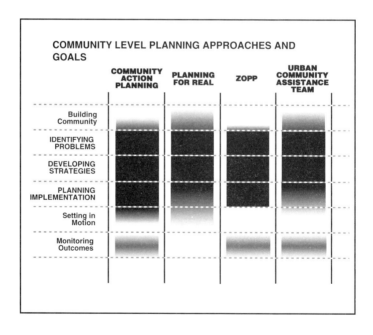

Figure 4.17 Comparison of the four families of participatory planning.

- *Planning implementation*: Tasks should be identified, responsibilities established, and an indicative timetable included in a plan of operation.

- *Setting in motion*: Specific steps should be outlined for starting the projects agreed in the plan of operations. Key individuals should be assigned direct responsibility, both in the community and in the municipalities. Intermediate "next steps" should be determined. The basic question that needs to be addressed is "What should we do tomorrow to get things going?".

- *Monitoring outcomes*: Agreed projects should be reviewed periodically to assess progress and to take remedial action if needed.

All of the tools are explicit in "identifying problems" and "developing strategies". For "building community", Planning for Real and UCAT are the strongest since considerable time – up to three to six months – is spent by both methods in mobilisation of the community. By the nature of the process, Community Action Planning and ZOPP rely more on the workshop itself for strengthening community bonds and developing leadership.

"Planning implementation" is formally structured in considerable detail in the ZOPP, and to a lesser extent in Community Action Planning. Planning for Real and UCAT both rely more on the momentum of the workshop to define and shape implementation and assure flexibility in outcome. Planning for Real notes that residents must be involved in implementation to ensure continued "ownership" of project programmes, but how this is to be addressed is less explicit.

"Setting in motion" is explicit in the various stages of Community Action Planning and formal working teams are formed with immediate agendas and clear responsibilities. Planning for Real and UCAT implicitly include working groups – steering groups – and agendas for the next steps. The ZOPP ends with a detailed timetable and work programme including a period for mobilisation and set-up, but it is less explicit in answering the question, "what do we do tomorrow?".

"Monitoring" is noted in all of the tools and each indicates that there should be follow-up and continued review to assure progress. However, the "where, how and when" to monitor is generally not explicit and is left to the interpretation of the workshop team. Planning for Real suggests a community newsletter for feedback and follow-up.

Comparison of dependency, implementation and expansion of programmes

The four families of tools are here reviewed as to their potential in addressing the three key recurring difficulties of projects as identified from experience: dependency, implementation and expanding the programme. Figures 4.18, 4.19 and 4.20 compare the tools as to their relative effectiveness in these respects.

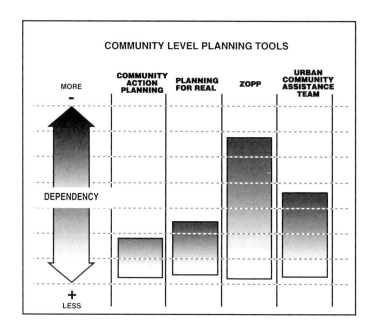

UCAP is not readily an independent process. Although it requires few special materials (only paper of any kind for charts and markers), some training, and a handbook or simple fold-out as guide to the process, and a moderator who needs little training to start the process in the first instance, it relies on outsider intervention to initiate, organize and manage and thus considerable costs may involved. Planning for Real requires more extensive preparation of special materials and a model, but this is a clear advantage in identifying problems and soliciting suggestions. A trained moderator – or at least one familiar with the process – is needed. A ZOPP workshop is most dependent on outside resources and support: it requires elaborate props and a specially trained (and highly paid) moderator to conduct the sessions, who is required to prepare a written report and to supervise a typed final documentation. Although the workshop materials could be improvised and the technique applied without the need of the professional moderator, it seldom is done this way. It can be expensive because of the requirements for sequestered venues. Community Action Planning is least costly in terms of materials, but requires a moderator. The availability of relatively detailed handbooks which include hints on technique allow less familiar users to run a workshop, and sometimes to initiate their own.

Figure 4.18 Tendency toward dependency.

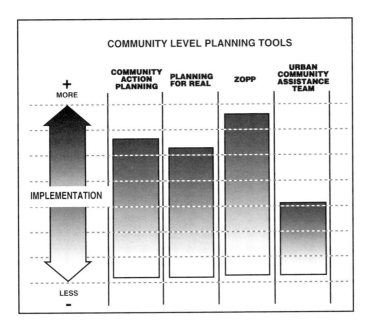

ZOPP places the most emphasis on implementation. It engages in elaborate detailed planning which includes specific tasks, man-months of effort, number of personnel needed, and a master matrix linking the overall goals with the specific activities and tasks. Planning for Real prepares a plan of action with "now, soon, later" groupings and with categories of "no help, some help, and done by others". This provides a simple yet clear structure from which to develop specific project plans. UCAT leaves in place a "Project Memorandum" which becomes a project brief including a funding proposal and a management guide. Community Action Planning at the minimum generates a "who, what, how and when" chart which structures and guides implementation. In capacity building workshops for technical staff a "Project Memorandum" is also prepared which formalizes specific projects for funding proposals.

Figure 4.19 Emphasis on implementation.

Dependency is inherently contrary to participatory programmes. The goal is equal opportunity to contribute from all participants. Some indicators of dependency include the following:

- The reliance on special materials. The supplier has power in controlling the event.

104 Action Planning for Cities

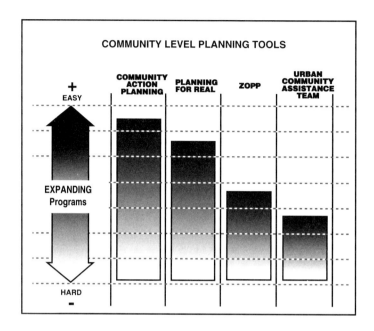

Community Action Planning requires the least effort in going to scale. It is explained in relative detail through handbooks and is simple to understand. Training of a cadre of moderators, or even having community members act as moderators and trainers, can be undertaken concurrently with community workshops. Very little funding is required, and no extensive community mobilization is needed. Planning for Real is essentially uncomplicated to organize. Again, familiarity with the process facilitates expansion to other areas. More mobilization time is needed for model preparation, but this is considered a requirement in organizing non-structured communities. Costs are low. ZOPP requires more planning and is often a part of a larger program because of the funding required. A moderator must be arranged, participants must be identified and acceptable dates for a workshop agreed. A venue must be located. Funding must be found to cover the relatively high expenses. The most expensive is the UCAT because of it outside professional team. Considerable time is needed to set up the event but this is seen as part of the process in mobilizing a community.

Figure 4.20 Ease in expanding participatory programmes.

- The necessity and degree of outside training required.
- The need for an outside moderator/leader to implement the process. When the community cannot carry out participatory programmes without outside direction, dependency is high. After an initial "push", communities should be able to continue on their own.
- The documentation of the activities should be locally produced and held, and understandable and available throughout the community.

The *emphasis on implementation* in participatory processes gives an indication of their priority in achieving a concrete goal. Successful participation must include an explicit and detailed outline of how to proceed and cannot rely on the euphoria of the moment. Indicators which support implementation may be structured around the following sequential levels:

- Clear, articulated and agreed objectives in overcoming problems.
- Specific strategies and agreed options.
- A development plan outlining what to do, how to do it, and when.
- An indication of people responsible for immediate next steps.

The relative *ease of expanding* a participatory programme allows scaling-up to reach many communities quickly. Factors to consider include:

- Ease of implementation. The process should not be complicated but rather easy to understand and execute. It should not rely on conceptual word-games but should stress practical method.
- Should require little extensive training.
- Should need little or no funding.
- Language, techniques and routines should use the local vernacular.

Which tool to use?

Each of the tools has its strengths and weaknesses, and the strengths may be exploited to best address the varied circumstances that a participatory process may confront.

The tools and their key characteristics are summarised in Figure 4.21, with their "best use" highlighted in the last column. For working with communities who lack existing organisational or social structures and who therefore need to mobilise and encourage the development of community, the UCAT and Planning for Real would seem best suited. At the other end of the spectrum, when dealing with more stable, cohesive communities, Community Action Planning allows quick entry in preparing a plan of action. The ZOPP equally tends to be more appropriate in defined and cohesive situations, with the added requirement of relatively sophisticated participants, probably those who have previously been involved in participatory workshops. Higher costs tend to parallel this relationship: it will cost more – in terms of all resources: financial, time, people – to mobilise communities and get them involved in preparing a development plan.

A "super tool" that combines the strengths of each of the tools would not do. You cannot reconcile quick entry with a deliberate, longer mobilisation period. It would be difficult to use the relatively sophisticated ZOPP concepts with the pictorial option cards of Planning for Real. Their underlying concepts differ considerably and are in any case intended for different purposes.

In short, practitioners and communities have available a range of tools that address many of the situations that arise. Proper selection is still required to best match tool and community, tool and desired outcome, and tool and resources available.

Community projects and city plans

How can community projects inform city plans? How best to build co-ordination amongst the many local programmes, so as to enable cities to allocate resources efficiently and equitably? What roles do communities play at the city level, and what roles do city authorities play at the community level?

A recent quote[4] commenting on the cancellation of the Reconstruction and Development Programme in South Africa rephrases these issues most appropriately: "And schemes have been stuck in a bog of arguments . . . should the state build a whole house, or just service a plot of land with water and sewerage and leave the resident to get on with it? If the whole thing, how big, and how solid?" Community action planning is a tool that effectively facilitates in these decisions.

As noted in the previous chapters, in the customary arrangement of initiating projects the city bases its actions on "master plans" or similar documents. The master plan, which becomes the overall planning guideline, is prepared under expert professional guidance, based on traditional "data-intensive" methods. Professionals collect data about communities and then filter and structure the information for use in the master planning process. Using the master plan as one input, the city then proceeds to develop and initiate programmes and projects for the communities. Although the process is cyclic, there is only limited involvement of communities and the cycle flows in one direction. The link is through professionals – outsiders – in the "none", "indirect", or at best in the "consultative" mode (see Figure 3.4: Participation in a typical project). Figure 4.22 indicates this general relationship amongst the key elements in a simplified form.

The primary difference in the proposed model is that it assumes a changed relationship between the communities and city authorities. The process is still a cycle, but the cycle now flows several ways and encourages activities outside of the

---

[4] From the article "South Africa Reconstructed", *The Economist*, April 6, 1996, p. 43.

	Distinguishing Methodology	Time Frame	Materials Required	Relative Cost	Best Use
COMMUNITY ACTION PLANNING	Simple hand-made charts provide frame for documenting and organizing issues in small group interactive workshop sessions.	*Preparation:* Short period to identify representatives and make basic logistic arrangements *Workshop:* 2 to 4 days	Simple, commonly available materials: • large paper sheets for documentation • markers, tape/pins	Low/moderate: Can be very inexpensive	Quick entry into relatively defined community to identify issues and develop plan of action
PLANNING FOR REAL	Community-built model is base to focus public inputs and to initiate workshop sessions with card and chart documentation techniques.	*Preparation:* Relatively long period to build model and mobilize community interest; recommend 3 months as ideal *Workshop:* 2 to 4 days	Simple, commonly available materials: • local materials for model making, polystyrene for base, etc. • markers, tape/pins • 'Planning for Real' kit is useful with custom charts	Low/moderate: Can be relatively inexpensive by drawing on community resources	Longer term approach for strengthening and mobilizing community interest
ZOPP	Rigorous approach uses cards to solicit inputs and to document issues leading to a 'logical project framework' which summarizes entire project	*Preparation:* Short period to identify participants, arrange for logistics, and secure moderator *Workshop:* 2 days to 2 weeks; 5 days most typical	Elaborate, custom 'suitcase' with varied cut paper, markers, pins, glue sticks, and cutter • large sheets of paper for affixing issue cards, easels to hold sheets also common *(Custom suitcase considered luxury and not necessary by authors)*	Moderate/high: Requires highly trained moderator Can be relatively expensive in venue costs and moderator fees	For seasoned and relatively sophisticated participants in detail structuring of projects
URBAN COMMUNITY ASSISTANCE TEAM	Community mobilization and project definition through outside professional assistance team working with local officials, volunteer agencies, and residents	*Preparation:* Long period of up to 9 months in some forms to identify counterparts, collect information and mobilize community for event *Workshop:* 2 to 4 days	Varied materials with generally high degree of sophistication for professional results in project delineation and report publication	High: Most expensive which requires fund raising efforts; costs can include transport of team, sophisticated audio-visual equipment, professional documentation and final publication	For initial entry which mobilizes and builds alliances in communities; for quick interventions

Figure 4.21 Summary of the four approaches for community-level action planning.

cycle itself. Interjected at the crucial juncture of community and city is a participatory relationship which acts as an information interchange and defines priorities and options. In effect the professional's role is replaced with an interactive action planning workshop. As noted in Chapter 2, this is where appropriate tools are needed which bring together all the actors in a partnership relationship. Community Action Planning, Planning for Real, ZOPP and UCAT provide the modality. These workshops should be formally scheduled to maintain momentum and lobby for city action. They should be well publicised and easily remembered by community and city alike. For example, the first weekend, in the second month for three days – as easy as 1, 2, 3!

Community types and appropriate tools

A simple model may be used to better understand the type of communities and their expected issues that may arise when deciding on the appropriate tool. In the "real world" these stereotypical types rarely exist, but such an approach offers a useful device with which to understand and to frame issues.

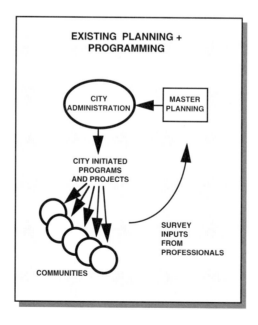

Figure 4.22 The existing community + city planning relationship.

From Chapter 2, three basic types of communities were identified:

(A) Those that are highly organized, cohesive and have a sense of identity, both spatially and socially. Two subtypes are noted:

- *Type A-1*: Lower income communities. They have much to gain in an improvement programme and would be eager to participate. These form the *ideal participatory* partnership.

- *Type A-2*: Higher income communities. They have little to gain in an improvement programme since they already have access to political power and often provide the professional cadre as well. They would most likely be *reluctant* to participate in any participatory process, other than to keep informed. However, their access to political power requires that they be brought into the process.

(B) Those that have little sense of neighbourhood. These are often seen as "stepping-stone" communities and highly *transitory*. The general stereotype suggests that families stay for a short time and then move to more stable

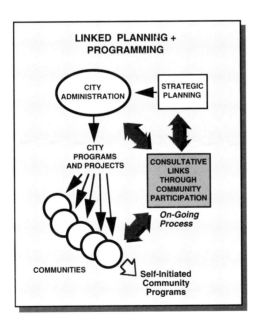

Figure 4.23 The proposed community + city planning continuum.

situations. These neighbourhoods require much effort to organise. However, through the participatory process a sense of community starts to form and a sense of shared interests develops.

A series of overlay maps is suggested to assist in defining community demarcations:

(1) Mapping of communities by social boundaries. This may be quickly done by listing existing community names as commonly identified. These maps can be prepared in rough sketches by local respondents and compared and correlated. Listing community organisations would be another input and knowing the organisations would be directly useful in the action planning process.

(2) Mapping of areas defined by similar physical characteristics. These may be grouped by house types, lot sizes, and even tenure and income which parallel the physical characteristics in many cases. These typologies tend to be biased toward physical factors. Streets are not considered suitable boundaries for communities. They may be convenient for drawing maps but they do not parallel utility servicing nor social groupings, since streets are often the centre of activity and not the boundary.

(3) Mapping of areas defined by population sizes, that is, number of people deemed to be a convenient size and manageable planning groups.

(4) Mapping of political and administrative boundaries.

(5) Mapping of facilities customary at the community scale. These include schools, clinics, religious buildings, and so on.

(6) Mapping of small local commercial centres. These are the clusters of corner stores and shops found in all urban areas, which service the neighbourhoods.

Once all the plans are prepared and overlaid, community demarcations become obvious. The overriding criteria, however, is the self-identity of the community as this indicates a degree of social cohesion. This may be most prevalent in the "ideal" type of community, and perhaps to a lesser extent in the "transitory" type. For "reluctant" communities the boundary decision would be taken largely based on physical characteristics and existing spatial boundaries. In very large communities it may be desirable to form subgroups to make action planning workshops more manageable.

The three general types are also related to the spatial pattern of an urban area. In the inner ring one tends to find the "ideal participatory partners" as well as "transitory communities". Both of these are typical targets of upgrading programmes. In the outer ring the "reluctant communities" may be more common following the typical flight to the suburbs by those with higher incomes. Squatter settlements are also found, which may be "transitory" or "ideal". Figure 4.24 is a schematic representation of the generalised spatial pattern.

In choosing the appropriate tool, the one which is responsive to the specific characteristics of the communities should be employed. For the "ideal" community, time available, ability to organise and desired goals determine the choice of tool, and several may be chosen. In "transitory" communities time is the key factor. For a quick entry to begin a mobilisation process, Community Action Planning is the choice. To continue and broaden the process Planning for Real is suggested. In the "reluctant" communities the UCAT is the recommended choice since it is not dependent on the active engagement of the community. Figure 4.25 illustrates desired links between the type of community and the appropriate choice of tool.

What problems could be anticipated?

There are several issues that may prove to be problematic at the city level and should be considered in an action planning process.

- The sudden demands imposed on city services may prove to be unmanageable as the priority projects filter up from the communities. In cities with

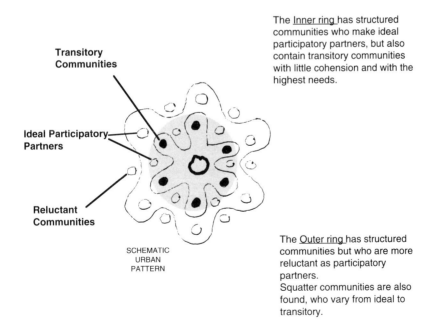

Figure 4.24 Spatial relation of communities and participatory partners.

already deficient and stretched administrative capacities, would projects prove to be impossible to implement resulting in a loss of credibility? In one sense the work of the city is simplified in that choices are narrowed already at the community level and less political manoeuvring need take place. In many cases projects can be combined into broader city-sector programmes. For example, a water supply improvement programme could be implemented for larger areas of the city if deficient water supply repeatedly arises in the communities.

- Cities must rethink the role of the institutions which become involved in action planning. Are the institutions seen as primarily a clearing-house for passing on information, or should they be "mega-agencies" with added implementation responsibilities?

- Does the model encourage counterproductive competition amongst communities? This already seems to be the prevailing situation and decisions are made on the basis of political access and the degree of community organisation. However, using a city-wide process defuses the politics and encourages the spread of programmes more equitably, and it becomes more difficult to show favouritism. And again, projects can be combined into

Type of Community	Characteristics		Appropriate Tool
IDEAL PARTICIPATORY PARTNERS: Cohesive, highly organized, lower income	Much to gain; supports their needs and assists in long term stabilization	Easiest in terms of effort	• Community Action Planning • ZOPP • Planning for Real
TRANSITORY COMMUNITIES: Non-cohesive, transitory	Much to gain, but need organizing; action planning starts stablizing community	Requires much effort; customary target of community development inputs	• Community Action Planning • Planning for Real
RELUCTANT COMMUNITIES: Cohesive, highly organized, higher income	Little to gain, already in the power system	Difficult to work with: may not need workshops since already access to power and experts come from this strata: they can use the indirect or consultative level of participation with sufficient confidence to reflect community	• Urban Community Assistance Team

Figure 4.25 Characteristics of communities as participatory partners.

	CLEARNING-HOUSE ROLE	MEGA-AGENCY ROLE
Primary Role	• Liaison: interface betweencommunity and city • Pass-on and coordinate	• Liaison: interface between community and city • Implement
Key Concerns	• Assure sufficient power	• Assure reponsiveness
Alternatives for Setting It Up	*Establishing New Agency*	
	• Fresh start, no hinderance from past practices	• Resentment by other agencies • Possible duplication • High cost
	Restructuring Existing Agency	
	• Loss of power	• Expand on proven base • Possible duplication

City agencies supporting community-level action planning must deal with broad, cross-sectorial issues. The staff act as a "clearing-house" and interface between city and community. Staff are reluctant in taking responsibility for these concerns, but nevertheless are held responsible by the community for the success or failure. Where should action planning agencies be institutionally located?

Two institutional models are suggested: In one implementation functions are eliminated with a focus on linking community organizations with city agencies, identifying programmes and agencies that could be of assistance. The agency's role is non-partisan and it must be assured sufficient power to carry-out implementation.

The alternative model is a mega-agency: the mandate would be broadened and portions of water, sewerage, education, social services, health, transportation would be incorporated into its responsibility. The agency would have an implementation role and a strategic role to coordinate and prioritize programmes. However as a result from its size and power the agency may no longer be content with providing service to communities. Duplication with other agencies would also be a concern.

Regular monitoring is important in both models to provide strategic direction for the agency and to set priorities at the city scale.

Existing agencies could be restructured or a new agency established. Existing agencies would now share power with communities – traditionally considered as dependent, lacking skills, and with no understanding of broad issues – and this may prove to be a difficult transition. New agencies must compete for scarce funds and skilled personnel.

Figure 4.26 Implications on urban institutions

114 Action Planning for Cities

programmes reaching more communities. A city would need to make explicit the criteria for decisions, agreed with the communities. For example, communities who put more of their own resources into a project could receive higher priority.

- Would the communities be too involved in their own struggles to participate effectively? The workshop format requires little time, but follow-up pressure on the city would require more involvement which may not be forthcoming.

- Transparent and widespread access to information is vital to ensure informed choices with a higher chance of implementation. Communities consider their own capabilities when identifying projects and development options, but they also must be aware of the capacity of the city. The action planning process of deciding priorities and courses of action would allow communities to take this into account, focusing on the tradeoff between

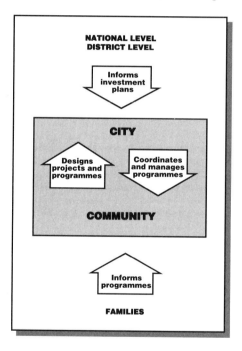

Community-level projects inform investment planning at city and national levels. And conversely, national-level programmes and policies inform city and community projects. The link is provided through action planning.

The box above illustrates the general relationship between the various development partners. The box to the right illustrates the specific case in South Africa.

Figure 4.27 Local-level and national-level information flows.

Time	April 22-May 4	April 28	May—August	Mid-September
Phase	**TOWN LEVEL PROJECT**	**PROVINCIAL LEVEL PROGRAMME COORDINATION**	**PAPER ON POLICY**	**NATIONAL LEVEL INVESTMENT PLANNING**
Location	Schweizer-Reneke	Mmabatho	Durban	Pretoria (tentative)
Aims	PROJECT PLANS AND ISSUES	RDP ISSUES AND NEXT STEPS	LESSONS/ AGENDA FOR NATIONAL SEMINAR	POLICY DISCUSSIONS AND FUTURE DIRECTIONS
Participants	• S-R Interim Development Committee • S-R Community Representatives • S-R Town Council Representatives • University of Natal • CSIR Representative • Oxford Brookes • Ridge Development • MIT (See Note A)	• MEC (Local Govt. • RDP Provincial Coordinator • RDP Local Coordinator • Community Representatives • Oxford Brookes • Ridge Development • University of Natal • MIT	• University of Natal and Housing)	• University of Natal • Project Team • RDP representatives as necessary • RDP Coordinators • Funding Agencies • NGOs • Provincial MECs • Oxford Brookes • National RDP Coordinator • Minister of Housing
Objectives	"Jump-start" the development process Produce a Community Action Plan Expose strengths and weaknesses of method	Presentation of S-R findings Expose provincial -level issues Links to RDP objectives	Review other projects Document S-R experience Prepare agenda for National seminar	Assess applicably of S-R experience at national level Review likely constraints to broader implementation To define further projects and decide next steps
Responsibility	*RDP Officer:* invitations, venue *Brookes University:* workshop timetable, methods, documentation *University of Natal:* technical assistance	*RDP Officer:* setup meeting	*University of Natal* with other project teams *Ridge Development* (Re: Dept. of National Housing	*RDP Office/ Ministry of Housing:* invitations, venue *University of Natal:* background paper, agenda, logistics, etc.
Outputs	Community Action Plan Methodology issues	Issues to consider consider Next steps	Background paper Seminar agenda	Further pilot projects Policy recommendations

Phases of Work
The Schweizer-Reneke Pilot Project Programme, South Africa

Acronyms: MEC: Member of Executive Chamber; BESG: Built Environment Support Group; ANC: African National Congress; RDP: Reconstruction and Development Programme; SR: Schweizer Reneke; CSIR: Centre for Scientific and Industrial Research; PAC: Pan African Council

Note A: Also included are the following: Local government co-ordinating committee, Civil Association, PAC Representative, ANC Representative, Women's League, BESG - NGO Representative, and the SR Hospital

Figure 4.27 *(continued)*

time, funding, and outside and internal resources. For example, communities may choose a faster option, which implies more community contribution and less support from the city, or they may choose a delayed option with little community input and heavy reliance on city provisions but also riskier since situations can change rapidly.

Information flows must also be established between the community–city and the national levels. Community projects inform investment planning at urban and national levels and conversely national and city policies and programmes inform choices made by communities. One example of the process of feeding information up to policy and investment planning is illustrated in Figure 4.27 using the case of South Africa.

Further reading

Community Action Planning

Goethert, R. & Hamdi, N. 1988. *Making MicroPlans: A Community Based Process in Programming and Development*. London: Intermediate Technology Publications. A Spanish version is available from the Economic Development Institute (EDI), the World Bank, Washington, DC.

Hamdi, N. & Goethert, R. 1995. *Community Action Planning: A Manual for Technical Staff Working with Communities*. Prepared for UNCHS (Habitat) for the Government of the Peoples Republic of Bangladesh.

Planning for Real

Gibson, T. 1988. *Planning for Real: Users' Guide*. Telford, UK: Neighbourhood Initiatives Foundation.

Neighbourhood Initiatives Foundation, 1995. *A Practical Handbook for "Planning for Real" Consultation Exercises*. Telford, UK.

Neighbourhood Initiatives Foundation, 1995. *Planning for Real Kit: A Tool for Community-Led Neighbourhood Improvement*. Telford, UK.

ZOPP

GTZ (Deutsche Gesellschaft für Technische Zusammenarbeit), 1987. *ZOPP in Brief*. Eschborn.

GTZ (Deutsche Gesellschaft für Technische Zusammenarbeit), March 1987. *ZOPP Flipcharts*. Eschborn.

GTZ (Deutsche Gesellschaft für Technische Zusammenarbeit), March 1988. *ZOPP (An Introduction to the Method)*. Eschborn.

Norad (Norwegian Agency for Development Co-operation), 1990(?). *The Logical Framework Approach (LFA)*. Handbook for Objectives-Oriented Project Planning. Oslo.

Urban Community Assistance Team

AIA Regional Urban Design Committee, 1985. *R/UDAT Handbook*. Washington, DC: American Institute of Architects.

AIA Regional Urban Design Committee, 1990. *Creating a Design Assistance Team for Your Community: A Guidebook for Adapting the American Institute of Architects' Regional/Urban Assistance Team (R/UDAT) Program for AIA Components and Chapters*. Washington, DC: AIA.

Wates, N. 1996. *Action Planning: How to Use Planning Weekends and Urban Design Action Teams to Improve Your Environment*. London: The Prince of Wales's Institute of Architecture.

Selected recent references on techniques

Fisher, F. & Tees, D.W. 1994. *Training for Elected Leadership*. Prepared for the International Development Institute, Nairobi. UN Centre for Human Settlements (Habitat) Training Materials Series. It includes 12 training handbooks, and a companion Trainer's Guide for Training of Elected Officials. See also the Training Materials Series on *Designing Human Settlements Training in Africa*, Vol. 1: Case Study, and Vol. 2: Trainer's Tool Kit. There is a similar series for Europe and Latin America.

Gosling, L. & Edwards, M. 1995. *Toolkits: A Practical Guide to Assessment, Monitoring, Review and Evaluation*. Development Manual 5. London: Save the Children.

Kroehnert, G. 1991. *100 Training Games*. Sydney: McGraw-Hill.

Nilson, C. 1993. *Team Games for Trainers*. New York: McGraw-Hill.

Townsend, J. 1985. *The Instructor's Pocketbook*. Management Pocketbooks. Hampshire, UK: Conifer Press.

References

Beaudoux, E., Crombrugghe, G. de, Douxchamps, F. Gueneau, M.-C. & Nieuwkerk, M. 1994. *Supporting Development Action: From Identification to Evaluation*. London: Macmillan Press.

Chambers, R. 1983. *Rural Development: Putting the Last First*. Harlow: Longman Scientific & Technical.

GTZ (Deutsche Gesellschaft für Technische Zusammenarbeit), March 1988. *ZOPP (An Introduction to the Method)*. Eschborn.

Goethert, R. & Hamdi, N. 1988. *Making MicroPlans: A Community Based Process in Programming and Development*. London: Intermediate Technology Publications. A Spanish version is available from the Economic Development Institute (EDI), the World Bank, Washington, DC.

Hamdi, N., Goethert, R. & Mongold, N. 1988. *Planning Assistance Kit: A Planning Guide for Community Based Organizations*. Boston: Massachusetts Housing Partnership Challenge Grant Program.

Lampkin, M. 1981. Intervention in the city building network: an evaluation of the AIA's R/UDAT Program, MCP and SM Arch thesis, MIT, Cambridge, USA.

Neighbourhood Initiatives Foundation, 1995. *A Practical Handbook for "Planning for Real" Consultation Exercises*. Telford, UK.

Wates, N. 1996. *Action Planning: How to Use Planning Weekends and Urban Design Action Teams to Improve Your Environment*. London: The Prince of Wales's Institute of Architecture.

SECTION 3
Training and Education

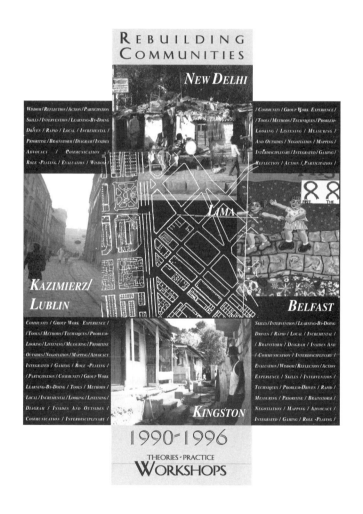

CHAPTER 5
Designing a Programme

Many training efforts are begun without any reason, continued with no purpose and end in no results.

McGehee & Thayer

In 1991, both the World Bank and UNDP published strategy papers setting out a new agenda for their assistance programmes for the 1990s.[1] Both documents aligned themselves to enabling strategies which would change the focus of aid away from capital projects in housing, infrastructure and urban upgrading, toward enhancing urban productivity, alleviating poverty and protecting the environment. Both documents were complementary in their objectives. Whilst the World Bank would continue to promote economic development at the core of its activities, UNDP would emphasise an agenda linking GNP to human and social development. Both organisations would adopt a style of technical assistance based on pragmatism rather than ideology, recognising the new realisms discussed in Chapter 2. Their technical assistance would be based on facilitating private organisations, municipal institutions, local authorities, community groups and NGOs to supply, manage and own urban housing, services and utilities. The principal task for planners would be to create "a regulatory and financial environment in which private enterprise, households and community groups can play an increasing role in meeting their own needs".

Both the World Bank and UNDP encapsulated ideas originally set out in the UN Global Strategy for shelter to the year 2000. This report had come to the conclusion that neither public nor private sectors on their own could sustain providing enough of housing, services and utilities to match demand in fast growing cities. The poor performance of governments in implementing their programmes at a scale which makes any difference was associated increasingly with dysfunctional policies and with a lack of institutional capability to manage urban change effectively. Poor performance, it was concluded, had much less to do with technical capabilities which were generally abundant in developing countries and more with enabling the market to perform more efficiently. It followed, therefore, that if urban institutions were to adopt facilitating policies, if private organisations, including CBOs and

---

[1] The World Bank policy paper (*Urban Policy and Economic Development: An Agenda for the 1990s*) and the UNDP strategy paper (*Cities, People and Poverty: Urban Development Co-operatives for the 1990s*) are both summarised in Harris (1992).

NGOs, were to be empowered as partners in development, then they would need the means, the political will and the professional know-how to turn development theory into development action. Market enablement, for development agencies, was their principal role for the 1990s. Urban management and with it human resource development through training and education was to assume high profile if the enabling paradigm were to be promoted and if planners were to become skilled and competent in practice.

Underpinning these revised agendas for policy development would be a revised theory of practice based on a profound body of academic and theoretical enquiry illustrating the need for new professional roles and responsibilities which training and education will have to supply. No longer would planners frame their professional roles according to centralist planning theories and idealised futures, nor to the interests of established government institutions, powerful landowners or development banks. Instead, advocacy planners would practise "in relation to a growing variety of special interest groups and regulatory systems" (Schön 1983) working more often as intermediaries between the interests of local groups and governments, between regulators and regulated, and with a role frame which is open to discovery based on "shared patterns of enquiry" and decision making on open learning, on action and reflection. What is called for is a kind of "professional pluralism" not easily taught in schools, designed to confront practice situations which are interdisciplinary, complex, uncertain, unstable and unique (Schön 1983, 209).

In this chapter, we will review the kind of competencies and skills which this pluralist stance demands, as well as modes of training and education best suited to development practitioners in general and action planners in particular. We will review what it takes to get started when preparing a programme, as well as what to consider in its design and in the preparation of training materials, in particular trainers' guidebooks. Whilst a variety of training modalities are outlined and illustrated, the principal tool here is field-based training for professional staff and conducted mostly in group, or workshop settings. The focus is on training which runs parallel to project development and in which communities play a strategic role.

What action planners need in competence and skills

Each of the conventional disciplinary fields – planning, architecture, engineering, social science – have at their core bodies of specialised knowledge designed to ensure professional competency and to enable professionals to organise "messes" into understandable plans. Architects are taught to design buildings, shaped in part by an understanding of the performance of materials and the use of appropriate technologies. They develop an understanding of the cultural, climatic and political norms which shape the physical and spatial organisation of the built environment. Structural engineers know what it takes to design efficient structures, whether of buildings, roads, dams, or bridges. Whilst much of this core knowledge is constantly adapted to new innovations and demands, disciplinary knowledge is principally about being competent as an architect, engineer or planner as judged by a variety of professional bodies and institutions. It is now known that this core knowledge does not translate easily into effective development practice. Disciplinary, or "category one" knowledge, made rigorous by scientific or social theory and technique, is more easily taught because it is easy to codify with numbers, routines and language and because it assumes operational processes to be explicit, technically rationalisable and single-disciplinary. It assumes a context for learning and practice which is relatively certain, stable, easy to measure and model, which is precisely what cannot be assumed in development work. In what Shanahan & Ward (1995, 73) term as tendency one in their analysis of university adult education, disciplinary teaching "is characterised as 'academic' in the sense that it would appear to be 'cut off' from everyday life and is not deliberately aimed at changing society in any way".

In schools, disciplinary skills and disciplinary values are the basis around which curricula are designed. Students are taught inside to bring these same values uncompromisingly to projects, only to find outside that few care much about these values. They are taught that innovation is the prerogative of their profession and earn their grades for the new, the unfamiliar, the extraordinary.

Projects are more important than processes, understanding divorced from action, rigour more rewarded than relevance, single or single-body clients more familiar than multiple clients. In academia, clients are usually "on your side", supportive and well-off. They know what they want and have the means, the connections and the political savvy to get it. They are usually literate, articulate, speak the same language and are unthreatened by the professional elite. Information is abundant, time is on your side, and comprehensive surveys and statistical modelling of trends and futures are all a measure of good practice. To be in control is to be professionally competent (Hamdi 1996).

If we now refer to Figure 5.1 with its two columns of characteristics, those taught "inside" and those demanded "outside", we come to understand three seemingly key issues which it raises. First, on the left and "inside" we see an agenda which is principally convenient for *teaching*. It fits timetables, results are easily assessable against well-tried formal academic criteria, it promotes authority of teachers and fits the orthodox definition of rigorous enquiry. On the right and "outside" we find an agenda more suitable for *learning*, but which involves activities on the doubtful side of academic enquiry. Teaching and learning become disparate activities with competing objectives and divergent routines. We must, it seems, distinguish what can be taught, from what must be learnt, and then search for settings and pedagogy which craft a better balance between the two.

Second, these same divisions point to modes of acquiring knowledge which are legitimately distinguishable in their ideals and objectives. The first, "inside", in search of universal truths and principles; the second, "outside", in search of locally appropriate practices. What is needed are modes of teaching and acquiring skills and knowledge which at once have universal value and local relevance. Are these two realms irreconcilable? How can the demand in education for freedom to innovate with theory and explore ideas be made more compatible with that of practice and of developing the necessary skills? How can we break the prejudices of

INSIDE: ACADEMIC/PRACTICE AGENDA	OUTSIDE: URBAN REALITIES
INSTITUTIONAL TRUTHS	SOCIAL/ECONOMIC TRUTHS
IDEALISED GOALS (DISCIPLINARY)	DESIRED GOALS/NEEDS (PEOPLE)
PROFESSIONAL ORIGINALITY	POPULIST INNOVATION
EXPERTS AS LEAD AGENTS	EXPERTS AS CATALYSTS
UNDERSTANDING	ACTION
POLICY MAKING	POLICY IMPLEMENTATION
RATIONALIST THOUGHT/PROCESS	INFORMED TUITION
SINGLE DISCIPLINARY	INTER/MULTIDISCIPLINARY
SPECIALISTS	GENERALISTS
SINGLE CLIENTS	MULTIPLE CLIENTS
END STATES (PROJECTS)	INCREMENTAL/PROGRESSIVE (PROGRAMMES)
STRICT TIMETABLES	OPEN-ENDED PROGRAMME
CERTAINTY/CONSISTENCY	UNCERTAINTY/TRANSITION/CHANGE
DEFENSIVE	ACCOMMODATING

Figure 5.1 A divided agenda. (Source: Hamdi 1991/1995).

academics who view training with some disdain – it is vocational, hands-on, experimental, skills-oriented, and viewed as not the legitimate business of universities; and conversely break the prejudices of practitioners who view education as preoccupied with theorising and talk-shops, none of which is the business of practice.

Third, if we compare both agendas – "inside" and "outside" – we find one further uncomfortable alliance, that between rigour and relevance, which is best summed up by Donald Schön (1983, 3):

> In the geography of professional practice, there is a very dry, high ground where you can practise the techniques and use the theories on which you got your PhD. Down below, there is a swamp where the real problems lie. The difficulty is to decide whether to stay on the high ground, where you can be rigorous but deal with problems of lesser importance, or go down into the swamp to work on problems you really care about but in a way you see as hopelessly unrigorous. It is the dilemma of rigour or relevance. You can not have both, and the way in which people choose between them sets the course of their professional lives. One consequence is that [professionals] who stick to the high ground become not only separate from practice, but increasingly divergent from it.

Later, in practice, young professionals find themselves threatened by the very principles which they were taught as fundamental to good practice, and search security through a repertoire of defences. The risk of surprise, of being wrong or ignorant, admitting uncertainty, changing your mind or taking second place to non-professionals encourages at best more *specialisation*, at worst more jargon and abstraction. Furthermore, it encourages *simplification*, reducing complex problems into single objectives, measures and criteria; *rejection*, of situations which are not easy to explain, excluding knowledge and information from those outside professional circles; and *assimilation*, normalising differences, denying the unique, the one-off, transforming and incorporating problems into safe and well-established disciplinary routines. "In ways, like these, normal responses maintain or enhance professional power. Reproduced through training and rewards, conservative and well defended, normal [or disciplinary] professionalism is very stable." (Chambers 1993, 6).

In real life, it seems, "we are bound to an epistemology of practice which leaves us at a loss to explain, or even describe, the complexities to which we now give over-riding importance" (Schön 1983, 20). These complexities demand competencies which enable us to cultivate responses to change, diversity, uniqueness and uncertainty which today are the norm. They include socially rather than professionally biased behaviour, continuous adaptation of ideas, methods and techniques, improvisation, experience and intuition. Disciplinary, or "category one" knowledge is lacking in these respects. Not all these competencies can be taught, but most can be nurtured during education and developed in training. They demand experiential as well as didactic training – a "category two" knowledge acquired in practice or simulated practice, through open-learning, promoting wisdom, good judgement and optimal ignorance. Schön (1983), Chambers (1993), Dudley (1993), Edwards (1996), Slim (1996), and others argue these competencies to be important characteristics of a new enabling professional role and a new paradigm for professional development.

In contrast to the orthodox, technically rational role of "instrumental problem solving" and in response to these new demands, Schön (1983, 50) argues for practice based in knowing-in-action – a knowledge base latent in the minds and practices of experts and ordinary people, but which is not easy to describe or make systematic.

> *Once we put aside the models of technical rationality which leads us to think of intelligent practice as an* application *of knowledge to instrumental decisions, there is nothing strange about the idea that a kind of knowing is inherent in intelligent action. Common sense admits this category of know-how, and it does not stretch common sense very much to say that the know-how is in the action . . . Although we sometimes think before acting, it is also true that in much of the spontaneous behaviour of skilful practice, we reveal a kind of knowing which does not stem from a prior intellectual operation.*

Schön argues that intelligent practice cannot be wholly dependent on disciplinary theories and techniques taught in schools which, once learnt, we then assume can be successfully applied. Rather, "much of the knowledge relevant to practice is inherent in intelligent action." Technical rationality, which is the foundation to disciplinary knowledge, depends on agreements about ends, which is precisely what cannot be assumed in practice. In practice, most ends are confused and uncertain. They have to be sought "in action", articulated and agreed, and then often corrected and modified as work proceeds, through monitoring and reflection.

Important to Schön's alternative to technical rationality, therefore, is his concept of reflection-in-action – or of "thinking about doing something while doing it". He argues that much "reflection-in-action hinges on surprise", on making mistakes, on "open learning". We want to reflect on things that go very well or very badly, in order to apply corrective measures as we go to our plans, or indeed to modify the norms and methods of enquiry and action for next time. As such, reflective practice qualifies or disqualifies the assumptions we make, and the values we apply when defining problems, setting priorities or evaluating alternatives. It tells us about the value and appropriateness of the norms and standards we apply, the procedures we adopt, patterns of behaviour we assume to be correct or acceptable, about attitudes – about wisdom and good judgement. "If they are to be effective catalysts for change, practitioners must develop wisdom, that combination of skills, abilities and attitudes which will enable them to operate successfully in a messy and unequal world" (Edwards 1996, 18). Reflection nurtures wisdom and is a "corrective to overlearning" in schools.

In this new, reflective, "open-learning" role, information about the negative impacts of proposals is not withheld from other participants. Assumptions are tested publicly and negotiation about priorities, responsibilities and possible courses of action is conducted in open forum. The objective throughout is to learn about what is most likely to work and who is most likely to be affected and how, rather than to push through pet ideas or idealised solutions. Thus, in a reflective or open-learning contract between practitioners and clients, "the client does not agree to accept the practitioner's authority, but to suspend disbelief in it. He agrees to join the practitioner in inquiring into the situation for which the client seeks help . . ." (Schön 1983, 296–297). This shared pattern of inquiry leads to a restructured understanding about needs, desires and goals, as well as about the nature of problems, the aspirations of people, the constraints imposed by culture, politics and those who hold power. It follows "the Freirian concept of 'Conscientization', calling for raising the self-reflected awareness of people (including experts) rather than educating or indoctrinating them, for giving them power to assert their 'voice' and for stimulating their self-driven collective action to transform their 'reality' . . ." (Rahman 1995, 25).

Thus, in practice and in what PRA methods call "triangulation", broad policy objectives for improving health, education and housing, for example, or even discrete proposals for building schools, health centres or houses, can be confronted and modified by the values and perception of others who may have a better knowledge of conditions and a better understanding of what is likely to work. Representatives from the variety of interest groups and disciplines involved have the opportunity to review the interests of other groups who may have different interpretations of the symptoms and causes of problems, not only to see *what* they see from those others' point of view, but also to understand *why* they see it in the way they do. It leads to agreement that one interpretation may be more adequate than another, even in the opinion of those who originally held the less adequate interpretation. It leads to new questions and, therefore, new lines of inquiry (Hamdi 1991/1995).

Training and education: deciding on focus[2]

Wisdom, good judgement and reflective practices are not easily taught through curricula or classroom instruction. We need instead to provide a variety of connected learning settings in which competencies can be developed, skills taught, topics explored, decision-making processes self-evaluated, techniques invented, new practices devised. We need to engage trainees in a multiplicity of pedagogic forms and training modalities and across disciplines in ways which teach skills important to practising locally and thinking globally – skills in organisation, negotiation, group work, participatory planning, advocacy, mediation, facilitation, listening, evaluation. The enabling professional will need to moderate the demands of equity with efficiency, understand the field of actors and vested interest groups whom they will have to satisfy, and learn to communicate with a variety of techniques suited to the different clients they will have to involve and satisfy, and the different cultural settings in which they will have to work. We need to ensure that the instructional setting in which training and education take place (see Figure 5.2) is conducive to learning and to sharing the knowledge which professionals acquire in ways which empower their clients. We need to understand that "learning is not usually an outcome of formal teaching. Instead it comes from a process of self-development through experience" (Pretty et al 1995).

In the first place, we need to distinguish between the methods and ideals of training and education, and then look to their synergy in building competencies and skills for development practitioners in general and planners in particular.[3]

In simple terms education has to deal with principles; and if principles are by definition "fundamental truths which form the basis to reasoning", then it follows that they must, at the same time, have universal application and local relevance. Education, then, should have universal value outside a specific context (unlike training), and many would argue must by necessity be free of context in order for students to explore and develop the field of ideas – to model the world according to the fundamental truths of their business.

In one sense, then, educators need not rely for their teaching on practice, and are free to invent their own field of constraints and opportunities. (Note we are not saying: educators need not make their teaching fit reality!) In that setting, students are taught the kind of professionalism which enables them to operate in any context (note again we are not saying *irrespective* of context) to *see*, *understand* and *respond*. They will need, therefore, during their education, to acquire wisdom and good judgement, and to appropriate the kind of universal tools with which to respond quickly and effectively to any given set of circumstances – which enables them to work locally and universally.

Training, on the other hand, has to do with the development of skills, and must combine *instruction* with *practice* or simulated practice. Practice outside the setting in which it is to apply, would make little sense. It follows, in general terms, that the objective and value of training can only be described on the basis of local needs and

---

[2] For a comprehensive review on the education and training of development practitioners, in particular planners, urban designers, engineers and architects, see Hamdi (1996).
[3] These themes are further developed in Hamdi (1986).

culturally-specific practices, and its successes be measured against improved performance for local projects and programmes. It is, as distinct from education, a process in which we teach *how to do* – in which local needs, practices and policies are predominant. The purpose of training, then, is to mobilise a cadre of skills to *craft the implementation* of these policies. Education informs the field of ideas; training follows to build the skills to implement these ideas. In education we teach how to make tools; in training we teach how to use tools, and modify these to fit local practices.

Now all this is not to say that in education we do not teach skills (communication, for example, or analysis), nor that in training we do not teach how to think! Educators are of course concerned with practice, as trainers are concerned with principles. Educators need context as vehicles for learning, just as trainers need principles as vehicles for teaching. But the objectives and foci of the two activities differ distinguishably, and so do the constraints which operate and the methods and techniques we therefore bring to bear in teaching. Each have differing sets of demands placed on them, and for that matter differ considerably in the length of time each takes to enact. Each will affect our choice of setting in which to teach and learn, as well as our choice of pedagogy and instructional technique.

Deciding on setting

Time-honoured practice in teaching suggests two settings in which learning about practice can be nurtured, each offering their own constraints and opportunities for both training and education: *learning from practice* (and with practitioners) and *learning in practice* (and with communities) (see Figure 5.2). Many times these are combined into single programmes whose content and direction will vary according to the focus of the programme (training, education), its objectives (topics, skills, methods) and according to the time available and for whom it is intended (policy staff, technical staff, students of development).

In *learning from practice* instruction is in short, interactive, thematically discrete, issue-focused workshops using case studies or simulations as the principal vehicle for inquiry. In the short time available (three days to one week) participants are introduced to a problem set which is either modelled on or taken from practice. They are asked to review the social, economic and physical context before their analysis and before deciding on a plan of action.

Whilst each case study and each workshop offers a broad range of issues and instructional opportunities, each is designed to illustrate discrete themes or topics with varying emphasis. These will be grouped, typically, into three often overlapping categories: *skills-related topics* (e.g. data collection, data analysis, participatory techniques, interviewing, communication, negotiation, mapping); *planning methods* (e.g. planning for self-settlement or for urban improvement, or using PRA methods); and *decision-making processes* (related to project preparation, roles and relationships of decision makers, assessing tradeoffs, dealing with constraints, as well as deciding the physical, social and political environment in which project work takes place). As such, learning from practice is akin to what Shanahan & Ward (1995, 74) describe as "tendency three" in university adult education (UAE).

	LEARNING *FROM* PRACTICE (and with practitioners)	LEARNING *IN* PRACTICE (and with communities)
PURPOSE	• teaching principles • subject or topic led • doing by learning • understanding derived from action	• teaching practices • programme or project led • learning by doing • action derived from understanding
PRINCIPAL VEHICLES OF INSTRUCTION	• case studies • simulations • role playing	• live projects • community programmes
KNOWLEDGE/ COMPETENCIES	• principles • best theories • approaches/attitudes • topics	• best practices • best judgement • behaviour • reflection • advocacy • improvisation • optimal ignorance • adaptation
SKILLS	• decision making • programme formulation • project preparation • evaluation • communication • interdisciplinary know-how • methods (planning, participation, PRA) • negotiation • data/survey	• decision making • enabling • looking/listening/interviewing • measuring • communication • reflection/evaluation • applications (of methods, principles) • project/prog implementation • mapping • trouble-shooting • negotiation • diagramming • analysis
LOCATIONAL CHARACTERISTICS	• in-house (non-region specific) • overseas (or on site)	• on site • in-country (or in close proximity to project area)
MODALITIES	• clinical instruction (workshops/seminars)	• field-based project development workshops • field-based evaluation • shadow programmes • secondment • partnerships
PRINCIPAL INFORMANTS	• practitioners • researchers • community leaders • trainees	• community leaders • other stakeholders (experts, government officials, development agency staff) • trainees

Figure 5.2 Designing a programme: deciding on settings.

"This is characterised by professional education/training whereby the adult student is trained to act on other people's environments, not his/her own. This is UAE for professional development. It is oriented toward changing environments but the environments it aims to change are those of other peoples – the clients who will pay for the services."

Skills development, planning methods and decision making often combine into case studies directed to four principal areas of exploration. First, *sensitising students and trainees* to the political, social and economic context for decision making and project work. Second, and subsequently, for *programme formulation and policy development*. For example, making urban-level structure plans, targeting localities for investment, reviewing the role of urban institutions. Third, for *project development* – for urban upgrading, for example, or new site development. Fourth, for *project and programme monitoring and evaluation*, offering rules of thumb and other techniques with which to self-assess the strengths and weaknesses of plans and planning and so to decide corrective measures for existing projects and build experience for new ones.

Unlike case-study-led training, *learning in practice* demands that students/trainees become involved on location, in the practice setting itself. The objectives of learning in practice are less to do with preparing people in project tasks or routines and "more to do with facilitating social change through some form of collective – personal learning . . . by attempting to create an educational environment which enables individuals – and through them, the 'excluded groups' to which they [may] 'belong' – to empower themselves. . . . In this way, 'learning', teaching, training becomes capacity building". (Shanahan & Ward 1995, 74). Often referred to as "on-the-job" training, learning in practice typically involves, therefore, field-based work or workshops, and is based on site and in communities. Trainees may be attached to a project or programme and in various capacities and relationships. In this respect, there are a variety of training modalities, often used in combination, but whose application depends largely on the purpose of training and on who is being trained. Field-based workshops, field-based research, live studios, shadow programmes, partners in research and field-based secondments are all examples, some of which we will return to later in this chapter. Each, in different ways, offers insights and experience into the spectrum of development issues and settings which trainees are likely to confront in practice. The intermixing of these is paramount in curriculum development and course planning.

Planning a programme for field-based instruction

During the preparatory phases, the purpose and objectives of training have to be decided and, on that basis, decisions made about the appropriate setting in which it is to be conducted – its location, participants, costs, materials, sorts of training materials and schedules (see Figure 5.3).

During the course of field-based project development workshops, additional training needs will become evident "in action", and supplementary clinical or topic-based training workshops will need to be designed – for example, for interviewing techniques, site planning or infrastructure design. The tasks, responsibilities and

OBJECTIVES	LOCATION	COSTS	PARTICIPANTS	MATERIALS/ EQUIPMENT	SOURCE OF TRAINING	SCHEDULING
• urban improvement • infrastructure planning • new settlement design • capacity building • teach skills • change behaviour • change attitudes • change methods	• school house • church hall • community centre • local planning office	• materials • training • trainee replacement • trainees' per deums • travel • accommodation • catering • space rental • special events • reporting	• community leaders • technical staff from each of the disciplines involved in project (principal trainers) • management staff • NGOs • representatives from each of the authorities responsible for planning and implementation	• rough large paper for charts • tape/pins/ markers • mapping materials (card, paper, scissors, etc.) • modelling materials (card, boxes, tape, etc.) • tables, chairs • base plans and base information • programme/ schedules • certificates • audio-visual	• community leaders • local university staff • local consultants • government staff • NGOs	• phases of training • length of each training phase • timing • timetables

Figure 5.3 Planning a programme for field-based workshops.

relationships between expatriate consultants and local trainers (from local universities, government departments, NGOs or local consultants) need to be worked out, as well as the means by which the results of training will be evaluated. In most cases, universities are involved to prepare and manage programmes, evaluate results and ensure a programme of continued training and evaluation services to the various government departments. Students and professional trainers are, therefore, often involved together in workshops which serve both training and educational objectives.

Before training can start, preliminary meetings with communities and trainers will need to record the commitment of all parties to training. Participants will *need* to be motivated and, furthermore, convinced, that training will serve their purpose, that they will be better off after training in doing their work. "Lack of motivation is one of the main reasons why learning fails", and this may be due to a variety of reasons. It may be that trainees attend training sessions because they have been instructed to do so and may not know why they are attending. Others, if they are in practice, will be fearful of the backlog of work at their offices which may develop whilst they attend training programmes. Participants may be uninvolved due to the teaching style of training programmes (lectures, talked down at, culturally unfamiliar techniques such as gaming or role playing). Some will know it all from before and yet others may be suspicious or resentful of the trainer or their organisation. In all cases where motivation is low, the rewards are likely to be unclear. Trainers will be looking to tangible signs of promotion, new working opportunities, better jobs, or more marketable skills (Pretty et al 1995). In all these respects, the benefits of training will need to be made clear, so that the relevant government departments can become committed, and properly resourced to support. Changes in routine and procedure within these departments which emerge after training will have to be accommodated, changes which may imply new terms of reference for operatives, once they return to their respective jobs. In these respects, training will have a profound influence on institutional reforms generated *from inside* by that institution's own operatives.

Typically, training programmes will adopt a combination of objectives, some more emphasised than others. These are likely to include the desire to *change behaviour* amongst administrators, institutions or professional staff in order to adopt new planning routines which are more participatory, more adaptive or decentralised, for example; to *persuade* people such as managers to adopt a flexible approach to standards or development controls; to *inform* on latest methods, techniques or technologies; to *stimulate thought* about needs, objectives or priorities; to *motivate* action where there has been intransigence; and to *change attitudes* and *shift paradigms* about the delivery of housing, services or utilities (Pretty et al 1995).

During the planning phases of training programmes, careful consideration will need to be given to training materials. These will need to be prepared in ways which enable trainers (and potential trainers) to adapt training material into formats, language and visual material which are easily understood, culturally appropriate and simple to produce. Wallcharts, postcards, models, Planning for Real packs, theatre and video are all common media. Most common, perhaps, for training technical staff is the trainer's guidebook which today proliferates in all fields of development work.

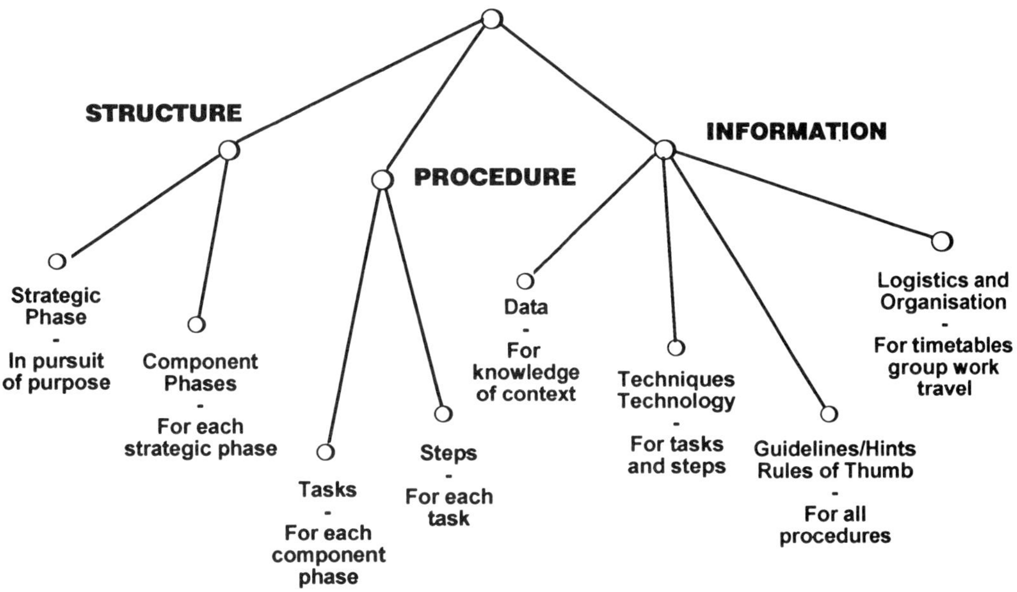

PURPOSE / OBJECTIVES

Figure 5.4 Designing a programme: structure, procedure and information for training materials.

Figure 5.4 illustrates at least four levels of information and activity which are usefully contained in the trainer's pack and which give structure (without content) to the design of training materials. Figures 5.5–5.9 illustrate one way of setting out this structure in guidebook format, derived from field work in Bangladesh.

Assuming the value of guidebooks, and accepting the limitations of "book" formats (see Dudley 1993, Pretty et al 1995), a number of premises are worth noting when preparing their format and content, and those of other training materials.

First, guidebooks should avoid assuming correct solutions, or guaranteed outputs. Philosophy, process and method are the principal means with which to structure programmes, rather than strict instructions. A menu of formats and techniques, fact sheets, help cards and project planners which can be used in a variety of combinations, tailored to the task at hand, is useful. Strict instructions, sophisticated diagrams and jargon block innovation, subordinate the role of trainers and assume guidebooks and manuals to be substitutes for professional competence.

Second, guidebooks will need to strike a balance in their content between information which is transferable from place to place, and information which is place specific. They will need, in other words, to be both generally useful and locally relevant. Both trainers and trainees are encouraged to contribute to the content of training. Trainers bring method, structure and principles based on best practices, guiding trainees toward outputs which are formulated during and after training and which can include information and examples of work which trainees themselves provide to illustrate processes.

Third, it follows that the content of guidebooks is best derived after training and with trainees, drawing on their experience and technical understanding of

COMMUNITY ACTION PLANNING

SUMMARY

STRATEGIC PHASES	COMPONENTS	PLANNING TASKS
Statement of PROBLEMS and OPPORTUNITIES *Page II–1*	**IDENTIFYING URBAN ISSUES** *Page II–2*	1. Review Topics *Page II–5* 2. Summarize Issues *Page II–7*
	UNDERSTANDING COMMUNITY CONTEXT *Page II–9*	3. Review Community Issues *Page II-8* 4. Make Community Observations *Page II-9* * Review Problems *Page II-11*
Documentation of KEY INFORMATION *Page II–13*	**ASSEMBLING INFORMATION** *Page II–14*	5. Prepare Base Plan *Page II-16* 6. Identify Spatial/Physical Elements *Page II-18* 7. Identify Non-spatial Elements *Page II-19*
	MAKING COMMUNITY MAPS *Page II–18*	8. Complete Base Map *Page II-22*
	IDENTIFYING CHARACTERISTICS *Page II–24*	9. Prepare Typologies *Page II-26*
Set of ACTIONS & Related TASKS *Page II–29*	**DETERMINING ACTIONS** *Page II–30*	10. Decide Actions *Page II-32* 11. Gather Prioritized Actions *Page II-33*
Plan for IMPLEMENTATION *Page II–35*	**CONSIDERING IMPLEMENTATION** *Page II–36*	12. Identify Tasks *Page II-38* 13. Consider Constraints *Page II-39* 14. Establish Responsibilities *Page II-40* * Consider Roles *Page II-41*
	SYNTHESIZING PROPOSAL *Page II–42*	15. Prepare Coordinated Plan of Action *Page II-44* * Supplementary Tasks

HAMDI – GOETHERT

Figures 5.5–5.9 Samples from a manual on Action Planning prepared in Bangladesh (Hamdi & Goethert 1995).

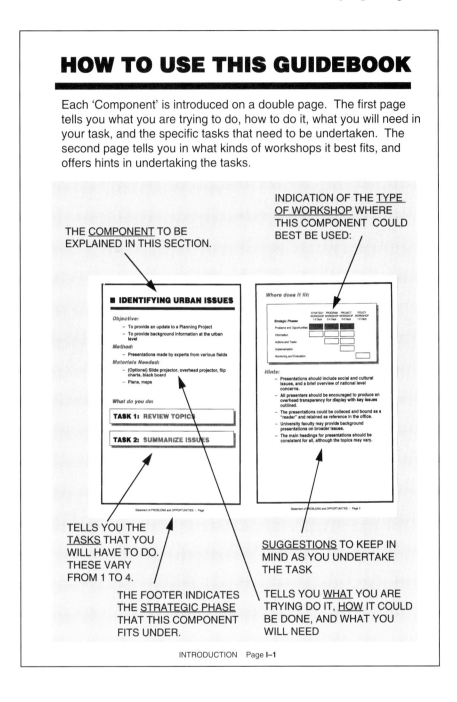

Figure 5.6

136 Action Planning for Cities

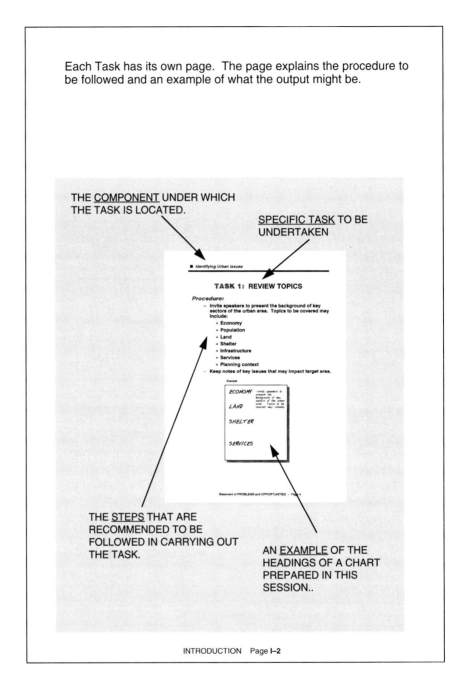

Figure 5.7

■ IDENTIFYING CHARACTERISTICS

Objective:
- To document plot types as a basis for assessing deficiencies in infrastructure, plot uses, densities, and growth potential

Method:
- Family profiles, plot surveys through interviews and plot measurement
- Graphical representation, numerical calculations and description text

Materials Needed:
- Plans, measuring tape, pencil, paper
-
-

What do you do:

TASK 9: PREPARE TYPOLOGIES

Hints:

Prepare a checklist for interviewing families.

Ensure that you have the right equipment before going out to the community.

A clipboard may be useful for taking notes in the field.

A Polaroid camera is helpful to record information.

Plan for IMPLEMENTATION Page II–1

Figure 5.8 Component phase: Identifying characteristics (strategic phase: Documentation of key information).

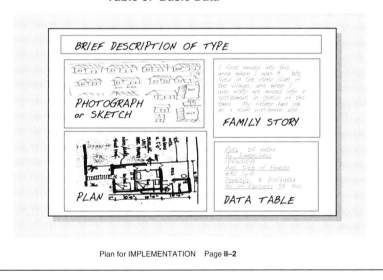

■ *Making Community Map*

TASK 9: PREPARE TYPOLOGIES

Procedure:

- Identify key types of dwelling/plot situations found in area. Types are determined by a combination of:
    » Use (commercial, mixed, residential)
    » Plot sizes (large, small)
    » Tenure (ownership, rental, squatter)
    » Building type (multi-story, single floor, shack)
- Prepare the following for each dwelling/plot type:
    » Description of <u>type</u>
    » Description of <u>development process</u> in the form of a "family story" highlighting past, present situation and future expectations
    » Description of <u>physical characteristics:</u>
        • Plot plan with dwelling, plot uses, and dimensions
        • Photograph or sketch of dwelling
        • Table of Basic Data

Plan for IMPLEMENTATION   Page **II–2**

Figure 5.9 Tasks to undertake component phase with steps to follow in undertaking each task.

community leaders, government staff, local practitioners and NGOs, all of whom are likely to contribute to the training programme.

Finally, guidebooks and training programmes will need to cater to at least two additional demands: those of managers and their institutions, and those of project staff. Managers will be concerned with effective co-ordination and accountability and will want to minimise risk and exert control over project development. They will, therefore, look to the means by which training will help their purpose in this respect. They will want to know "what their staff are learning and why" (Davidson et al undated). Field staff, on the other hand, will want flexibility in their routines and relative autonomy as decision makers, so that they can respond as they see fit to local problems. They will need to be taught, during training, how to adapt routine procedures and invent formats which suit their purpose. Training programmes will, therefore, need to balance the need for a co-ordinated and planned response to planning, with an equal demand to be adaptive. Too much procedure will inhibit the ability of field staff to act quickly and spontaneously; too little will lead to responses which are *ad hoc* and unaccountable. It will threaten the status of managers who will see their capacity to manage undermined by the training programme.

Deciding modalities

The choice of learning modality will be governed by its aims, the setting in which training will take place, who is to be trained and in what.

Clinical workshops and seminars are common modes of instruction. Typically, participants through case studies role play the key actors who are likely to be involved in response to a problem set – government officials, community leaders, municipal engineers, development agency staff, consultants – and learn how each will focus the issues, protect their vested interests and interpret their responses to problems and opportunities. Case studies and simulation "encourages students to synthesise, evaluate and select material from knowledge, skills and methods courses, and apply it to policy formulation and plan making" (Rakodi 1996, 52). Participants are drawn from the major disciplinary fields that are likely to impact project development – planning, engineering, social development, health – and learn how each set of disciplinary interests is likely to contribute to the programme, and how each set of disciplinary demands and decisions may be modified, made relevant or irrelevant by the demands and decisions of others. It is in this interactive environment that interdisciplinary learning is nurtured to add to the more clinical settings of disciplinary teaching where trainees learn about health, planning or engineering. Proximity to location, under this modality, whilst useful, is not essential to instruction.

Field-based project development workshops sometimes referred to as charettes, or planning weekends, incorporate many of the characteristics of running a live project, but differ in three important respects. First, sessions are short, lasting from three days up to two weeks. Second, the emphasis is away from project delivery and instead toward methods and techniques for project preparation for rapid assessment and collaborative and community decision making. Issues, attitudes and best judgement are all emphasised and nurtured. Results tend to be more strategic than detailed. Third, sessions are conducted entirely in the field. Where these workshops serve an educational function, trainee students return to their universities and develop their field-derived proposals in more detail. Field-based workshops are a good vehicle for fostering collaboration amongst government departments and partnerships amongst development agencies who are invited to review the results and contribute as discussants. They are a useful way of getting projects started and for training. On site, trainees confront real constraints and conflicts in values, priorities and timetables, with changes of mind, with client members who appear and disappear, often randomly, with no access to office equipment like photocopying machines or drawing tables. Trainees are charged to innovate culturally appropriate forms of communication, non-reliant on client literacy or on slide projectors, or overhead transparencies or flip-charts. Instead, street theatre, puppetry, painted murals and community models are the norm. Later, this same group will be charged with "selling" their ideas and projects to government officials and other experts.

Workshop programmes are clustered into three typical phases: getting information, developing a strategic plan or "over-arching" concept (sometimes referred to as "taking a position"), and preparing action plans. A variety of examples, taken from throughout the world, are illustrated in Chapter 6.

Unlike clinical or in-house case-study-driven evaluation, *field-based evaluation* involves learning from communities and community projects, with a view to institutionalising lessons learnt, and building a broader understanding of development processes, whether in housing, health, enterprise development or credit schemes. Evaluation is based on information derived and mapped directly with operatives and beneficiaries. Oral testimonies, story gathering, social mapping and programme diaries, as well as interviewing, listening and mapping, are all useful techniques with which trainees become familiar. Field work varies in time, length and style. Evaluation workshops can last one to two weeks, where all involved reflect on the processes which shaped or hindered development. Often, lessons learnt form the basis to new programme formulation – and offer a point of departure for next time. For students of development practice, extended field-based postings or research are an additional modality. In this case, trainees spend time in and with communities, observing and mapping production and distribution processes of goods and services, building and decision-making processes, the effect of government subsidy and credit system on enterprise development, and inter-community partnerships, amongst others.

Of the numerous other modalities, the following are the most common. *Shadow programmes* involve trainees being attached to an organisation or a unit of that organisation. Trainees track the activities of a single operative throughout the life of a specific programme and learn by observation. *Partners in research and project development* is a modality clearly allied to the shadow programme. Unlike the former where trainees remain principally as observers and documenters rather than integral team members, partnership programmes involve trainees in work which is productive to a programme and learn by apprenticeship. Two modes are common. The first, with an educational focus, involves students of development practice as research assistants allied to academic staff, and the students gain instruction by doing. The second is where in-country staff or Southern NGOs are partnered to expatriate consultants or Northern NGOs who, *de facto*, become trainers. Over the period of the project, in-country staff and organisations acquire the skills and know-how for conducting their own subsequent programmes and assume self-sufficiency. Two issues impose severe limitations to this mode of training: first, most consultants are paid according to a specified schedule of outputs. The lengthy process of training often disrupts the practitioner's schedule. As a result, trainees are often marginalised from mainstream work and assume subsidiary and routine roles. Second, self-sufficiency for expatriate staff is an unprofitable ideal. Consultants, especially, depend for their livelihood on ensuring their continued involvement with projects and may often mystify planning processes. *Field-based secondments* are increasingly popular for students and young professionals alike. Many of the bilateral development agencies now offer training opportunities to newly qualified professionals through secondments to their field or regional offices. Others are experimenting with secondments for students in mid-training. One example is the British Voluntary Services Overseas (VSO) programme. Under this programme, students seek their own field placements within communities for periods of 6–12 months, based on their interests and disciplines. On their return, they are required to organise their experience in ways which can be communicated to schoolchildren. Information packs, slide presentations and development games involve children in the experience of the student trainee and, at the same time, encourage the trainee to develop training/teaching skills.

Underlying principles

In their different ways, all training modalities, as well as the examples illustrated in Chapter 6, embody a number of fundamental principles which underpin their design. First, training programmes, particularly those which are field based, are *trainee led*. Trainees are asked to a build a programme around a problem set, and to identify what needs to be considered – what information and know-how will be needed, and then how to get it before making proposals for its resolution. Unlike subject-driven enquiry (we need a new road from A to B, this is how to design and provide it), trainees set their own parameters and develop their own criteria (we need to improve access from A to B, what do we need to think about when doing it?). The answer is not assumed in the question, the limits of enquiry are not pre-set, the programme is structured but not prescribed, curricula are avoided. Trainees are encouraged to reformulate the problem in terms which are holistic and inter-disciplinary, reflecting on their own experience and expertise and those of the environmentalists, anthropologists and administrators with whom they are likely to be working. In this way, trainees act as informants to the programme, and become themselves a resource to the training sessions. Second, programmes are *active and interactive*. The general consensus is that more learning takes place by doing, and by doing it with those who have most knowledge about the setting in which training is taking place. "It almost doesn't matter what you do so long as you do something. If your first idea is a good idea then that's fortunate, but even if it is not, it may provoke a response or suggest another potentially constructive avenue for [work]." (Dudley 1993, 69).

Participants are encouraged to perceive problems and opportunities, issues and interventions through the eyes of the various actors with whom they will have to deal after training by interacting directly with those others, or through role playing.

Not all will share a common view of how to proceed, nor will they necessarily agree on the value or even existence of the problem. Each disciplinary position, and each set of vested interests, are presented and assessed in so far as how they might influence the nature of the enquiry, and later the design of the project or programme itself. In the process, trainees develop analytical skills for problem seeking and problem solving, for finding questions and answers and, in this way, find gaps in their own knowledge and know-how. The enquiry, in this respect, is trainee led. Training needs are developed "in-action", based on what trainees themselves identify as difficulties in their capability to understand the context and to develop the skills it demands to be competent.

As a result, and thirdly, programmes are designed where *trainee needs are linked to trainer demands*. Most times training programmes are initiated "from outside", in response to projects which governments with development agencies will have agreed. Training needs assessments are, therefore, conducted by trainers following a pattern of enquiry which considers potential trainees instrumentally in respect to the proper functioning of the project. Trainers sort out what needs to be done, whether the skills to do it are available and, if not, what training is needed to fill the gap in skills and know-how. Trainer demands, therefore, dominate the planning of training programmes.

These demands, if they are to be assimilated by trainees, will have to be transformed into needs which trainees identify as *tangible and concrete*, a fourth important principle in programme design. Unless they are, trainees will remain passive observers and will lack commitment. They will be there because they were told or are paid to be there.

Fifth, training programmes are usefully designed to maximise the opportunity for *improvisation and chance learning*. Whether programmes are designed around case studies or field work, trainees are encouraged to discover questions to shape their investigations, with opportunities for observing the unexpected, coming across information by chance, stumbling upon good ideas, and pursuing lines of enquiry which may not have been part of the initial programme. In this respect, Dudley (1993, 60) suggests the principle of maximum serendipity: "Seek out situations which increase the chances of (trainer and trainee) discovering something which the other knows. Do things together. Create a tangible focus and an understood context."

Finally, training will need to be easily *scaled* and know-how *widely disseminated* if it is to have effect. A number of criteria are important. For example, those trained can often themselves become trainers, even when they are not specifically trained in this respect. Communities can train other communities, technical officers other technical officers and managers other managers, thus encouraging a *horizontal transfer* of know-how. Urban institutions will have to incorporate training into their operational routines, and not see it as a series of one-off events into which they occasionally step out. This demands a preparedness amongst policy makers to institutionalise programmes, even though those trained may demand their institutions to adapt to new routines and new work habits. Training programmes cannot therefore demand large outlays of resources (training centres, specialised training staff, sophisticated technology), nor can they rely on outsiders for extended periods. Except in special circumstances, overseas training should be minimised and in-country training maximised, through national and regional universities and training centres. Training techniques and technologies should be simple and transferable, where sophisticated equipment and complex procedures are avoided, as they should be in action planning programmes themselves.

How then do these principles and modalities combine in practice? In Chapter 6 we illustrate a variety of examples.

References

Chambers, R. 1993. *Challenging the Professions*. London: Intermediate Technology Publications.
Davidson, F., Teerlink, H. and Mengers, H. (undated). Training for integrated infrastructure development. Rotterdam: Institute for Housing and Urban Development Studies. (Unpublished.)
Dudley, E. 1993. *The Critical Village: Beyond Community Participation*. London: Routledge.
Edwards, M. 1996. The getting of wisdom: educating the reflective practitioner. In Hamdi, N. (ed.), *Educating for Real: The Training of Professionals for Development Practice*. London: Intermediate Technology Publications.
Hamdi, N. 1986. Training and education. Inventing a programme and getting it to work. *Habitat International* 10 (3): 131–140.
Hamdi, N. 1991/1995. *Housing Without Houses: Participation, Flexibility, Enablement*. New York: Van Nostrand Reinhold; London: Intermediate Technology Publications.
Hamdi, N. (ed.) 1996. *Educating for Real: The Training of Professionals for Development Practice*. London: Intermediate Technology Publications.
Hamdi, N. & Goethert, R. 1995. *Community Action Planning: A Manual for Technical Staff Working with Communities*. Prepared as part of the project: Government of the People's Republic of Bangladesh UNDP/UNCHS (Habitat) Project BGO/88/052. Preparation of Strategic Plan, Master Plan, Detailed Area Plan – Metropolitan Development and Plan Preparation and Management. Dhaka and Chittagong.
Harris, N. 1992. *Cities in the 1990s: The Challenge for Developing Countries*. London: UCL Press.
McGehee & Thayer, In: UNCHS 1987. Manual for Training Needs Assessment in Human Settlements Organisations. Arlington USA. Institute of Urban Studies, the University of Texas.
Pretty, J.N., Guijt, I., Thompson, J. & Scoones, I. 1995. *Participatory Learning in Action*. London: International Institute for Environment and Development. Participatory Methodology Series.
Rahman, M.A. 1995. Participatory development: toward liberation or co-option? In Craig, G. & Mayo, M. (eds), *Community Empowerment: A Reader in Participation and Development*. London: ZED Books.
Rakodi, C. 1996. Educating urban planners. In Hamdi, N. (ed.), *Educating for Real: The Training of Professionals for Development Practice*. London: Intermediate Technology Publications.
Schön, D.A. 1983. *The Reflective Practitioner: How Professionals Think in Action*. New York: Basic Books.
Schön, D.A. 1984. The architectural studio as exemplar of education for reflection-in-action. *Journal of Architectural Education* 38 (1): 2–9.

Shanahan, P. & Ward, J. 1995. The university and empowerment: the European Union, university adult education and community economic development with "excluded groups". In Craig, G. & Mayo, M. (eds), *Community Empowerment: A Reader in Participation and Development*. London: ZED Books.

Slim, H. 1996. Practical wisdom and the education of today's relief worker. In Hamdi, N. (ed.), *Educating for Real: The Training of Professionals for Development Practice*. London: Intermediate Technology Publications.

CHAPTER 6

Learning in Practice: Field-Based Project Development Workshops

I hear and forget
I see and remember
I do and understand
           Confucius

The followings series of field workshops, under the theme "Rebuilding Communities", were organised as part of the SIGUS[1] and CENDEP[2] *Learning in Practice* programme. These workshops, typically situated in Third World communities, share several characteristics:

- The freedom and responsibility of the workshop participants to define their own areas of exploration and subsequently agendas for action within the framework of concerns derived from the field and with local participants.

- The review and revision of these programmes and proposals by members of the community as well as by members of the various organisations brought into contact with the activities of the workshop.

- The very real and immediate nature of the problems and opportunities discovered by the workshop participants in their encounter with the everyday-reality of the community. Here, what is possible and/or desirable in theory confronts what is possible and/or desirable in practice, resulting in a powerful cross-fertilisation of both.

- The integration of host institutions (typically local schools of architecture and/or planning) into the pedagogical aims and structures of each workshop. By bringing together an international group of participants, a range of perspectives is generated.

---

[1] SIGUS: Special Interest Group in Urban Settlement, School of Architecture and Planning, Massachusetts Institute of Technology, USA.
[2] CENDEP: Centre for Development and Emergency Planning, Schools of Architecture and Planning, Oxford Brookes University, UK.

In addition, all workshops share the following learning outcomes:

- The emphasis on developing methods for participatory planning, field surveys and conflict resolution, and on working in multidisciplinary and multicultural groups.
- The need to identify community leaders and other stakeholders as working partners for project development and implementation.
- The need to reflect on the concept of community and on the relationship between "outsider" and "insider" when deciding interventions.
- The importance of building experience of working in an often divided society.
- The necessity to identify an effective institutional framework for project development and to look to ways of influencing policy through community-level projects.
- The development of presentation skills to suit a variety of complex settings and client groups.

The Five Workshops[3]

Each of the workshops reviewed in this chapter typically follows the schedule illustrated in Figure 6.1. The examples reflect the specificities of each setting as developed during the workshops. Accordingly, a variety of presentation formats are used (project outlines, journal excerpts, reflective narratives, context descriptions) although the structure of each workshop is similar throughout. The text has been retyped and arranged to form an overall presentation on the workshops, but the words themselves and the illustrations come directly from the workshops.

1. *"Something is Happening in Southside"* – *The Jamaica workshop* targeted a low-income and marginalised community in Kingston, the capital city. The Southside community is located in a prized expansion zone of a revitalising downtown. Examples from the workshop illustrate the following: the site and the community context; learning from other examples; understanding the community; identifying strengths, opportunities and problems; structuring an approach; projects for implementation.

2. *"Reach out to the Moon"* – *The India workshop* addressed issues of a poor squatter community located in the midst of an older, long-established neighbourhood, which itself had developed incrementally. A reflective

---

[3] The workshop in Jamaica was sponsored by the Overseas Development Administration, those in India and Poland were partially sponsored by the US Agency for International Development, and that in Peru by the British Council.

FIELD WORKSHOP						
TYPICAL PROGRAMME - WEEK 1						
Sunday Day 1	Monday Day 2	Tuesday Day 3	Wednesday Day 4	Thursday Day 5	Friday Day 6	Saturday Day 7
ARRIVAL	1. INTRODUCTORY TOUR of host city 2. WELCOME RECEPTION with community	3. PRESENTATIONS of urban area context and the community by leaders and invited guests	4. FIELD SURVEY Identification of topologies of housing projects, public and private developments, and neighbourhoods (low, middle, high)	5. FIELD WORK Teams focus on three activities: collection of family stories, building a large-scale neighbourhood model and making tentative assessment of problems and opportunities		6. COMMUNITY FEEDBACK Display of neighbourhood model for community identification of problems and opportunities (all day)
TYPICAL PROGRAMME - WEEK 2						
Day 8	Day 9	Day 10	Day 11	Day 12	Day 13	Day 14
7. FREE DAY Optional tour to points of interest	8. ELABORATE STRATEGIES Teams tackle and develop specific issues as identified by initial assessment and community feedback. Each team to include a participating expert			9. PRESENTATION to community and invited guests (evening)	10. INTERNAL MEETING to discuss next steps 11. CLOSING PARTY	DEPARTURE

Figure 6.1 Typical workshop schedule.

account entitled "Architects and Planners in Low Income Settlements: Agents of Change or Development Tourists?" by one of the participants offers an insight into the issues facing development practitioners working in this setting.

3. *"The Bird Can't Fly" – The Belfast workshop* was arguably the most complex and difficult, despite the overwhelming amount of information, the misleadingly familiar setting, and the common language. The workshop was located in the divided and contested areas of West Belfast, in the Springfield Road and Falls Road area, and focused on issues of housing, security, employment, youth relations and community development. The workshop was favoured by a lull in the 25-year conflict which was interrupted on the last day of the workshop by a bombing in London announcing the end to the sectarian ceasefire. It made real the difficulties facing communities in situations of conflict. The examples outline the following: the programme; the context of West Belfast and "The Troubles"; projects developed by participants; a Belfast journal; an essay on community development work in other people's wars.

4. *"With/In Formal Development" – The Peru workshop* tackled the complexities of deteriorating inner cities and the on-going conflicts of interests amongst

its multiplicity of uses. The basic issues addressed revolved around the questions of "Whose city" and "Is there a common ground?". The examples illustrate the following: information gathering and method; learning from other examples; structuring an approach.

5. *Housing in Transition – The Poland workshop* was held in the first year of the transition to a market economy and explored options for rethinking the physical, economic and institutional aspects of the existing housing complexes. The case study, located in the city of Lublin, highlights the variety of activities built around the workshops, which included seminars, classroom work, special research projects, and summer research. The examples shown include: a background to housing in Poland; methods of work and presentations of participant projects; follow-up activities and workshops.

Learning in Practice: Field-Based Project Development Workshops

Rebuilding Communities — New Delhi, Lima, Kazimierz/Lublin, Belfast, Kingston — Workshops 1990–1996 — Theories · Practice

REBUILDING COMMUNITIES DOWNTOWN
KINGSTON, JAMAICA

THE SITE, THE COMMUNITY

Downtown communities are often characterised by conflicting vested interests, high densities, multi- and largely rental occupancy, absentee landlords, low levels of formal employment, high rates of crime and generally dilapidated housing and infrastructure. These areas are often marginal to city systems despite their prime central location. Despite these characteristics, these communities are highly resourceful. They often hold a strong sense of community and have a long-standing history in the development of cities. At the same time they are constantly under pressure to be redeveloped and present significant challenges to the urban management efforts of government planning authorities.

This two-week workshop focused on a typical downtown area – Southside – in Kingston, Jamaica. It focused on issues and development options culminating in research initiatives urgent to Kingston and relevant to Jamaica and the Caribbean region. It identified issues which are likely to have a bearing on the thinking, practice and education of architects, planners and urban designers.

✦ OBJECTIVES

The workshop programme focused on generating action plans as part of a broader range of proposals to improve the physical, social and economic fabric of the downtown community of Southside, Kingston. The emphasis was on minimal displacement to existing communities which would be achieved through small-scale strategic interventions and with the maximum participation of the broader residential and commercial community. The workshop had three overriding objectives:

▌ To propose improvements relevant to the Southside.
▌ To demonstrate methods which have relevance to other similar communities in Kingston and which can become integral to urban development practices.
▌ To prioritise an agenda of collaborative research relevant to the larger Caribbean region.

✦ VENUE

Participants worked on location within the Southside area with members of the business, commercial and residential community. Small theme-related groups which included planners, architects and social scientists prepared action plans to implement proposals identified in the workshop.

REBUILDING COMMUNITIES DOWNTOWN
KINGSTON, JAMAICA

LEARNING FROM OTHER EXAMPLES
FIELD TRIPS TO SELECTED AREAS

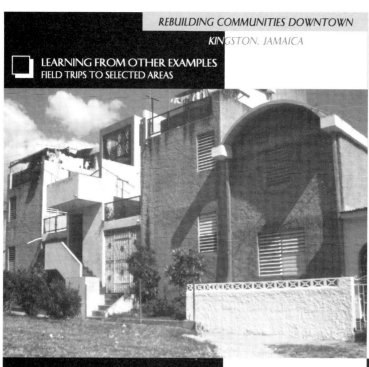

McIntyre Lands (left)

McIntyre Lands is a prize-winning housing project built in the 1970s under the support of Michael Manley, Prime Minister at the time. The project was designed by the Design Collaborative.

The project contains a total of 411 units with a mix of the following types:
- Single-storey expandable 1-bedroom units.
- Single-storey expandable studio units.
- Two-storey 2-bedroom units.
- One-bedroom apartments.
- Studio apartments.

Expansions to single-storey houses were partially implemented, in that walls on property boundaries were built. The project used a team design approach which included the community in the formation of the detailed brief and the design process.

Portmore (right)

The Greater Portmore Project is a new township targeting a wide range of income groups and encompassing some 1300 acres of marginal lands adjacent to the old Portmore in the Kingston Metropolitan Region.

The first phase of the development, to be constructed between 1990 and 1994, comprises the construction of 10 000 houses at an average rate of 2500 houses per year. There will be 800 3-bedroom and 3400 2-bedroom townhouses as well as 5800 studio houses or starter homes, consisting of a core unit with bath and kitchen, and organised in groups of fours. Residents are expected to build additions and improve on the core units.

REBUILDING COMMUNITIES DOWNTOWN
KINGSTON, JAMAICA

UNDERSTANDING THE COMMUNITY
IDENTIFYING KEY ISSUES, QUESTIONS, AND CONCERNS

The community has a population of approximately 6000 residents who are predominantly low income. Unemployment, which ranges from 60% to 85%, and low skill levels are major issues within the community. Residents earn much of their income through informal economic activities such as trading, small-scale manufacturing, catering, hustling, etc.

The Southside neighbourhood has a very poor reputation, associated with theft, drugs and violence. The stigma causes additional problems to the residents because they claim they are often not hired simply because of their home address. Because of its reputation, middle and upper-income groups generally avoid the area.

Physically, the area is in very poor condition. With the exception of one apartment complex consisting of 165 two-room units, the housing stock consists of houses in varying degrees of disrepair. The majority are in a derelict state and many are unsafe. Approximately 6% to 7% of the houses are owner-occupied and these are generally the best maintained houses in the community.

The typical house is based on the "yard" model. Each room is occupied by separate households. A survey revealed that the number of households occupying a yard varied from one to twenty and the number of persons per household varied from one to eighteen with the majority residing in small units of two to four persons.

The area is characterised by absentee ownership and informal or non-existent tenancy arrangements. There is a high level of squatting (called "capturing"). The area also has a large number of vacant lots and derelict abandoned buildings.

✦ IDENTIFYING KEY ISSUES

After information-gathering exercises, the workshop participants began to identify several key areas of concern for the community:

- Employment structures / patterns and disposable income.
- Accessibility of target population to basic social services such as education/training/advice, recreation, health care, etc.; also, the organizations that ensured such access and the degree to which members of the community were integrated into those organizations.
- The composition of the target beneficiary population in terms of income level, education, age, gender, etc. Then what are appropriate strategies for intervention given these characteristics?
- The links between new development and upgrading: what are the socio-economic processes that relate housing upgrades to overall quality of life? How can the housing industry generate employment and economic multipliers? What kinds of pricing structures are most appropriate for this situation?
- Realizing opportunities for economic advancement using skills already existing within the community. Many residents possess little or no formal vocational training, and therefore typically maintain multiple occupations, such as farming, raising goats/chickens, cottage manufacturing, recycling bottles, jobs with an employer, thieving, trading, hustling, agent shopping for funding, drugs sold to outsiders, etc. Would it be worthwhile to propose formal vocational training programs in areas such as concrete block manufacture, tile manufacture, mechanics, carpentry?

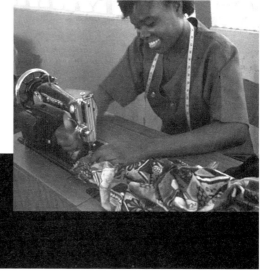

REBUILDING COMMUNITIES DOWNTOWN
KINGSTON, JAMAICA

TAKING A POSITION
IDENTIFYING STRENGTHS, OPPORTUNITIES AND PROBLEMS

Organised into five teams, the workshop participants proceeded to delineate, according to the major areas of concern, characteristics of the community that could be called either problems or opportunities, as either obstacles to further development or as potential resources upon which to build. Some characteristics, such as the predominance of communal child-care and the generally higher share of everyday work shouldered by women, were seen as potentially both a problem, due to the social inequality fostered, and an opportunity, due to the resilient matriarchal network and support structures it promoted. Other characteristics, such as those pertaining to absentee and negligent landlords, the lack in some cases of land tenure, and the poor sanitation, were seen almost exclusively as problems; still other characteristics, such as the physical proximity to workplaces, and the general spirit of resourcefulness amongst some members of the community were seen almost entirely as opportunities.

What emerged from these analyses was the realisation that, in the absence of plentiful material resources, the formation and maintenance of strong and representative community organisations was central to any prospects of medium and long-term development. Several schemes were then proposed that would both satisfy some short-term need as well as provide an impetus for community organisation. The projects were seen as areas through which the community could come together and work jointly with NGOs, local government and other "exterior" organisations so as to take an active role in its own development.

Learning in Practice: Field-Based Project Development Workshops

REBUILDING COMMUNITIES DOWNTOWN
KINGSTON, JAMAICA

STRUCTURING AN APPROACH
PROJECTS FOR IMPLEMENTATION

The projects proposed included:

✦ Empowerment Through a Community Development Organisation

Southside and Tel Aviv are communities threatened by external development interests. In order to prevent mass dislocation, community members must obtain land tenure rights. Currently, much of the land is of unknown ownership or held by absentee landlords. Of particular importance is the securing of rights for especially vulnerable segments of the population, such as women and the elderly.

Housing authorities have found it politically difficult to expropriate land from low-income people. Community-based action needs to take advantage of this political opening and complement it with reforms that address problems including access to credit, legal obstacles to title transfer, lack of adequate municipal sanitation services, and access to training and job-creation programmes.

✦ Lane Living and Street Selling

Lane Living principally is working from the inside out: relating the house to the yard, the yard to the lane: encouraging interaction by living.

Street Selling is working from the outside in, relating the city to the community, using the street by encouraging interaction by commerce. Both are needed to make for a strong and viable community.

✦ Uses of Vacant Lots

The objective was to show the potential of vacant lots in improving the social structure and eventually the economic activities within Southside. The following were examined in addressing this goal:
1. Context of vacant lots
2. Dimensions of lots
3. Tenure
4. Needs of community in relation to lots
5. Previous use
6. Infrastructure
7. Viable use

It was found that approximately 53% of the lots were vacant – defined as lots which had no structure on them and lots with derelict buildings. Some had facades of notable architectural quality which could be renovated and adapted to various uses.

It was also found that the needs and wants of the people in Southside were community based, such as housing, community training centre, schools, clinics, etc. However, these were in conflict with location and value of the property.

✦ Microenterprises

OBJECTIVE

▌ Market Outreach
- outreach to new customers
- product upgrading
- clearing house/intermediary
- group sales

▌ Training
- financial management
- skills development

▌ Credit
- outreach to microenterprises
- alternative collateral
- on-going monitoring and support

▌ Capital: Stock Material and Support
- savings
- supplies for labour

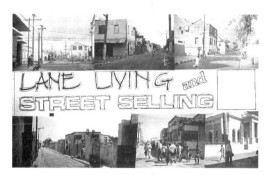

Furniture / Baking / Sewing / Vending / Craft / Tailoring / Carpentry / Beauticians / Upholstery / Electricians / Fishing / Welding / Masonry / Mechanics / Leatherworking / Repairs / Shoes / Restaurants / Garment Production

156 Action Planning for Cities

REBUILDING COMMUNITIES DOWNTOWN
KINGSTON, JAMAICA

✦ Upgrading of Houses

Principles for Proposed Housing Upgrading
- Providing tenure of housing to the occupants.
- Rebuilding with minimum relocation of occupants.
- Revitalisation and improvement of services.
- Attaining lower densities per room, while retaining existing densities per plot.
- Enabling people to participate in design and construction of their houses.
- Intervention of professionals to educate people about building for themselves.
- Revitalisation and reorganisation of open spaces within the plots.
- Creation of a viable maintenance programme and educating the community to participate in it.

Strategies for Housing Upgrading
1. Identification of specific dwelling units for immediate consideration.
2. Establishment of training and technical assistance centre for:
    - building model dwelling units;
    - suggesting methods for expandability;
    - educating the community in construction and self-management.
3. Building courtyards and transforming courtyards of old buildings.
4. Organisation of communal areas on the basis of use.
5. Provision of services that require low maintenance.
6. Exchange of courtyard spaces and dilapidated covered spaces wherever possible.

✦ Recreation and Community Facilities

The design of the central facility would follow the concept of a yard: a courtyard surrounded by a series of different buildings and spaces. Security is a major concern in its concept. However, the facade should not be fortress-like, but should be lively, interacting and inviting to the street. The catering facilities should serve the street as well as the interior. A community notice-board should be located on the outside wall. The internal courtyard should become a focus for surrounding activities. Spaces should be flexible: the large spaces should have subdivision possibilities. A variety of spaces would allow the potential for phased development.

Learning in Practice: Field-Based Project Development Workshops

REBUILDING COMMUNITIES DOWNTOWN
KINGSTON, JAMAICA

Physical

Social/Political

Income and Spending

Existing Edge Conditions

✦ EDGES AND ECONOMIC DEVELOPMENT

Strategy for Development

The relatively higher mobility of women out of the community for economic reasons suggests that this population group could lead the way to even better linkages. Additionally, the "hole-in-the-fence" represented by the Palace Theatre could be exploited to further weaken the social barrier at East Queen Street. Perhaps the area surrounding the theatre could be targeted for sorely needed additional recreation/entertainment development. The imminent rerouting of crosstown traffic onto soon-to-be-completed Airport Highway should be expected to impact life patterns at Southside's north edge.

But the more pressing need is to develop the linkages into Southside rather than the ones out. This is because public and private developers are seeing and acting on Southside's valuable locations - walking distance to both a stunning waterfront and downtown economic and institutional activities. Development is especially on-going along Harbour Street, with apparently no plans for residents to benefit. Lack of land ownership leaves them with no legal power. A major developer, for example, is known to offer squatters J$ 2000 (about $100 US) to move off commercial development sites.

To what extent can the community organise and require government to tie development plans to housing upgrading, community amenities and local employment? Untangling Jamaican land ownership seems a long-term process. Can voters who are not landowners form enough clout to keep Southside their residential neighbourhood? The Kingston Restoration Company's education programme and civic relationships seem to be the beginnings of community employment.

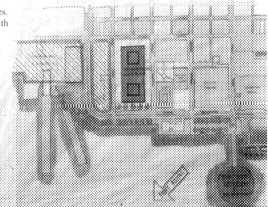

REBUILDING COMMUNITIES DOWNTOWN
KINGSTON, JAMAICA

✦ Bringing Life to the Waterfront

The waterfront and its environs were chosen as a prime area of concern with regards to the local communities and commercial activities. Seen as an area of vast resources, the waterfront appeared to invite interventions along three main axes:
- Commerce and Community
- Transport
- Tourism

Our findings on these issues can be summarised as follows:
- Vacant lots should be targeted for multi-use commercial complexes, apartments (low rise) and sporting and entertainment facilities.
- There exists a need to increase the variety of commercial activities, thus providing opportunities for individuals already in the "market" as well as encouraging creativity amongst new entrepreneurs.
- More interaction between the communities and the corporate world could occur through the creation of more "people places" such as parks, a promenade along the waterfront, sports and entertainment facilities, and outdoor restaurants.
- New transportational links need to be established from the waterfront to the rest of the city.
- The relocation of the ferry pier and the craft market to a more central location would enhance its accessibility to both tourists and office workers.
- A tourist booth/information centre is needed to begin to activate a tourist industry.
- Ridding the harbour of pollution, especially sewage, would make the promotion of water sports such as fishing, scuba diving, wind surfing, etc. more feasible.

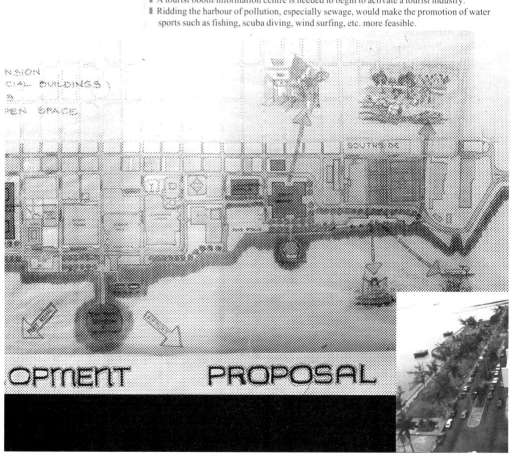

Learning in Practice: Field-Based Project Development Workshops

THEORIES
PRACTICES

REBUILDING COMMUNITIES:
RECOVERING THE GHETTO
"REACH OUT TO THE MOON"

SIGUS   CENDEP
TVB SCHOOL FOR HABITAT STUDIES
DAKSHINPURI, NEW DELHI, INDIA
1994

REBUILDING COMMUNITIES
DAKSHINPURI, NEW DELHI, INDIA

ON ARCHITECTURE + PLANNING IN DEVELOPMENT
A FRAGMENT

ARCHITECTS AND PLANNERS IN LOW-INCOME SETTLEMENTS: AGENTS OF CHANGE OR DEVELOPMENT TOURISTS?

AN ESSAY BY KAREN KHOR, MASTER OF CITY PLANNING, MIT, 1995
DAKSHINPURI, NEW DELHI WORKSHOP PARTICIPANT, 1994

As we entered the bustling world of Dakshinpuri with wide eyes, jeans and backpacks, I felt very much part of a conspicuous tourist group. We were aspiring architects, planners, urban designers and development professionals of the SIGUS Workshop representing three different academic institutions from three continents (MIT, Oxford-Brookes, and New Delhi's TVB School of Habitat Studies). We had converged into this unlikely corner of New Delhi to learn if and how we could apply the skills and knowledge of our professional training toward low-income community development. As a foreigner, another nagging question that followed me throughout my stay in Delhi was what constructive role, if any, can foreigners play in the development of human settlements unfamiliar to them.

Our intent was to learn through doing, and our action plan involved conducting rapid appraisal methods to identify problem areas and opportunities for improving community life for the squatter settlement in Dakshinpuri. In particular, we set out to conduct a rapid reconnaissance of the key issues within the community, get feedback from community members on our findings, engage in further field research and inquiry into specific problem areas, and, finally, present our recommendations to the community and influential institutions.

While we had a plan of action, we soon realised

REBUILDING COMMUNITIES
DAKSHINPURI, NEW DELHI, INDIA

that our ability to implement it would not be entirely within our control. There was a prevailing sense of uncertainty each day about what the particular logistical circumstances of the moment would allow us to do. An unpredictable assortment of activities took form: fleeting group gatherings, prolonged waits, *ad hoc* interviews and data collection, and intense bursts of preparatory activity for presentations....Amidst this bewildering environment, I found that my ingrained conditioning in thorough and systematic inquiry became almost an impediment to action. Efforts to engage in concerted planning and co-ordination inevitably seemed to disintegrate each time. Instead, spontaneous, impromptu decision making and action became the mode of group interaction. I came to realise that rapid adaptation to these new rules became the key to being an effective player.

Following a one-day exercise of data collection in Dakshinpuri, we held an information and feedback session with local NGOs and community members. As we proceeded to describe the community's need for physical and socio-economic reorganisation, the women in the audience broke out into complaints about the rampant substance abuse and wife beatings within their community. The meeting gradually dissolved into cacophony as each of the two monologues sought earnestly to prevail.

The issues that the women raised about the pervasive domestic problems did not seem to affect our final selection of topic areas to further pursue. After having identified the topic areas we wanted to work on and grouping ourselves accordingly, we spent a few days doing further data gathering, primarily by interviewing community members, government officials and NGO leaders. As part of the water sanitation group, my group focused on developing a more adequate water supply system for the squatter community. Lack of water supply had been one of the most common complaints that we had heard from our initial information gathering. In fact, there had been some previous organised effort at

REBUILDING COMMUNITIES
DAKSHINPURI, NEW DELHI, INDIA

upgrading the existing system, although with no apparent success.

The problems of the water supply that had been enumerated included the distance of the available water pumps from the community as well as the failure of most of these pumps to function. We decided that a reasonable solution would be to install several new water pumps interspersed within the confines of the squatter homes to increase both water supply and improve access. However, we faced the challenge of determining a feasible layout of the system of water pumps within a densely built area. We drew up what seemed a necessary redesign of the built community where the alleys between the tightly bunched mud homes would be widened to accommodate the hand pumps. It also appeared necessary to relocate a few of the mud homes in order to enable the most efficient design for water supply. In addition, we had identified several potential strategies for obtaining the new water pumps: communal pressure on the Municipal Corporation of Delhi (MCD) to fix the broken pumps; communal pressure on the MCD to install more water pumps within the settlement; or communal action to finance and contract a private company to establish the water pumps.

We sought out a sample of communal feedback on the alternatives we had identified and found a mix of conflicting opinions. Some people seemed agreeable to the idea of installing the water pumps even if it meant relocating homes and expressed willingness to pay a fee for the maintenance for such a system; others claimed that their neighbours would monopolise the pump if located near their homes and opposed the idea of maintenance; others seemed indifferent altogether.

Finally, we conducted presentations on our proposed action plans to two separate audiences: one audience being the local NGOs and members of the Dakshinpuri community, and the other audience being academics, government officials and other NGO representatives (in Hindi and English respectively). The feedback from the community members

REBUILDING COMMUNITIES
DAKSHINPURI, NEW DELHI, INDIA

and local NGOs (which did not actually include any squatter inhabitants although they had been invited) seemed to sum up to polite acknowledgement and appreciation of our efforts but also recognition that our proposals did not reflect community representation in the ideas and actions proposed. Likewise, the elite audience also pointed out the lack of linkages between our proposed ideas and the existing constraints. Someone commented that while we had devised projects to improve the living conditions for the squatters, we had surprisingly not addressed the fundamental uncertainty regarding how long these people could even expect to enjoy such improvements since they had no legal title to the land they occupied.

As I sat amidst the professional and academic audience in our final presentation and wondered about the relevance of our prescriptions, I realised that, regardless of the soundness of our proposals, the fact that we had an audience of influential players before us – including high-ranking officials, respected intellectuals, business people and community leaders – reflected our ability to access influential decision makers. Access to power is powerful, and, thus, there is the potential for us development planners and architects to be a resource to low-income communities and link to the decision-making process. Moreover, nobody challenged the technical substance of our proposals and their relevance, which indicated to me the value of our technical skills as architects, designers and planners in enabling us to focus on critical aspects of need or threat to welfare in human settlements. However, we proved to be ineffective in shaping our perceptions of the community needs according to the priorities and values of both the targeted community and decision makers, thereby rendering the proposals socially and politically unviable. The experience reinforced the common lesson that a lack of understanding of the political and social context of proposed projects can undo or immobilise technically innovative plans.

Within our short stay in Delhi, more barriers rather than opportunities seemed to be exposed related to the question of what contribution aspiring development professionals can make toward squatter settlements. Yet, it seemed that our ability to identify physical and social constraints and devise alternative responses to these issues, combined with our ability to access the decision makers, highlighted our potential influence and value as professionals. In addition, I would like to think that as outsiders with different perspectives, naive as they may have been, we can contribute in compelling those who face difficult issues in squatter settlements in their daily work to reexamine their roles and the impacts of their own work in low-income community development.

THEORIES

PRACTICES

REBUILDING COMMUNITIES:
BRIDGING THE GAP

"The Bird Can't Fly"

SIGUS   CENDEP

THE QUEEN'S UNIVERSITY OF BELFAST
WEST BELFAST, NORTHERN IRELAND
1996

REBUILDING COMMUNITIES
BELFAST, IRELAND

INTRODUCTION TO THE PROGRAMME

The two-week workshop was hosted by the Queen's University, Department of Architecture, with its venue at the Springvale Training Centre, a new vocational training school located on Springfield Road in the centreof the "Peace Lines" area of Falls Road, Shankill Road and Springfield Road. About 40 students participated from MIT, Oxford Brookes University (UK); Universidad Nacional de Ingenieria, Peru; University of Natal, South Africa; and the Warsaw University of Technology, Poland; and divided into teams to tackle urban renewal problems. The teams worked with community groups from both sides of the "Peace Lines", and listened to the ideas of local people about possibilities for their areas and putting together proposals for housing, planning and economic regeneration.

The workshop was organised into three overlapping phases. During the first phase, students formed "first impressions" of the issues which provided the context for their work. They did this in three ways: First in small discussion groups with community leaders, second through informal interviews with community residents, third through formal discussions and presentations with various authorities. The second phase entailed project identification and programme formulation. In consultation with community leaders and other stakeholders, projects were selected for elaboration in Phase Three. During Phase Three, each project area was expanded in more detail offering alternative ways of dealing with the issues. Proposals were structured to include: Problem Statement, Project Proposal, Partners and Stakeholders, Output and Outcome, and were presented for feedback to a group comprised of community members, university staff, and local authorities.

166 Action Planning for Cities

REBUILDING COMMUNITIES
BELFAST, IRELAND

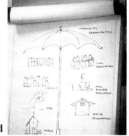

PROJECTS

Topics were determined by the workshop teams:

o **Community Redevelopment of the RUC Barracks, Springfield Road**
  Ben Hudson, Kiyoshi Kaneko, Lara Michael, Beto Ishiyama Nieto, Niel Pratt, Richard Wa Khweya
  Formation of community organisation to acquire and develop land. Training programmes will build structures which will house small crafts, shops and cafes. A museum is suggested to remind future generations of the troubles.

o **Regeneration of the Whiterock Industrial Park**
  Maria Elosua, Miguel Helbert, Moustapha Magumu, Monica Pinhanez, Anne Steffes, Tim Trevino
  Redevelopment of an existing British Army Barrack in West Belfast. The community hopes to have the area converted into a small/microenterprise industrial park.

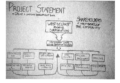

o **Community Development Bank**
  Maria Mulkeen, Catherine Preston
  Development of mechanism to channel finance and business assistance to micro and small entrepreneurs within the community.

o **The Ahlund Commission: A Way Forward for Policing and Security in Northern Ireland**
  Lance Anelay, Jim Brown, Charles Parrack, David Peppiatt, Seonaid Robertson
  A proposal for an independent, external Commission to act as a facilitator and mediator between concerned groups, aiming to assess the role of the police and enable community proposals for improved policing and security.

o **Strengthening Youth Relations to Build Trust**
  Malan James Amara, Alejandro Colom, Fred Gutierrez, Kristin Little
  Reinforcing "inter-community" links between youth centres on both the Catholic and Protestant sides of the Peace Line.

o **Sports Technology School**
  Anibal Pacheco Pico, Miguel Santiváñez Pimentel
  Development of sports facility as catalyst in bringing together Catholic and Protestant youth. Extensive training and sports programmes are intended to forge a common bond.

o **Mechanisms to Improve Housing in Beechmount**
  Francine Cadogan, Grace Guerrero, Veronica Naranjo, George Lubega Seguya, Karen Sewell, Danny Sokari-George
  Use of standard cul-de-sac housing pattern as a structuring element in redevelopment of deteriorated areas. Maintenance of community fabric, identification of focal elements, and economy of layout are key criteria.

o **Community and Identity: A Look at the Clonard Area and its Redevelopment**
  Rebecca Hegarty, Min Jung Maing
  Alternative redevelopment policies in rebuilding a deteriorated community through co-operative efforts. Suggestions included co-operative management of housing and housing issues, traffic calming, and preservation of the existing neighbourhood fabric.

REBUILDING COMMUNITIES
BELFAST, IRELAND

WEST BELFAST AND THE "TROUBLES"

The context for the Belfast workshop was grounded in "the troubles", the 25 years of armed conflict over whether Northern Ireland and its Catholic minority should rejoin the Irish Republic to the south or whether the North should remain a tiny British outpost with a Protestant majority. We arrived at a time of fragile hopes, a moment when a 17-month-old ceasefire had allowed daily life to resume a cautious normality: as one Oxford Brookes student described her first impressions, "The city seems to be holding its breath." British troops were off the street; an international commission had just proposed all-party talks; squabbling over Britain's preconditions for those talks had just begun. City officials and community activists were trying to take full advantage of the ceasefire, to make it a springboard both for a rising post-war economy and for the long slow process of reconciliation between Catholics and Protestants. We left two weeks later just as the ceasefire broke, and as the prospects for peace – and its "dividends" – appeared to falter.

Belfast was one of the great 19th-century industrial cities of the British Empire, built on textile mills, shipyards and machine-tool companies. The city increased its population sevenfold between 1840 and 1900, and housed that growth in two-storey brick rowhouses surrounding the factories and the waterfront. Catholics were relegated to the unskilled manufacturing jobs and lived largely in their own enclaves in working-class West Belfast, the target of periodic sectarian attacks from their Protestant neighbours. In 1969, in a wave of partisan violence, Catholics were burned out of their homes in the areas closest to Protestant quarters and fled into even more self-contained blocks behind barricades that became known, incongruously, as the "Peace Lines". Meanwhile, the long industrial decline that began with the Great Depression of the 1930s and worsened under the overlapping forces of civil war and capital flight has left a working class with almost no work.

Even before 1969, housing issues were saturated with the on-going political conflict. During urban-renewal efforts to clear substandard Victorian-era housing, Catholics claimed they got the most defective new housing in high and mid-rise towers (many of which since have been demolished and replaced with the low-rise townhouses that became the standard). The cul-de-sac design of modern "defensible space" also fed justifiable suspicions that new housing projects were planned with military security – rather than family security – in mind. In addition, some observers charge that housing policy has continued to reinforce residential segregation between Catholics and Protestants; housing officials insist that they have assigned tenants to new sites based on the tenants' own choices – and that it is preference of those households to live in separate territories. Moreover, the Catholic population of West Belfast has been growing while its Protestant counterpart has been shrinking, but it is politically impossible to add land to overcrowded Catholic areas from adjacent Protestant-identified spaces, even with no housing demand on the Protestant side.

REBUILDING COMMUNITIES
BELFAST, IRELAND

The so-called "Peace Lines" make West Belfast's social geography today painfully explicit: the once-temporary barriers have hardened into permanent structures between hostile neighbourhoods. Although the gates have been open during the ceasefire, communities on each side are in no hurry to pull the physical divisions down, and bureaucrats are in the awkward position of not only preserving the barricades but trying to soften their harsh presence with "environmental amenities:" replacing corrugated iron and barbed wire with variegated brickwork, landscaping the buffer areas. These cosmetic attempts to de-politicise the Peace Lines, however, are defied by the enormous partisan murals on the walls of housing developments, and by the aggressively political graffiti everywhere.

West Belfast has a strong network of community activists and, in spite of "the troubles", a portfolio of community-development activity: new enterprises incubating in an old mill complex; an Irish-language bookstore, cafe and school in a prominent church; plans for converting a heavily fortified police station (due to move to another site) into a peacetime asset. Funding increased substantially during the ceasefire, much of it from American and other international sources, but local agencies continue to have their access to capital complicated by the relationships (present and former) of staff and board members to the paramilitary organisations on both sides of the conflict. None the less, many agencies, activists and churches committed to "intercommunity" work were making links across the "Peace Lines", particularly between young people, and during the ceasefire these links seemed to be getting stronger.

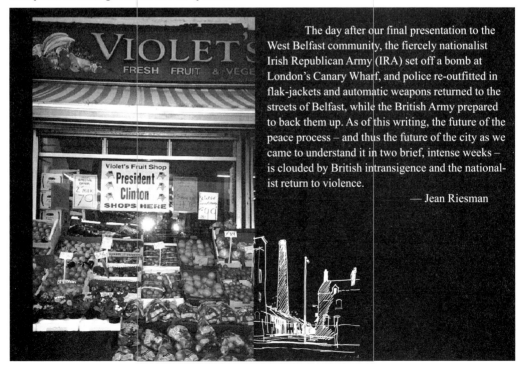

The day after our final presentation to the West Belfast community, the fiercely nationalist Irish Republican Army (IRA) set off a bomb at London's Canary Wharf, and police re-outfitted in flak-jackets and automatic weapons returned to the streets of Belfast, while the British Army prepared to back them up. As of this writing, the future of the peace process – and thus the future of the city as we came to understand it in two brief, intense weeks – is clouded by British intransigence and the nationalist return to violence.

— Jean Riesman

REBUILDING COMMUNITIES
BELFAST, IRELAND

BELFAST: A PERSONAL JOURNAL
— Catherine Preston

Sunday, January 28, 1996

...We were originally supposed to meet the group from Oxford Brookes today, but they aren't getting here until later, so I had the bulk of the day to myself. I wandered down to the Falls and the Shankill....Neither street was marked until you got way into the neighbourhood, away from the centre of town, which was odd....But I also saw the new high rise at Divis Flats, and the kerbstones painted red, white and blue, the tricolours, the political and sectarian graffiti on both sides. But otherwise, the neighbourhoods were strikingly normal. Sure, they were urban and obviously public housing, but they were lovely homes, with quiet side streets, children playing, people chattering and walking. Except at the border. The "Peace Line" turns West Belfast into a kind of maze, since you can't cross the streets and they dead end in places you don't expect. Its concrete, corrugated metal and barbed wire, more than 20 feet high, and on the Protestant side, more than half of the homes were empty and boarded up....It was just great, all in all. It made it all seem real. It wasn't like "coming home", but it wasn't like going through a war zone, either. I'm glad I went and saw it myself, before I get the sanitised version when we go out as a group.

Monday, January 29, 1996

Right, well, we've just spent about 2 hours with Gary, a lad from Youth Speak (a peer education group), getting a guided tour of Woodvale and the Shankill. It was really fascinating listening to him talk about the area in which he grew up and the times, events and people who affected him. He showed us the middle class estates where kids throw stones over the wall, the political head quarters, the history centres, where this bomb went off, where this murder occurred. Both kids and older folks stopped Gary just to say "howyeh" to him. He told us about friends who were in the paramilitaries, and we saw the RUC armoured rovers. But the problems really seem to be "normal poor" problems to a large extent, where the other groups are just the scapegoats....Its so sad, and so entrenched. And it was amazing, the ignorance of the other side, even among community workers. Gary was asked by one of the Oxford lads what "saoirse" meant, and despite having grown up around posters proclaiming it, Gary didn't know it meant freedom. I mean, if they had even a little bit of Irish history in school, he would know from "Saorstat Eireann" that the post-independence Republic was the Irish Free State. We talked about it afterward, and a lot of folks found the neighbourhood unsettling, even creepy, but though it was a bit depressing, it is so much more normal than I expected, the helicopters

REBUILDING COMMUNITIES
BELFAST, IRELAND

and patrols didn't bother me as much as the "Kill All Taigs" graffiti. But I guess I am a bit odd.

Tuesday, January 30, 1996

Just got back from dinner with everyone at The Greek Restaurant – a tiny, six table affair owned by Northern Irish Protestants – celebrating the birthday of one of the Oxford girls. The rambunctious, joyous mood provided a real contrast to the rest of the day, which we spent with the Housing Executive. They gave us a history of the executive and of the population and housing in Belfast, then took us on a tour of the public housing around the city and in particular in the "interface" areas. We all seem to agree that housing is not the real problem here – the Executive has shown that it can build quite lovely estates. But there is no room for expansion in the Catholic areas – and the new houses, to meet fitness standards, are about twice the size of those they tear down. And the Protestants, even though they aren't using their land, are unwilling to give it to Catholics. So the Catholics' housing stock is older and poorer than the Protestants', and the lines are not going anywhere – have even been institutionalised! Not only have millions of dollars been spent to build and landscape these monstrosities (offensive not to the eye, but to the soul), but they have a planning manual on them! The houses on either side are bricked up or have been torn down. Apparently an experiment with building the walls as back to back homes failed - ending in riots and burning. I know there's a reason - but I don't like it and it bugs me that the bureaucrats' attitudes are "solving the Troubles and territorial disputes are not our problem." I also find myself increasingly irked by the ignorance of the group, who seem to be illustrative of how this situation has been pushed to the back of our collective conscience. However, the ignorance is good for me, because it reminds me of my bias and shows up miscommunications. I think the best comment of the day came from a South African student who had come to understand that the problems here were far more entrenched than in his own country....The head of the INLA was killed today while we were just a couple of blocks away. They believe by his own. It just goes on and on.

Wednesday, January 31, 1996

...[The manager of the New Hill Community Centre] really feels that the walls are a necessity right now. The provide a "security" feeling that allows the communities to build themselves up. Only when they are individually developed can the societies grow together... She sees real, lasting peace a generation away, since to boost confidence, raise without prejudice and to disarm, etc. will take at least 20–30 years. And when those mental barriers are at last down, she said, the communities themselves will tear down the peace lines....

Friday, February 2, 1996

...We spent most of our time, thought, at a day centre for the mentally ill. The centre, which serves an area with about 11 000 people, has 111 members and a waiting list of many times that. Most suffer from schizophrenia, anxiety or depression, though the depression is often attributable to alcoholism. There is little stigma left about these mental illnesses, the manager said. People understand trauma-induced schizophrenia and a majority of the adult population is either on valium or prozac. Its good to know that there are facilities like this where people can get help, but unsettling to know there are so many people who need it. Should not surprise me, I suppose. Twenty-five years of shell-shock, three generations of unemployment. That said, it is an awfully large problem, one which makes solving conflicts or even getting stable employment difficult....

Monday, February 5, 1996

...One group spent today at the British Army Airfield hearing their side of the story. I was really struck by how many of them jumped at the chance to buy into the explanation and justification of their government's presence here. Some felt that we have been irresponsible in how much we have listened to the Nationalists. Others came back with a more balanced view but still were not much cynical about the military. There were apparently told that the Army's role in Northern Ireland was not at all political and it seemed that at least half of them swallowed that. Patriotism is a funny thing, I guess. Perhaps they are as biased as I am, after all.

Wednesday, February 7, 1996

Good day yesterday. Met with Kevin, a community activist we've been dealing with for the past week, to discuss plans for the RUC barracks. Kevin lives right across the street from the barracks and to make it even

REBUILDING COMMUNITIES
BELFAST, IRELAND

more interesting, he is a devout Socialist (bust of Lenin on his TV table) and an INLA man who has spent time in Portolaoise Gaol. He was fascinating to talk to, though he wasn't able to give much advice about funding. He took us on a walk around the site and up the hill to get a view of it. We soon became aware that we were being followed/monitored by a helicopter, which made us very nervous about taking photos, despite Kevin's assurances. Coming down, a half dozen RUC Rovers passed us and entered the barracks and then we heard a loud report which called all of us to attention as, thinking at first that it was a gunshot, we jumped about three feet in the air.

Friday, February 9, 1996

Well, I wish I had written about our presentations yesterday, when the mood was hopeful and forward-looking. That is no longer the case and now one wonders if what we did matters at all....Today, I went up the Whiterock Road to meet with the mural artist Mo Chara, aka Gerard Kelly. He told me about being in prison (for car bombing with intent) and being told to paint Mickey Mouse and such. Instead, he got a book of Celtic mythology and began to do Celtic designs. Then during the hunger strikes of 1980-81, he got the incentive to start doing murals (loyalists had been doing them since 1917, though Nationalists were barred from doing so) and stood up to the authorities who would try to intimidate him, even though the murals might be painted over the next day. Anyway, he wanted to talk to me about the contacts with the Irish–American business community because he has come up with an idea for a small enterprise. He wants to do Celtic design carved front doors, custom and standard, for domestic and export trade. I saw the prototype and it was brilliant, and he has fitted it out with Celtic hardware. He figures he could employ six people to start and eventually as many as 20. In an area where unemployment runs between 80% and 95%, 20 jobs are not to be sneezed at....

Which I guess brings us to today's disaster. Coming out of a movie theatre, we passed a TV crew interviewing a woman at a bus stop. I thought I heard them ask, "Have you heard the cease-fire has ended and what is your reaction?" I said I hoped I had heard that wrong. I hadn't. A bomb exploded in London's East End this evening injuring and perhaps killing many people. It was preceded by a message from the Provisional IRA saying that the cease-fire was over and including the ID password of the Army Council to prove that it was them, though there's speculation that this represents a division within the Provos.

I am so angry and frustrated. Yes, it was going slowly and painfully but we were closer to peace than we have been in 25 years – perhaps than we have ever been. It kills me to think that I may have been with people this week who knew that this was going to happen. I hate that my first reaction was "I'm glad I am leaving tomorrow." I feel like I am running away. The barricades and checkpoints are back already. The RUC are wearing flak jackets and the Army may be here by morning. We hope that there will be no rioting or revenge killings tonight, but we have no reason to have confidence in that. I could not walk tomorrow to the places I walked today and for the last two weeks, and know that I was safe. All the work that we, and the communities and many others, have done over the past 18 months may be lost, back at square one. Gerry Adams won't get one more concession without decommissioning. Clinton may get crucified for this. When we got here, few people had confidence in the peace process, and we had not faith that anything would change. By Thursday, a lot of us, including some we worked with in the community, had hopes. Now there is just sadness, frustration and despair. I can't put an up note on this. Right now, everything feels impossible, that they will never learn to live together. I hope I am wrong but how can you have confidence in that when the city is at war again?

Epilogue

It is now February 23 – two weeks since the bombing. There is perhaps more reason to be hopeful now. The communities of Ireland and the UK have in loud voices proclaimed that they want their peace back, at whatever price. They seem united on this alone, even in the face of another bomb scare and a bus bombing since. There is some disagreement on how to go about it, of course, but there is no question that everyone wants the cease-fire reinstated. One woman told the press, "I would talk to Satan himself if it would bring peace to our country." This is a truly Christian attitude – one which whether you are Catholic or Protestant, there is strong Biblical backing for. I hope that more people recognise this in the months to come.

REBUILDING COMMUNITIES
BELFAST, IRELAND

SIDE TAKING OR SIDE STEPPING:
AN ESSAY ON COMMUNITY DEVELOPMENT WORK IN OTHER PEOPLE'S WARS

There was a time when ribbons were only worn by little girls. But in recent years ribbons have been politicised and are now worn with conviction by ardent activists as a sign of solidarity. A red ribbon remembers those with AIDS, a pink one makes a stand for women with breast cancer. In West Belfast, there is a green ribbon which remembers IRA prisoners and demands their immediate release.

The green ribbon poses some interesting questions for those arriving as strangers in this part of the city to work with community groups and local activists. Should we wear the ribbon as we go about our business here? In other words, should community development workers identify with the cause of those amongst whom we work? Or can we navigate a more detached path through the bitter politics and factional alignments of this society?

Such questions are thrown into stark relief in societies which are, or have recently been, divided by violent conflict such as Northern Ireland. But it would be a mistake to think that such dilemmas only arise in times of open conflict. Every society is a divided society. Matters of class, wealth, gender, race and ability all create divisions and alliances wherever human beings organise themselves. The idea that violence can be structural as well as weapons-based is now received wisdom in much social theory. The particular question of alignment which we faced in Belfast was simply a more acute form of a dilemma we would face anywhere.

To some people there is no dilemma but simply a question of taking sides. For them there is no doubt that even if it is not entirely right, one group in Northern Ireland has at least been more wronged than the other. Under this analysis, any development initiative should identify with and prioritise the efforts of this group. Such a position might be characterised as solidarity-based development. Others are more uneasy with the notion of alignment. Instinctively they tend toward some position of neutrality or impartiality. Their feeling is that poverty in Belfast is a priority which transcends sectarian politics and unites both sides in a common purpose. They also recognise that every conflict needs some people who do not

REBUILDING COMMUNITIES
BELFAST, IRELAND

stake their identify and reputation on one side or the other. For it is often these people, when the time is ripe, who have the flexibility to go between and bring together the more entrenched activists.

Sooner rather than later – and on the basis of each particular conflict – the community development worker must make his or her position known. As outsiders, the great majority in the workshop chose the path towards neutrality and impartiality. In just two weeks we were hardly put to the test of sustaining such a position but had at least made a decision. While such a stance may be due as much to personal temperament as to political or ethical analysis, it is a legitimate one. Often accused of denying or avoiding conflict, the position of the impartial activist in fact seeks maximum mobility within a conflict. From this freedom she or he hopes to be just as creative as the solidarity-based activist.

— Hugo Slim

174 Action Planning for Cities

REBUILDING COMMUNITIES
CAQUETÁ, LIMA, PERÚ

CAQUETÁ: THE COMMUNITY AND THE SITE

Caquetá is a large sprawling district located in the north-west of Lima in the two districts of Rimac and San Martín de Porras. The site began to grow substantially from the early 1960s. Today there are some 20 000 slum dwellers and squatters, informal and formal market vendors and small businessmen.

For the purpose of the project, the site was defined according to the following areas:

1. Formal Co-operative Housing (el Barrio Obrero)
2. Shared Tenement Housing (Tugurios)
3. Consolidated (formal) Market
4. Informal Street Vendors (informal market)
5. The Clover Leaf - Trébol (the populated quarter of the Caquetá/Pan Americana intersection)
6. The Old Barrio (consolidated squatters)

METHOD

The workshop was carried out in several stages, each of which was carried out in small multidisciplinary teams:

Gathering information so as to understand the context and circumstances
Workshop participants were divided into groups assigned to each of the above zones. Information was gathered at two levels: at the *site* (macro) and at the *dwelling* (micro) level by *lookers* and *listeners*, who combined to identify *opportunities* and *problems*.

Developing strategies for intervention
After presentations by the six groups, a seventh group was created with one member from groups 1–6, with the task of collating and sifting information to form an overall strategic plan of action.

Preparing projects
Each group developed a project intended to illustrate, in a realistic, implementable manner, possible ways out of some of the most serious problems.

Formal presentations to the community and local authorities.

LEARNING FROM OTHER EXAMPLES
SEMINARS AND FIELD TRIPS TO SELECTED PROJECTS

The first three days of the workshop were spent in seminars covering basic necessary information regarding the site and its larger spatial and historical context. Architects, economists and historians introduced Lima's economic and social characteristics, as well as Caquetá's particular significance within those contexts. Due to the heavy presence of unregulated commercial activity in the area, much of the discussion revolved around the economy and culture of informal and ambulant merchants.

A series of visits to existing examples of housing projects aided further in introducing students to relevant precedents and lessons from the past:

Villa El Salvador
Villa El Salvador is the best known of the Lima Pueblos Jovenes, or young towns. Begun in the early 1970s as an organised land invasion, Villa was later organised into a series of zoned regions of superblocks consisting of blocks for individuals to develop. An on-site presentation was made by Miguel Romero and the leader of the local community organisation CUAVES.

CIDAP
CIDAP (Centro De Investigación, Documentación y Asesoría Poblacional) is an NGO specialising in slum renovation in Lima's historic centre. Participants visited several of its projects.

PREVI
PREVI was originally an international architectural competition for the design of low-income housing, although currently it is primarily inhabited by middle-income professionals. The group reviewed schemes by James Sterling, Aldo van Eyck and Christopher Alexander.

✦ **FINDINGS**

1. *FORMAL CO-OPERATIVE HOUSING (EL BARRIO OBRERO)* PROBLEMS UNSTABLE AND POOR BUILDING DESIGN . DISORGANISED PUBLIC TRANSPORT . DELINQUENCY AND DRUG ABUSE . LITTLE PUBLIC LAND . GARBAGE DISPOSAL 2. *SHARED TENEMENT HOUSING (TUGURIOS)* PROBLEMS DWELLING SECURITY . ACCESS TO LEGAL ADVICE . POOR WATER ACCESSIBILITY (WATER VENDORS AND/OR INFREQUENT SUPPLY) . OVERCROWDING . ELECTRICITY INSTALLATION INCOMPLETE . DRUGS AND DELINQUENCY OPPORTUNITIES PROVISION OF PUBLIC RECREATIONAL SPACE / INCREASED COMMUNITY ORGANISATION / ENCOURAGING MICRO-ENTERPRISE / RENTAL/SUB LETTING 3. *THE CONSOLIDATED (FORMAL) MARKET* PROBLEMS POOR INFRASTRUCTURE: UNPAVED STREETS, POOR CONSTRUCTION, ETC. / INSUFFICIENT SERVICES - WATER, SEWAGE, ETC. / POOR GARBAGE COLLECTION OPPORTUNITIES MAXIMISING LAND USE / CREDIT SYSTEMS ENHANCEMENT / IMPROVING MARKET SPACE, E.G. REMOVING MARKET WALLS 4. *STREET VENDORS* PROBLEMS POOR ROADS / W.C.S FAR

REBUILDING COMMUNITIES
CAQUETÁ. LIMA. PERÚ

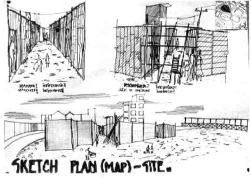

AWAY FROM SITE / NO ELECTRICITY OR WATER / FIRE RISK / CHILDREN IN DANGER, E.G. PLAYING IN STREET / DELINQUENCY <u>OPPORTUNITIES</u> IMPROVE SECURITY / CHILD EDUCATION / IMPROVE COMMUNITY ORGANISATION **5. THE CLOVER LEAF (" EL TRÉBOL")** <u>PROBLEMS</u> WASTE DISPOSAL / SANITATION / SECURITY / DIRT AND DUST <u>OPPORTUNITIES</u> STRENGTHENING COMMUNITY ORGANISATION / UTILISING FREE SPACE, E.G. SANITATION, WASTER DISPOSAL / SHELTER UPGRADING **6. THE OLD BARRIO** <u>PROBLEMS</u> DELINQUENCY / SEWAGE (BROKEN PIPES) / LITTLE SPACE FOR RECREATION / LAND EROSION / LANDSLIDE BY RAVINES <u>OPPORTUNITIES</u> RELOCATING OF LANDSLIDE VULNERABLE AREAS TO VACANT LOTS IN OLD BARRIO / FIX WATER AND SEWAGE PIPES / CREATING COMMUNAL SPACES **7. OVERALL STRATEGIC PLAN** <u>PROBLEMS</u> FIRE RISK / CIRCULATION / UNEVEN ROADS / RUBBISH / DRUGS AND PROSTITUTION / TENURE / LANDSLIDE/EROSION / SEWAGE/ PEST CONTROL <u>OPPORTUNITIES</u> COMMUNITY ORGANISATIONS / MAXIMISING OPEN SPACES / POLICE PRESENCE (POLICE STATIONS) / ENVIRONMENTAL IMPROVEMENT / COMMUNAL KITCHENS / PUBLIC

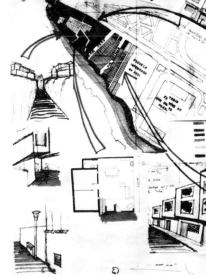

178 Action Planning for Cities

REBUILDING COMMUNITIES
CAQUETÁ, LIMA, PERÚ

STRUCTURING AN APPROACH
SELECTED PROJECTS FOR IMPLEMENTATION

Out of the analyses of existing conditions, the workshop participants decided to focus on the following projects, two of which are detailed below:
- Revitalising public spaces
- Improving the consolidated market
- Family business development
- Credit: problems, opportunities and myths
- Alternatives for integration
- Organising for land and services
- Recreational and educational facilities
- Making legal advice accessible
- River erosion in Trébol-Bajo: An urgent problem
- Toward neighbourhood security
- Organising public space for employment generation and training
- Fast, low-cost community facility development
- Space, light and life

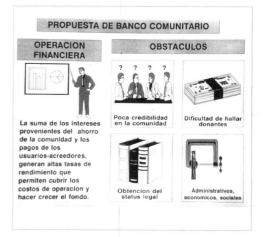

✦ IMPROVING THE CONSOLIDATED MARKET
Problems (due to the street vendors)
1. Blockade of secondary streets, creating an inconvenience for motor vehicles, especially for the neighbouring houses.
2. Fire hazards because of the inability of fire-engines to access the market in the case of a fire.
3. Creation of insecurity. For example, the creation of narrow street alleys with no light or vigilance between the street vendors and the residences which provides places for crime, drug consumption and delinquency. Additionally, the inability to lock up the market because it is on public land obstructs any security measures.
4. Inefficiency of the sanitation organisations has created an unfit environment that could easily spread disease.
5. The temporary nature of the stalls results in a sense of insecurity to the vendors since they may be evicted any time.

Strategy
Several options exist to improve the conditions of the street vendors, improving their immediate situation but, more important, promoting the long-term economic development of the area. If the economic environment is improved it could attract a wider clientele. The increased income generated would serve in turn to augment the social development of the area. Finally, were these alternatives to prove successful, the vendors would be encouraged to maintain and further improve their living standards.

Learning in Practice: Field-Based Project Development Workshops

REBUILDING COMMUNITIES
CAQUETÁ, LIMA, PERÚ

✦ River Erosion in Trébol-Bajo

Problems

Of all problems identified during site analysis – delinquency and drug-dealing mostly done by non-residents, the breakage of sewage pipes, the lack of public open spaces and inaccessible playgrounds – the erosion caused by the river appears as the most urgent issue. A few houses on the river front have already disappeared into the 20 m drop leading to the Rimac. Of the existing ones 20% are about to collapse and have already been evacuated. Another 20% are seriously damaged yet still inhabited and almost all the remaining 60% are in considerable danger.

Strategy

1. Temporarily relocate the families in the units in danger. This can be achieved in the empty sites and under-used units of Trébol-Bajo, and outside the area whenever necessary. This requires joint intervention at the municipal (via the *Defensa Civil*) and local level (community organisations and young professionals living in the area whose recognised influence at local and official level plays a major role).
2. Reinforce the riverside by a combination of a retaining wall and terracing. The FONCODES organisation (Fondo de Compensación y Desarollo) is capable of financing the project from its funds from the World Bank, BID (Banco InterAmericano de Desarollo), PNUD (Programa de Naciones Unidas para el Desarrollo) and similar institutions.
3. Build a second floor on top of the existing second row of houses in order to relocate the formerly evacuated families (most of the existing dwellings are single storey). Funding can come from FONAVI (Fondo Nacional para Viviendas); building materials from the Banco de Materiales (loans at low interest to local community organisations), and self-help construction by the community with the help of local masons, as already done in the past.
4. Leave a passageway of 2-3 m between the new first row of houses (Item 3) and the drop to the river. This will constitute an almost symmetrical solution along the Rimac. In addition to its safety, it could allow commercial activities on the riverfront similarly to what has been successfully done on the other side. The remodelling of the riverside needs to be financed at the Lima municipal level by INVERMET (Inversiones Metropolitanas) together with self-help construction by the community.

All of the strategies need to be administered at the three different municipal levels – Lima, Rimac, Saint Martin – jointly or independently as needed. Self-help construction can be supervised by LA ASESORIA of the Universidad Nacional de Ingeniería (CONSTRUCUNI).

REBUILDING COMMUNITIES
KAZIMIERZ + LUBLIN, POLAND

HOUSING IN POLAND

The transformation of Poland's economy and politics from a centrally planned to a market form is the critical general condition for all discourse on future housing development in the country. Central planning has affected every aspect of urban housing in post-war Poland, from financing and land acquisition through design, engineering, construction (materials and assembly), allocation and management. The challenge for the medium term is to address the problems and abuses of central planning institutions whilst retaining their more beneficial achievements. At issue is the precise balance between the degree to which public planning (probably at a more local level than traditionally executed) will continue to influence housing design and to what extent the "free" market will effectively replace government policy as the main determinant. Between the two extremes lies the realm of, for example, regulatory controls on individual enterprise, of "safety nets" for those inevitably cast aside under market capitalism, and of private but communitarian initiatives designed to use the market for the good of groups rather than individuals: in short, a set of institutions – public and private – which will balance and stabilise the expected surge in speculation and the increased mobility of capital and labour. Where a Soviet-style command economy and the more virulent strains of the "free market" coincide it seems, is in the profoundly non-democratic process through which investment decisions are made. What Poland will attempt at all levels, of which housing is simply one, is to integrate more points of view into policy; this will require in the housing industry, a more multidisciplinary approach to the organisation and management of resources and skills so as to avoid the replacement of one set of "experts" with simply another.

The deliberations of the workshops, therefore, were predicated on the desire to maintain a multidisciplinary approach which must never, in turn, be reducible to yet another special discipline; on the desire to strengthen contacts between academic and professional worlds; and, most importantly, on the desire to establish a collaborative effort to determine directions for future research, rather than a series of "problem-solving" sessions in which one set of experts tells another what to do.

REBUILDING COMMUNITIES
KAZIMIERZ + LUBLIN, POLAND

 METHODS AND PRESENTATIONS BY STUDENT GROUPS
KAZIMIERZ FORUM / JANUARY, 1991

One of the strongest impressions from this group's week of study at LSM was the difference in perceptions that existed between groups on exactly what "the housing problem" is. Depending with whom one spoke (planning professionals, co-operative managers, adult residents, or children), one would be left with significantly divergent impressions of the current housing situation (physical, political, social and economic) and would be led to equally different planning and design responses.

Therefore, the first part of the presentations focused on identifying the different perspectives that had been observed during the course of study and considering the implications for policy decision making.

❖ A PLURALITY OF PERSPECTIVES

In the case of LSM, we observed three distinct areas of perceptions which varied according to the unique position and vantage points of three distinct groups – professionals, adult residents, and children. Several drawings were made by the latter group so as to demonstrate their views of their environment.

Not surprisingly, housing problems as perceived by professionals tended to focus on larger-scale issues (e.g., the panel construction system, parking, transportation, etc.), while the problems perceived by adult residents tended to be more immediate (more telephones and play-fields, security, larger apartments, etc.) Children's perceived problems were the most small scale (need for bike racks, open space, safe pedestrian routes, etc.).

REBUILDING COMMUNITIES
KAZIMIERZ + LUBLIN, POLAND

✦ Structuring Choices

Given the inevitable need to compromise on finding common solutions to divergent perceptions of exactly what constitutes the problem, the group proceeded to explore how such tradeoffs could be considered. Taking adult resident perceptions as an example, the group structured them according to two scales: one focusing on needs and the other on costs. Arranging the issues raised by the adult residents on each scale, one begins to see the tradeoffs that will need to be made in choosing which problems to address.

Other scales could be developed. For example, a scale of "political feasibility" or a scale of "level of resident participation". Structuring choices in such ways, decision makers can begin to understand the tradeoffs being made and can identify a strategy that maximises benefit while minimising cost.

184 Action Planning for Cities

REBUILDING COMMUNITIES
KAZIMIERZ + LUBLIN, POLAND

 MULTIPLICITY OF LEARNING SETTINGS

A linked series of seminars, workshops, courses and research followed the workshop:

The November Symposium: Exploring Critical Housing Issues in Poland.
30 NOVEMBER 1990, MIT.
The symposium – open to the Cambridge community – provided a background to housing issues in Poland, and began to identify and debate key areas for effective housing interventions. Speakers and panelists were drawn from the World Bank, USAID, local professionals and MIT faculty.

The Kazimierz Forum: New Housing, Rehabilitation and Political Reconstruction.
14–25 JANUARY 1991, KAZIMIERZ, POLAND.
A seminar and workshop which explored housing issues in the context of the new market orientation with local authorities, academics, students and professionals from Poland, the US, United Kingdom, Lithuania and Japan. Approximately 79 participated over the two-week period.

The Lublin / LSM Workshop.
JANUARY 1991, IN LUBLIN.
A one-week-long, hands-on workshop in Lublin, focused on housing issues of the 50 000-member LSM Housing Estate and the City of Lublin. Three areas were targeted: understanding the informal market sector, with the goal of mobilising informal sources as initiators of market centres; understanding the pre-war housing typology, with the goal of developing a context for informed design decisions; and participatory planning in the LSM Estate.

Transformation, Innovation and Opportunity: A Two-day Workshop on Housing Rehabilitation in Poland.
19–20 APRIL 1991, MIT.
An exploration of the institutional and spatial approaches of public housing in Boston which may be appropriate in the Polish context. Approximately 47 people attended, including faculty and student members from the Warsaw University of Technology, professionals from the Lublin local authority, Boston professionals from government and private practice, and MIT faculty and student members.

The Poland Joint Studio and Workshop.
SPRING SEMESTER, 1991, POLAND.
Focus was on design explorations in the rehabilitation of the LSM Estate. Offered to 18 upper-level students.

Preparatory Field Research in Lublin.
SUMMER 1991, POLAND.
One and a half months of effort focused on identifying areas of assistance in the development process, the construction sector, and in participatory planning. Funded largely by an USAID grant, six graduate students and four faculty members participated from MIT with nine students from the Warsaw University of Technology, Tony Gibson of the Neighbourhood Initiatives Foundation in England, and with financial and technical support by Lublin local authorities and the Institute of Physical Planning and Municipal Economy in Poland.

CASE FILES

PHASE II: STRATEGIES, OPTIONS AND TRADEOFFS

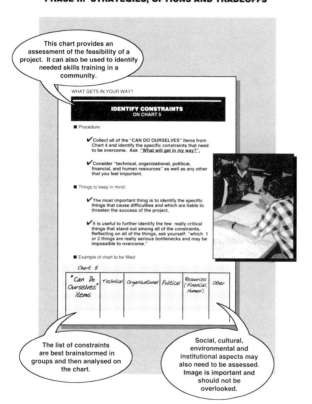

Introduction

How does a Community Action Planning workshop "look and feel" in practice? Given the limitation of presenting the dynamics of action planning in "report form" (spontaneity, improvisation, interactive work are difficult to present), this section illustrates three examples of Community Action Planning workshops undertaken by the authors. Each is undertaken in a different context designed to show how the basic principles have been maintained given the diverse conditions and goals. Together they offer a resource of ideas, and techniques and format for planning and running an action planning workshop. The examples include a "site planning" workshop in Colombo, the capital of Sri Lanka, a "capacity-building" workshop for community development corporations (CDCs) in Boston, and an "urban upgrading" workshop in a small rural township in Schweizer-Reneke, South Africa. The reader may secure the complete handbooks (see Reference list) from the authors, or from the institutions where the workshops were held. The examples presented follow three of the fundamental phases of action planning (see Figure CF.1): Phase I: Problem Identification and Prioritisation of Problems and Opportunities; Phase II: Developing Strategies, Options and Assessing Tradeoffs; and Phase III: Planning for Implementation.

The workshops were documented in the form of handbooks. These handbooks provide the reference for explaining the activities, and pages have been selected and annotated by us to highlight issues, principles and recommendations. The annotations highlight four areas of consideration: the procedure followed, the sources of information, useful techniques and cautions or "things to watch out for". The pages illustrated from the handbooks provide some of the information, whilst the notations in "bubbles" add supplementary considerations as necessary for a better understanding of the process and the "spirit" of the sessions.

The handbooks incorporate several basic principles in their preparation:

(1) All are simple in format. Artistic embellishment has been minimised.

(2) The procedure provides the structure for the handbooks.

(3) Tasks are broken down into single, discrete steps, and include objectives, procedure, hints and the output, usually with a sample chart as guide.

(4) Examples are included drawn from the workshop itself and help clarify the process.

SITE PLANNING FOR NEW COMMUNITIES Colombo, Sri Lanka	BUILDING CAPACITY Boston, USA	URBAN UPGRADING Schweizer-Reneke, South Africa
PHASE I: PROBLEM IDENTIFICATION AND PRIORITISATION		
What Do You Need • Identify Area Problems and Opportunities • Undertake Community Survey • Identify Community Problems and Opportunities • Determine Goals and Priorities	*Setting Objectives* • Identify and Clarify Concerns • Prioritise Concerns and Identify Conflicts • Set Objectives • Prioritise Objectives	• The Site • Physical Programming • Socio-Economic Programming
PHASE II: STRATEGIES, OPTIONS AND TRADEOFFS		
How to Get What You Need • Allocate Resources • Identify Proposals *What Gets in Your Way* • Identify Constraints • Review Sequence of Proposals	*Building a Programme* • Consider Options • Prioritise Options • Identify Conflicts and Opportunities • Select Viable Options	• Objectives and Issues • Circulation Networks • Utility Infrastructure • Dwelling Considerations
PHASE III: PLANNING FOR IMPLEMENTATION		
Building a Plan of Action • Identify Proposal/Tasks • Develop Schedule • Design Proposals *Getting Projects Going* • Identify Project Teams • Decide Immediate Tasks	*Building a Programme* • Assess What You Have and Where to Get What You Need • Decide When and Where to Get What You Need • Decide Who Does What, When and How • Decide Where to Put It *Information Sheets* • How to Pay for It? • How to Own and Manage It? • How to Build It? • Approvals • Resources	

Figure CF.1 The three case examples and the phases of Community Action Planning.

(5)   Text is held to a minimum, and prepared in an active style.

Current technology, which is widely available and which has become relatively inexpensive, allows "instant" on-site documentation. Community-specific examples with people, places and work sessions can be incorporated into the handbook, which make understanding easier and clearer, and encourages its continued use with less dependency. Portable computers and printers make on-site preparation feasible, and hand-held scanners, instant photography and digital videos provide the inputs. Only electricity is required, and even this can be provided by solar panels and batteries to assure portability.

References

Centre for Development and Emergency Planning, Oxford Brookes University; Department of Property Development and Construction Economics, University of Natal, South Africa, May 1995. *Pilot Project Schweizer-Reneke: Executive Summary, Workshop Procedure, and Workshop Documentation.* London: Overseas Development Administration Dissemination Project Report, No. D139.

Hamdi, N., Goethert, R., Jayawardena, D., Sirivardana, S. & Weerapana, D. 1983. *A Chronicle: Workshop on Programming and Design of Low Income Settlements, Colombo, Sri Lanka.* Colombo: Publication of the NHDA/MIT Joint Program of Research, Colombo.

Hamdi, N., Goethert, T. & Mongold, N. 1988. *Planning Assistance Kit: A Planning Guide for Community-Based Organizations.* Boston: Massachusetts Housing Partnership Challenge Grant Program.

CASE 1: SITE PLANNING FOR NEW COMMUNITIES

A CHRONICLE: WORKSHOP ON PROGRAMMING AND DESIGN OF LOW INCOME SETTLEMENTS, COLOMBO, SRI LANKA

Introduction

The handbook from which the information in this case file is taken highlights the activities in a special workshop held in Colombo, Sri Lanka, 18–23 July 1983, hosted by the National Housing Development Authority (NHDA). It was held in the Summitpura community, a low-income settlement on the outskirts of the city.

The focus of the workshop was on programming and design, and training of junior technical officers of the NHDA. Preliminary plans had already been prepared by government agencies for the site, and clearing efforts were under way as a prelude to starting construction.

From a training point of view, the use of the real site provided the opportunity for the participants to confront and explore timely, actual issues without penalty, and to exercise full freedom in exploring alternative ideas and approaches.

The site is an expansion of an existing low-income settlement, Summitpura, and is intended to provide additional houses for the growing population and for relocating families required to move because of upgrading activities. Summitpura was in the early stages of an upgrading programme, and provided a ready reference for assessing strategies in action.

Participants were largely drawn from urban housing agencies in Sri Lanka: architects, planners, engineers, administrators and economists were represented.

The housing programmes of Sri Lanka

The two paradigms discussed in Chapter 2 and illustrated in Figure 2.1 are clearly seen in the recent history of housing policy in Sri Lanka. Immediately prior to 1982, Sri Lanka was very much a provider, but one in a state of transition. Its Million Houses Programme launched in 1978, which was to consume some 12% of total public sector investment from 1979 to 1983, did include a substantial amount of direct construction (36 000 units) albeit with a large share of aided self-help units (50 000) (see Sirivardana undated, and also Weerapana 1986 and Marga Institute). Its National Housing Development Authority (NHDA) was set up in 1979 to deliver subsidised houses and to co-ordinate the national efforts. Policies, however, shifted considerably with the election in 1982. This was partly due to the pressure of party policies (the pledge of one million houses which the new government had made with only 3% to 4% to be allocated out of gross public expenditures would be difficult to achieve without a new paradigm), partly due to the influence of international trends (notably, influential funders and prestigious universities), but mostly due to a number of key Sri Lankans who saw it both correct and expedient to shift substantially to support policies. These same people saw an opportunity to attract international visibility to their programme, to endorse their national status in a wider intellectual and political community. All of this, of course, is perfectly legitimate. A small country willing to experiment needs the cushion of international respect, needs to have its successes and its mistakes, if and when they occur, legitimised in the interest of learning.

By January 1985, various subprogrammes were well under way as a part of the Million Houses Programme, including rural housing, urban housing, plantation housing, fisherman housing, and housing for the Mahawelli development area. Whilst the urban and rural subprogrammes fell dominantly under the support paradigm (rural housing being largely its target), others, Mahawelli for example, would continue under the provider paradigm.

Sri Lanka is significant for study, however, because its objectives follow those which we have stated in Chapter 2, and because of its effort to translate a number of theoretical and somewhat abstract ideas into policies. And having done that, then to embody these policies not only as significant parts of its national programme (rather than as isolated "demonstration projects") but also as parts of its national development ideology. Most significantly, it had a housing authority staffed with people who were enthusiastic, if sometimes uncertain, about what they were doing.

Despite its poverty, Sri Lanka has a high literacy rate, a low mortality rate, and a zero rate of urbanisation. It has a well-established and well-developed welfare system reaching out into the smallest villages.

Sweeping land reforms were initiated between 1972 and 1976 which enabled nearly one million acres to be placed in public ownership which later enabled the NHDA substantial flexibility and control of development. In addition, the ceiling on the housing property law of 1973 transferred some 12 347 properties or 71.6% of all tenements to state ownership.

Most significantly, the Sri Lankan programme has avoided, it seems, simplistic "problem-solving" techniques, recognising the complexity of shelter as a "system" (L. Peattie, 1986, informal discussions, Colombo) involving people, actions, intentions and events. Sri Lankans recognised that their programme, if it was to work as a support paradigm, had to strike a careful balance (always shifting from place to place and from time to time) between community needs and government objectives; between adequate off-site preparation and on-site development and implementation; between the need to know, to inform action (information) and the desire to act to build knowledge and experience (implementation).

It is perhaps less significant in our discussion here, whether these objectives have been met, or whether the Sri Lankans can claim successes (which they clearly can), but more that they exist at all. This offers the case value for research. It is indeed the dynamics of the process which are worth observing and evaluating, more than the categories under which the programme is being enacted (houses built, monies disbursed, costs recovered, etc.).

Key features of the programme

Perhaps the overriding and most significant feature of the Sri Lankan "support" programmes is embodied in the psyche of those operating it. This is, to respect the everyday and sometimes cumbersome way in which people confront problems, and who one way or another, and sometimes with a little help, improvise and solve them. It is a psyche respectful of existing institutions committed to building on what they had, and yet confident in making changes, and innovating where and when it is needed.

It entailed asking: what is the least we need to do to get things going? It entailed learning how to leave things alone. From these attitudes – which indeed are fundamental to the support paradigm – a number of programmes emerged.

First was the shift away from the wholesale redevelopment and toward upgrading. Both rural and urban integrated upgrading programmes were initiated, with the emphasis on small-scale, piecemeal additions and improvements in health, sanitation and housing. Where new construction was demanded, sites with services were provided mostly on a small-scale infill basis, in inner urban areas (see Hamdi & Goethert 1984a).

Second, to fuel small-scale private enterprise and provide direct assistance to poor people a "Housing Options and Loan Package" was developed for each of the urban and rural subprogrammes (NHDA 1984). This provided small loans for a variety of construction investments for utilities, upgrading, building a new core house at interest rates around 6% over a 15-year repayment period. The sizes of loans varied from rural to urban programmes and from item to item (5000 rupees to upgrade houses and latrines in rural areas and 7000 for the equivalent in an urban area). The package was a tool which enabled the household to negotiate a personalised solution on its own terms. It was also a device by virtue of its size for the housing authority to have a say about (rather than directly control) standards of construction and types of technology. By July 1988, 22 454 rural and 9572 urban families had benefited from these loans.

Third, enormous emphasis was placed on local and largely existing traditional institutions to manage the programme. In the rural programme, both district (Pradashya) and village (Gramadoya) councils, assisted through local offices of the housing authority, took on various administrative and decision-making tasks such as disbursing loans, collecting repayments, evaluating completion schedules and trouble-shooting. The programme, in other words, was substantially decentralised with much of the work conventionally done in offices (regulating land, approving standards, making plans) now being done on-site, with very few drawings, with rapid surveys and in close collaboration with residents.

In urban areas, where the existing traditional structure of institutions was more fragmented than in rural ones, community development councils were set up (hence, they were often seen to serve the housing authority's interests) who were to establish, with no legal powers, "community standards" tailor-made to local needs, rather than dictated centrally. Even existing thrift societies were bolstered and formalised as official lending institutions, and so providing a local banking service for savings and loans not just for housing, but for small businesses and so on. This kind of support of the private sector went down well with both the conservative policies of the lending agency and the more grassroots policies of housing authority ministers and officials.

Government assistance or "support" for all these local initiatives not only came in the system of financing, however. It also came in building local capacities to organise, build and manage. On-site training was therefore the fourth key feature of the programme, building, then transferring, the skills, the tools and the methods with which to implement the programme. These tools, as with the training programmes, came in various forms. The "homeowner's file", for example, was an attempt to assist individual families in book-keeping. It was an attempt to empower families to control the construction and management of their houses. The file contained, amongst other things, various schedules for recording expenditures and repayments in the hope that better book-keeping would balance the family budget more effectively and indeed would ensure regular repayments of loans, but moreover gave them control of the process. For the authority it supplied an open book on expenditures and therefore some measure of control over how and where borrowed money could be spent. Other tools included the National Housing Development Authority's *Implementation Guidelines for the Rural Housing Sub-Programme*, setting administrative and financial criteria and communicating the ideological message of the programme. Various training of trainers handbooks provided a basic structure for deciding on details of programmes, design and implementation of upgrading projects (see Goethert & Hamdi 1988 and Hamdi & Goethert 1984b). Design guidelines for sites and services projects were directed at technical staff to enable them to consider basic criteria in planning these projects. Various more technical "how to build" books emerged, and so on.

Training also assumed various forms. The emphasis, however, was to shift training out of the classroom and into the field. It included not only those who would do the work but also those who funded the work and others who might be affected by the work. Training, therefore, was seen not as something one person teaches another, but as a process in which each actor brings specific knowledge to a given situation, and in co-operation can discover more knowledge – with which to affect both the programme and the outcome.

Some of these training activities were directed at building the capacity of local government to manage local programmes and to discover appropriate ways to disburse loans and recover costs. Others were directed more at the project scale, sometimes in upgrading (services, utilities, employment, health improvement, etc.), and sometimes at teaching basic skills in preparing sites and services programmes. In all cases, learning was coupled closely with doing – the results were not only a cadre of better informed individuals, but also a plan of action *vis-à-vis* the subject or site in question.

The case presented here is one of many Community Action Planning programmes conducted in Sri Lanka.[1]

Summary of the Summitpura workshop programme

The workshop was divided into four parts: context definition, socio-economic programming, physical programming and design explorations.

The *first day* was directed at familiarising the participants with government policies, understanding the administrative framework for implementation of projects, and familiarisation with the site. Presentations were made by Ministry officials, and an initial "walk-through" of the site was undertaken.

The *second day* focused on the understanding of the socio-economic context. The morning was spent in the field, with teams surveying families to determine their priorities, perceptions, characteristics, family trajectories and aspirations. The afternoon programme revolved around the definition of the socio-economic parameters for a project programme.

The *third day* focused on the development of a physical programme. In the morning, the participants again surveyed families in the adjacent low-income urbanisation. The goal was to review and to evaluate first-hand the situation of the physical environment: streets, walkways, open spaces, utilities, services, dwelling/lot, construction procedures and materials. In the afternoon the physical programme for the site was defined.

The *last two days* were directed toward the exploration of designs for the expansion site adjacent to Summitpura. One day was spent on design explorations of the critical circulation elements, and the design of the lot and block layouts. The remaining day included design investigations of the basic utilities – water supply, sewage disposal, street paving, electricity and street lighting – and design considerations for dwellings options.

References

Goethert, R. & Hamdi, N. 1988. *Making Micro-Plans: A Community Based Process in Programming and Development*. London: Intermediate Technology Publications.
Hamdi, N. & Goethert, R. 1984a. Guidelines for Navagampura Project Planning and Design. MIT/NHDA unpublished document.
Hamdi, N. & Goethert, R. 1984b. Physical upgrading of settlements in Sri Lanka: A trainer's guidebook. MIT/NHDA.

---

[1] Since 1983, in addition to Community Action Planning's wide dissemination to rural communities, it is now adopted by 14 of the country's 51 urban local authorities. In the seven years between 1988 and 1994, it is estimated that community action planning activities have reached some 50 000 families in 450 low-income settlements in Sri Lanka. More recently, in 1992–1994 alone 670 workshops of various types had been organised, according to April 1996 issue of *Urban Voices*, the publication of the Urban Management Programme for Asia and the Pacific (UNDP, ESCAP, UNCHS, World Bank). Efforts are now being made to multiply the successful experience to the other countries throughout the region.

Marga Institute, Housing Development in Sri Lanka 1971–1981. Colombo: Marga Institute.
NHDA, 1984. Implementation Guidelines for the Rural Housing Sub-Programme. Colombo.
Sirivardana, S. undated. Housing mainstreaming – a case study in learning. National Housing Development Authority, Colombo, internal report.
Weerapana, D. 1986. The evolution of a support policy for shelter: the experience of Sri Lanka. *Habitat International* 10 (3).

Case Files **197**

COLOMBO
SRI LANKA

SITE PLANNING FOR
NEW COMMUNITIES

PHASE I: PROBLEM IDENTIFICATION AND PRIORITISATION
The Site

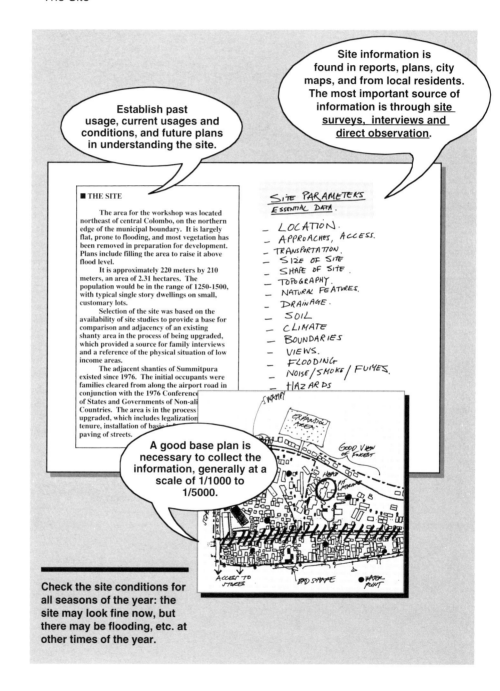

Establish past usage, current usages and conditions, and future plans in understanding the site.

Site information is found in reports, plans, city maps, and from local residents. The most important source of information is through site surveys, interviews and direct observation.

A good base plan is necessary to collect the information, generally at a scale of 1/1000 to 1/5000.

Check the site conditions for all seasons of the year: the site may look fine now, but there may be flooding, etc. at other times of the year.

PHASE I: PROBLEM IDENTIFICATION AND PRIORITISATION
Physical Programming

> Family surveys and site observations provide two sources of information for assessing dwelling design and the site layout.

■ **PHYSICAL PROGRAMMING**

The physical programming again focused on identifying the different viewpoints, one from asking the families, and one based on the observations and assessments by the survey team.

Teams were asked to assess physical elements at the individual dwelling scale and the community scale. Questions to be addressed included: What existed? What was provided? What is the use and what activities do actually take place? Is what was provided adequate or inadequate: does it meet the demands place on it?

For the dwelling, the physical elements surveyed included rooms, materials (roof, walls, floors), and windows and doors. Families were asked to determine what they liked best and what they liked least; what they were planning to change, and what is their incentive to do so; and a tradeoffs assessment between a large lot with no house vs a small lot with a complete house.

For the site elements, each of the physical components were reviewed: lot, street, open-play areas, community centers, toilet blocks, water standpipes, and garbage services.

SUMMARY PHYSICAL DATA
IMPLICATIONS FOR NEW DESIGN

DWELLING - IMPACTS ON LAYOUT & SIZING SPACES.
- SMALL HOUSE SIZES IMPLY MULTI-USE OF SPACES
- SIZES OF DWELLINGS RANGED FROM 26-48 SM
- N° OF ROOMS RANGED FROM 2-4.
- TEMP. ADDITIONS USED FOR BULK STORAGE.
- COMMERCIAL SPACES AT FRONT - TRADING OCCUPIABLE SPACE FOR INCOME EARNING SPACE
- SIZES IN GENERAL CONSIDERED ADEQUATE (?)
- SEPARATE QUARTERS FOR MEN & WOMEN.
- KITCHENS OCCUR LARGELY INSIDE (LACK OF SPACE ON ? LOTS) SOMETIMES OUTSIDE - (UNCLEAR AS TO PREFERENCE?)
- FRONT ROOMS FOR DISPLAY - PHOTOS/FURNITURE

> Families are asked about their preferences and their intentions about changes to their dwelling, and their incentive to do so.

PHASE I: PROBLEM IDENTIFICATION AND PRIORITISATION
Socio-Economic Programming

> Interviews should be unrushed and conducted in familiar settings. Questions should be open. Individual interviews and focus group interviews are useful.

> Conclusions from the surveys are summarised on a chart and displayed for validation and reference.

■ **SOCIO-ECONOMIC PROGRAMMING**

The first two days were intended to serve several roles: to learn how to program, to learn to identify what the key issues are, and to identify methods and procedures which can be used to achieve desired programmatic goals. In addition, a site-specific program was to be developed for the area adjacent to the Summitpura community.

Family interviews were carried out by each group, from which were extracted critical issues as identified by the family. These were compared to observations of the survey team. Afternoon sessions were devoted toward discussions correlating the two viewpoints, the one from the family and the one from the observers. Conclusions were subsequently drawn, identifying the socio-economic issues which impact project formulation.

Families were interviewed with regard to their perceptions of the following: family composition, family trajectory, employment/income, expenditures, aspirations, use of community facilities and priorities.

Story-telling is an effective and quick technique for understanding process.

PHASE II: STRATEGIES, OPTIONS AND TRADEOFFS
Objectives and Issues

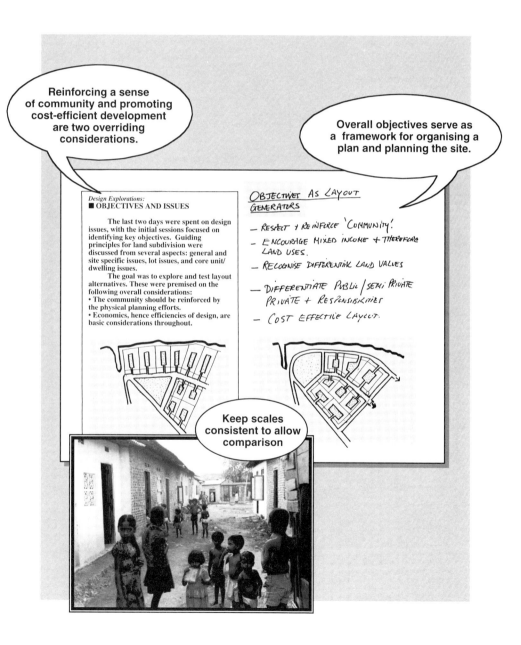

202 Action Planning for Cities

PHASE II: STRATEGIES, OPTIONS AND TRADEOFFS
Circulation Networks

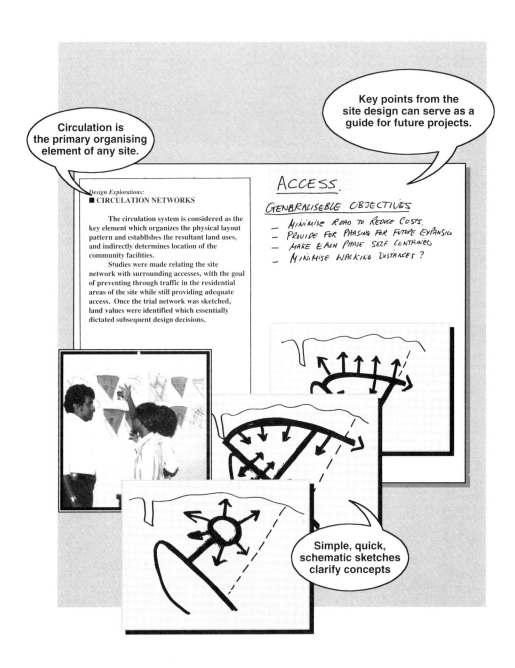

PHASE II: STRATEGIES, OPTIONS AND TRADEOFFS
Utility Infrastructure

> The <u>procedure</u> in providing utility services is the most important fact to convey, as well as alerting the planner to other non-design issues such as maintenance and the necessary administrative framework.

Design Explorations:
■ **UTILITY INFRASTRUCTURE**

The sessions dealing with the design of the utilities focused on general provision levels and technical concerns as well as specific design elements. Discussions were held on deciding levels of service, installation issues, maintenance and layout considerations. Considered were water provision (individual vs communal), sewage disposal (individual vs communal; pit latrines, septic tanks, or waterborne pipe networks), and electricity.

From a layout standpoint, utilities were concluded to parallel the circulation layout. Therefore, the networks were essentially determined, and discussions focused on the technical implications of each utility.

Design evaluations were made in three areas: general layout issues, length issues (the network), and node or intersection issues. Lengths and nodes comprise the critical costs elements of utilities and stress was on their evaluation and quantification. For example, the number of nodes reflects costly manholes, joints in the water network, and the poles in the electrical network. The length parallels the sewer and water pipes, as well as the electrical lines.

UTILITIES.
- CONSIDER MAINTENANCE IMPLICATIONS OF PROPOSALS
- POSITION OF WATER + SEWERS FOLLOW ROAD NETWORK.
- DECIDE LEVEL OF UTILITIES REQUIRED
- CONSIDER FUTURE INCREMENTAL EXTENSIONS / ADDITIONS
- DECIDE WHO INSTALLS WHAT + WHEN.
- PROVIDE ADMINISTRATIVE FRAMEWORK TO ENABLE INEVITABLE FUTURE CONNECTIONS / EXTENSIONS / ADDITIONS.

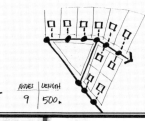

| NODES | LENGTH |
| 9 | 500. |

> Deriving simple numeric values from the sketches provides a reference for comparison to other projects and a basis for determining costs.

PHASE II: STRATEGIES, OPTIONS AND TRADEOFFS
Dwelling Considerations

> Tradeoffs between demand and feasibility are important issues to consider for low-income families.

Design Explorations:
■ **DWELLING CONSIDERATIONS**

The last working session reviewed possible dwelling options. Each team prepared varied core unit designs and identified for who and where on the site the different types would be most suitable.

Criteria for decisions were discussed, but in all cases the provision of complete direct constructed units were considered as inappropriate.

BASIC DWELLING PROVISION

- DECIDE WHAT, FOR WHOM + WHERE ON SITE.
- TENDANCY FOR LOW INCOME TO PREFER SITE WITH A BASIC PROVISION - CAN MOVE IN IMMEDIATELY.
- TENDANCY FOR OPEN SITE + 'FINISHED' DWELLING TO BE MORE APPROPRIATE FOR HIGHER INCOME GROUPS.
- OPEN SITE APPROPRIATE FOR LOW INCOME FAMILY IF: - LIVE WITHIN WALKING DIST.
  - LIVE RENT FREE
  - CHARGES WILL NOT BE LEVIED ON NEW SITE UNTIL OCCUPIED
- CONSIDER LOCATION OF DIFF TYPES IN TERMS OF LAND VALUES.

> The preparation of <u>options</u> should be strongly encouraged in exploring designs, and <u>criteria</u> for deciding amongst the alternatives should be made explicit.

> The lot should be as big as possible to readily allow expansion of the dwelling.

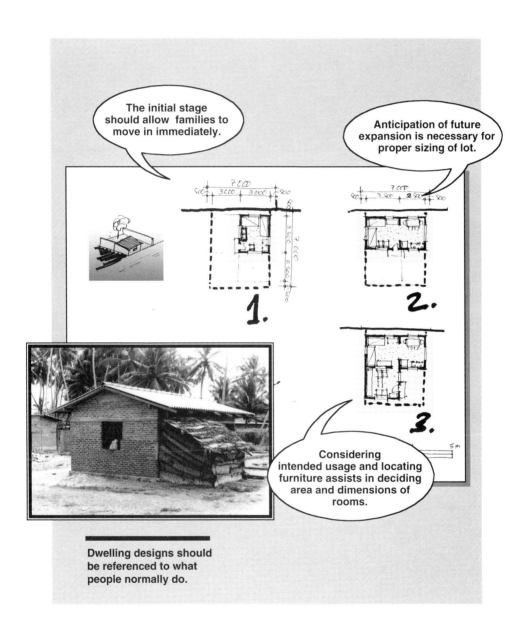

Dwelling designs should be referenced to what people normally do.

CASE 2: BUILDING CAPACITY

PLANNING ASSISTANCE KIT: A PLANNING GUIDE FOR COMMUNITY-BASED ORGANIZATIONS, BOSTON, MASSACHUSETTS, USA

Introduction

The Planning Assistance Kit (PAK) is a series of worksheets designed to assist community organisations in physical planning, implementation and management of their housing. It is designed to be used to structure planning workshops and as a source for understanding housing development issues and procedures. It is an active, collaborative and quick approach to planning and design where community organisations learn what is required in planning new housing developments. In a broader sense, it is a process of "going to scale" based on building the capacity locally to act and guide development. It is a tool for empowerment.

PAK is intended to assist local community players in the housing field in Massachusetts and its principles are largely applicable throughout the United States. Community players include community development corporations (CDCs), tenant organisations, homesteaders, co-operatives, labour unions and land trusts.

The "Planning Assistance Kit" was developed with funding from the Massachusetts Housing Partnership (MHP) Challenge Grant Program in 1988. The Challenge Grant Program supported efforts which foster innovation in affordable housing development across the state of Massachusetts. It emphasised working partnerships between non-profit groups, businesses, state, region and local officials, and other individuals and organisations who are working to increase the supply of affordable housing in Massachusetts.

The PAK workshops are typically held in a minimum of two sessions: the first for setting the objectives of a project (PAK-I), and the second focused on building a programme (PAK-II).

During the production of this guide, several test workshops were conducted to refine various stages and parts of the method. Workshops were held with staff of the City of Boston Public Facilities Department and a local community development corporation – the Riverside Cambridgeport Community Corporation – together with a group of tenants living in buildings owned by the CDC. Several workshops were also held with students to test and develop specific details of the planning guide.

Background

During the 1980s non-profit and community-based groups in the United States had an increasingly important role to play in the provision of housing for low and moderate-income people. The cutbacks in federal funding, the growth of neighbourhood movements and the inability of the private market to provide adequate opportunities for low-income people to purchase or rent houses, have led neighbourhood-based organisations to focus strongly on developing affordable housing. In order to achieve this goal effectively, these organisations have had to structure their staff, their advisory board and the community itself to deal with a wide range of new issues.

In preparing a plan of action, it was seen that community groups often lack the following:

- Know-how and resources to achieve their goals.
- Knowledge of alternatives that are available.
- Information in the form of tradeoffs, technical, financial, etc.
- Negotiation, technical, financial and managerial skills to move from one stage to the next.
- Consensus amongst key actors about which steps to take, about what the problems really are, and about what priorities to adopt.
- Knowledge of hurdles likely to be encountered on the way and the experience which enables hurdles to be avoided or overcome.
- Organisation and leadership to achieve their objectives.

In this context the Planning Assistance Kit was developed as a tool for local organisations to confront and manage new projects. It was primarily seen as a way for community organisations and the technical staff of the authorities to effectively interface and dialogue. It was seen as particularly useful given the increasing number of non-profit CDCs which have been set up with city and state support. The local CDCs were increasingly given control of the development of publicly owned land and assistance in this task was imperative.

Two basic premises drive the planning guide:

- Objectives are usually well known by community-based organisations. However, communities often need considerable assistance to become effective producers of housing and often lack the technical and procedural know-how and management skills.
- Solutions are more likely to be appropriate and problems are more likely to be tolerated when design and development decisions are made by those closest to the situation and/or by those who will be affected by those decisions.

With these premises in mind, the Planning Assistance Kit (PAK) provides the following for communities:

- It is a tool for promoting clarity about objectives and defining problems, and assists in structuring the most appropriate or feasible way of meeting communities' objectives.
- It helps communities to become familiar with logistics, procedures and potential hurdles.
- It provides a structure for expanding the range of options with the potential of more effective solutions.
- It helps communities to stumble on "good ideas", to become aware of the investment required, and to get a sense of risks involved.

For public authorities, PAK provides:

- A means for securing effective community participation.
- A teaching tool for staff.
- A means for more structured decision making.

Throughout, the following basic principles apply:

- The workshop setting brings together conflicting interest groups for negotiation as a prelude to planning.
- The format provides a structure for positioning and defining problems and issues more effectively.
- The planning guide avoids telling people what to do, but it helps them to find out what to do and how to do it.
- It helps communities to discover alternatives based on an informed understanding of prevailing circumstances.
- The planning guide is structured incrementally, with each step informing the next.
- It helps prioritise problems and options and provides a means for dealing with problems as they emerge.
- It provides a means to move ahead even with incomplete information.

The PAK contents

The PAK consists of five elements. The first four are contained in a three-ring notebook – the Planning Guide – and the last is packaged separately.

- *PAKMAN*: This is the introduction to the kit and tells how it can be used. It is principally directed to those who will moderate the planning workshops. It covers both how the kit can be used as an instruction tool as well how it might help community-based groups develop specific proposals for a given site. It outlines what needs to be done and known before planning can begin.

- *PAK-I and PAK-II*: The two sections "Setting Objectives" and "Building Programs" are directly concerned with the building of a proposal. PAK-I sets procedure and suggests ways with which to clarify concerns, prioritise needs and resolve conflicts of interest. PAK-II introduces methods for identifying realistic options for the financial, construction, location and management components of a programme, and subsequently suggests ways of preparing schematic proposals. Worksheets (which may be used as wallcharts) are used to make the steps and concepts of community development more accessible to a wider range of people. Each step includes a statement of goals, an outline of the steps, an explanation of techniques and helpful hints. A sample workshop is included as well as a blank for the participants to fill in as the workshop progresses. The filled blank provides a record of the session which provides a means to monitor compliance.

- *INFOPAK*: This section is a directory of information about agencies, printed materials and other resources in the housing and development field. Each entry includes a brief description of purpose and the characteristics, addresses and telephone numbers of relevant organisations. It also gives information, where applicable, on the approvals and resources needed, for example if preparing a rehabilitation project.

- *GAMEPAK*: A game board, packaged separately (see Figure CF.2), is designed to sensitise participants with the housing development process and to familiarise them with terminology in the housing field. The game uses hurdles, gates and tradeoffs which players have to negotiate as they proceed through the four stages of the planning process. The INFOPAK section of the planning guide is an active element in the playing of the game and requires participants to refer to the planning guide to answer questions from "quiz cards" as the player moves through the game. The game is intended to be played informally in the first part of the planning workshop and often serves to "break the ice" between participatory partners before planning begins.

Case Files **211**

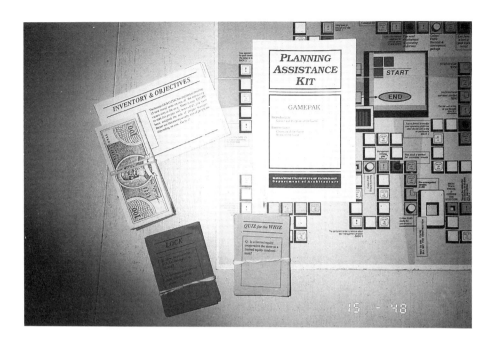

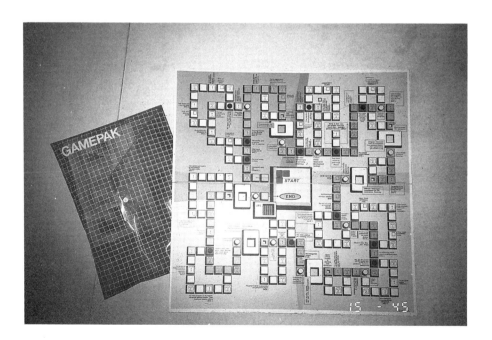

Figure CF.2 GAMEPAK in the Planning Assistance Kit.

212 Action Planning for Cities

GETTING STARTED
Preparing the Workshop Schedule

Prepare the Workshop Schedule

Goals:
To produce a schedule that lists all the activities that will take place in a workshop situation and to assign time allocations to each activity.

Steps:
1.1 Decide what the scope of the workshop will be, based on the workbooks and stages of each workbook that are presented in the PAK.
1.2 Find out what may be the best schedule for the potential participants in the workshop.(e.g. evenings, weekends, etc.
1.3 Use the chart provided here (or make up your own) to schedule the activities and time allocations for each. Once the schedule is assembled, circulate it to all who will participate.

Techniques:
It is important that the schedule be followed as closely as possible to maintain the morale of the group. If changes become necessary during the workshop, make sure that everyone is aware of the revised schedule. Some improvization will typically be necessary.

It is a good idea to assign a person as a timekeeper so that everyone knows that there is a person responsible for keeping things on track.

Allow "slack time" so that people can socialise a bit and get to know each other.

> Start the process informally by focusing around a common interest; for example, use an aerial photograph of the community or a model to identify boundaries and talk about special features or play *Gamepak* to familiarise the group with planning terms and procedures.

Worksheet to be filled in by moderator

Case Files **215**

PHASE I: PROBLEM IDENTIFICATION AND PRIORITISATION
Setting Objectives

> Consider carefully the reasons why others are affected by the concerns. These become the basis for negotiation with the varied interest groups.

> The first steps must quickly generate interest in the process and attract those who are hesitant to get involved.

> "Brainstorming" is a good technique in noting concerns of everyone.

Stage 1
Identify and Clarify Concerns

IDENTIFY AND CLARIFY CONCERNS ELM ST. MAY 1, 1984

WHAT ARE THE CONCERNS	WHO IS AFFECTED & WHY	WHAT OTHER OPPORTUNITIES
- NEED HOUSING FOR LOW INCOME FAMILIES	- CHILDREN OF HOMEOWNERS — MAY HAVE TO LEAVE N'HOOD - LOW INCOME RESIDENTS — MAY HAVE NO OTHER PLACE TO LIVE — PAYING TOO MUCH FOR RENT — WANT TO STAY IN THE NEIGHBORHOOD - BUSINESSES — NEED PLACE ...	

Stage 2
Prioritize Concerns and Identify Conflicts

PRIORITIZE CONCERNS & CHECK COMPATABILITY ELM ST. COOP MAY 1, 1989

CONCERN	INTEREST GROUP									AFFORDABLE HOUSING	PRESERVE OPEN SPACE	STRENGTHEN ECONOMY	REDUCE PARKING PROBLEMS	STOP CRIME & VANDALISM	INCREASE PROPERTY VALUE
	RESIDENT RENTERS	HOUSING ACTIVISTS	CITY GOV'T.	LOCAL BUSINESSES	PENSION	TOTAL								
AFFORDABLE HOUSING	5	0	2	5	3	15		◐	O	O	●	O	O
PRESERVE OPEN SPACE	1	2	4	6	6	19				O	O	O	O
STRENGTHEN ECONOMY	4	4	0	0	1						◐	O	O
REDUCE PARKING PROBLEMS	3	3	6	4	5	20						O	O
STOP CRIME & VANDALISM	6	5	6	2	4	23							O
INCREASE PROPERTY VALUE	2	6	3	3	3	17							

O = OK   ● = CONFLICT   ◐ = POSS. CONFLICT

PAK-I.12

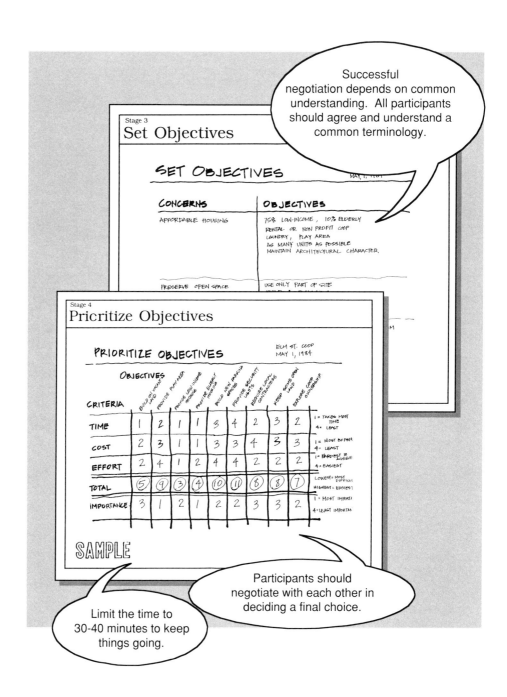

PHASE II: STRATEGIES, OPTIONS AND TRADEOFFS
Building a Programme

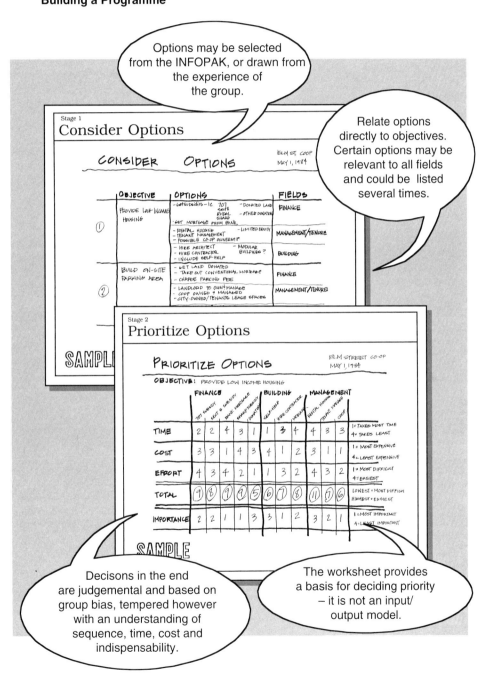

218 Action Planning for Cities

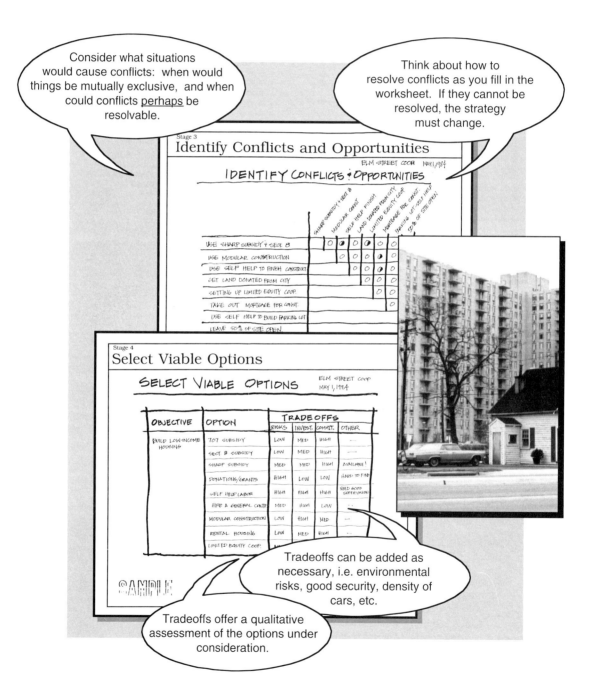

Case Files **219**

PHASE III: PLANNING FOR IMPLEMENTATION
Building a Programme

> Having resources is not enough: you must also be in compliance with permits in achieving what you want.

> Be warned: you may not be able to get what you need in all cases.

Stage 5
Assess What You Have and What You Need

ASSESS WHAT YOU HAVE & WHAT YOU NEED   ELM ST. COOP
                                         MAY 1, 1984

OPTIONS	HAVE		NEED	
	APPROVALS	RESOURCES	APPROVALS	RESOURCES
SHARP SUBSIDY	-NON-PROFIT STATUS -MUST BE NEWLY CREATED	-MIN. OF 25% LOW-INCOME	-UNITS TO BE APPROVED BY EOCD -MUST LOCATE	-CONSTRUCTION MORTGAGE

Stage 6
Decide Where to Get What You Need and When

DECIDE WHERE TO GET WHAT YOU NEED & WHEN   ELM STREET COOP MAY 1, 1984

(N) = NOW   (S) = SOON   (L) = LATER

	NEED	WHERE TO GET IT
APPROVALS	- UNITS MUST BE APPROVED BY EOCD (N) - MUST BE LOCATED IN HOUSING DEVELOPMENT AREA (N)	- EOCD, LOCAL HOUSING AUTH. - EOCD FOR CLASSIFICATIONS - LOCAL COMMUNITY DEVELOPMENT DEPARTMENT
RESOURCES	- CAPITAL TO INVEST AS EQUITY (N) - ABILITY TO ADMINISTER & HANDLE STATE PAPERWORK (L)	- FUNDRAISING FROM PRIVATE FOUNDATIONS - SYNDICATION - HIRE PROPERTY MANAGEMENT CONSULTANT

SAMPLE

> Be flexible in considering resources or approvals. Some skills can be best acquired by hiring specialists, enlisting friends, or by training.

> "Now" approvals may be the most urgent or critical because many other activities depend on them.

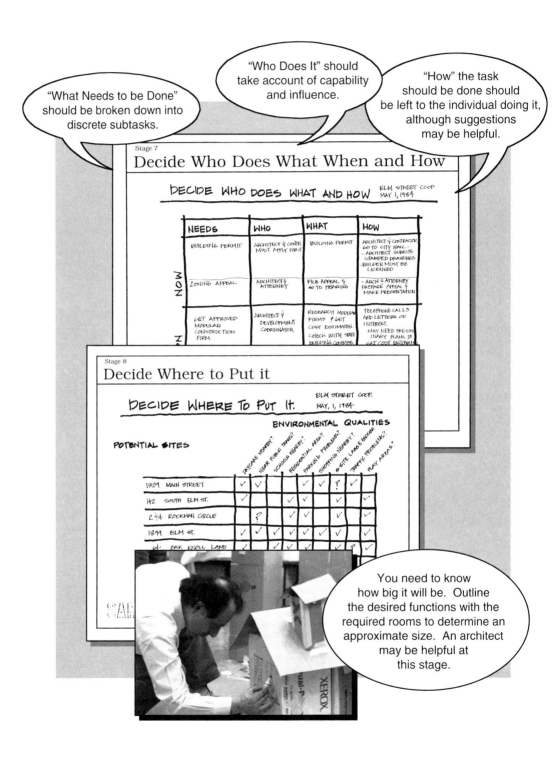

PHASE III: PLANNING FOR IMPLEMENTATION
Information Sheets

> The Information Sheets are organised around five topics:
> - How to pay for it?
> - How to own and manage it?
> - How to build it?
> - Approval
> - Resources
>
> Each sheet contains: a summary description, How to Get More Information, Approvals Needed, and Resources Needed.

Information Sheets

Building Permit

Most cities or towns require a building permit to be acquired for any construction or rehab work that is more extensive than ordinary [...] roof). Someti[...] the Commonw[...] building perm[...]

How To G[...]
Call or write:
Boston the bu[...]
describe the p[...]
permit.

Approvals

Resources

Greater Boston Community Development Corporation

Assists community based organizations in the development and management of affordable housing through technical assistance and management assistance.

How To [...]
Call or wr[...]
Corp., 79[...]

Approv[...]
-none

Resour[...]
-Technical [...]
basis nego[...]

Chapter 707 certificate Program

Rental Housing Subsidy

State subsidy program to renting families that pays the difference between 25% of their income and the fair market rental rate for a qualified apartment. Certificates distributed to families through LHA or CDCs under contract to EOCD.

How To Get More Information:
Call or write: Local housing authority or EOCD, 100 Cambridge St. Boston, MA, 02202, (617) 727-7130.

Approvals Needed:
- Certificates eligible to families and individuals with incomes less than 64% of area median incomes.
- Apartment must be inspected and built to meet 707 physical standards requirements.
- Tenants must be taken from local housing authority waiting lists.
- Tenants must be determined to be income eligible by local housing authority.
- Landlord cannot charge more than fair market rent for apartments.

Resources Needed:
- Residents must pay 25% of their income for rent.
- Landlords must do paper work to get subsidy portion of rent from government.

CASE 3: URBAN UPGRADING

PILOT PROJECT SCHWEIZER-RENEKE: EXECUTIVE SUMMARY, WORKSHOP PROCEDURE, AND WORKSHOP DOCUMENTATION, SCHWEIZER-RENEKE, SOUTH AFRICA

Introduction

Schweizer-Reneke is situated in the North-Western Province of South Africa, some 65 km south of Vryburg, and 158 km west of Klerksdorp. Its principal economic base is agriculture, with approximately 405 600 hectares of good farming land in its vicinity. Typical of many South African towns, its broader municipal area accommodates a population of 145 000, segregated into four distinct ethnic neighbourhoods. The town itself of Schweizer-Reneke is mostly white and accommodates about 8% of the total population; Roschunville, traditionally Indian in composition, has 3.5%; Charon, comprising a largely coloured population, accommodates 8.5%; and Ipelegeng, the focus of this project, with a mostly black population, represents the majority (80%) of the total.[1]

Conditions of housing, services and utilities vary considerably amongst each of the neighbourhoods, as do rates of employment. The population of Ipelegeng are mostly migrant workers. They find jobs in areas outside the province, or find employment as labourers in neighbouring farms. Despite a growing potential industrial base in mining and trade, over 50% of the neighbourhood's population are unemployed.

In housing, Ipelegeng is mixed in quality and standard. Of all housing, 95% is built through self-help community, using corrugated tin sheeting and recycled components (windows, doors, etc.). At least 45% of the housing stock is considered by residents to be lacking in space, or other basic amenities. The small number of houses built from permanent materials belong to policemen, teachers and other public officials. Some 2500 families have settled in the township informally, as squatters (without permanent status), 90% of whom live in shacks which are considered neither durable nor adequate in space, privacy or amenity. Many houses

---

[1] Statistics are taken from two memos prepared specifically for the workshop by Boyce Mpembe, RDP Co-ordinator, dated 13 January 1995 and 23 February 1995.

sit on generous lots, used often for cultivation or other income-generating activities. Until recently, few families owned their own property, although ownership is now strongly encouraged. "An integral part of apartheid planning involved undermining African tenure. In accordance with the notion of the African's temporary status in white urban areas, title to township property was reduced to 30 years in the early 1950s, and was revoked completely in 1968. The immediate result was that all African residents in the townships were reduced to being state tenants" (Parnell & Pirie 1991).

Connection to electricity is generally available to most houses, whatever their condition, and street lighting is adequate – part of the legacy of security provision during the apartheid era. Other utilities are rudimentary. About 75% of households use bucket latrines as their principal means of sanitation, and some 95% of households rely on standpipes for their water supply. Malnutrition, dehydration and diarrhoeic diseases are common.

Ipelegeng is also deficient in basic services. A small kindergarten provides day care and raises most of its funds through parent contributions. There is a parallel advisory centre run by community volunteers, with support from human rights lawyers from other parts of the North-Western Province. A small community hall provides space for meetings and other functions, with a capacity for about 150 people. The existing clinic is small, poorly equipped and understaffed. Access for blacks to the hospital, which is situated in white Schweizer-Reneke, has until recently been severely restricted. The hospital has now undergone "deracialisation".

Schweizer-Reneke, and Ipelegeng in particular, is typical of the kind of township targeted for improvement by the post-apartheid regime under its progressive Reconstruction and Development Programme (RDP published in 1994). The RDP, based substantially on the international definition of the "enabler paradigm", was designed to capture the spirit of the new era, in building a new democracy in South Africa, to address basic needs, and to tackle the failure (or lack of intent) of past policies in delivering adequate housing, service and utilities to its black majority. Furthermore, it recognised the importance of its urban area responsibilities, given that cities account for 80% of the country's gross domestic product, and accommodate approximately 60% of its population. It recognised that urbanisation, including the integration of townships, was inevitable and likely to increase.

The RDP represents an integrated socio-economic policy framework seeking to "mobilise all our people and our country's resources toward the final eradication of apartheid and the building of a democratic, non-racial, and non-sexist future." (RDP 1994). It contains six basic principles at its core:

- An integrated and sustainable programme of development.
- A people-driven process.
- Peace and security for all.
- A national programme of building.
- A commitment to link reconstruction with development.
- Democratisation in all areas of governance.

These principles are embodied into five linked policy programmes: meeting basic needs, such as for jobs, land reform, housing, water and sanitation, and health care; developing human resources, with the focus on education at all levels and on training; building the economy; democratising the state and society; and ensuring a progressive and sustainable programme of implementation.

Underpinning all these efforts would be a commitment to full local-level participation (people and organisations) in all programmes, not least in the governance and administration of its urban-sector reconstruction activities. To this end, the Local Government Transition Act made it "compulsory for every village, town, and city throughout South Africa (including the former homeland) to establish a negotiation forum ... to agree on the non-racial boundaries of the new local government for each area, plus its administrative structure, distribution of power, budget, and composition of the council and its executive body" (Switting 1996). This process culminated in the local government elections of November 1995. Full stakeholder participation, in policy development and programme implementation, mobilisation of resources from private and community sectors, partnership between community organisation and local authority and between private enterprise and government administration were all stated characteristics of the new effort. Community Action Planning seemed well suited to the RDP's new agenda and to exploring its implementation.

The programme

The action planning programme for Ipelegeng had two linked objectives, both of which were targeted toward assisting the Government of South Africa to implement the recommendations of its Reconstruction and Development Programme (RDP).

(1) *To undertake a pilot project* to demonstrate the methods and principles of Community Action Planning in a "learning by doing" setting. The pilot would serve:

- To "jump start" the development process for the selected community at Ipelegeng, Schweizer-Reneke.

- To expose strengths and weaknesses of methods and policies which will need to be considered if the process is to be expanded to other townships and provinces.

(2) *To disseminate lessons learnt* from the grassroots to provincial and national-level authorities and NGOs through a national seminar. Its objectives are:

- To assess the value of Community Action Planning and other approaches to other townships and provinces and to the RDP.

- To review what is likely to get in the way of implementing the RDP programme at the community level.

- To define a broader programme of projects for implementation and to decide next steps.

The programme was arranged under four phases as illustrated in Figure CF.4, culminating in a policy paper which would be discussed at a national level dissemination seminar.

The pilot Community Action Planning workshop was held between 24 and 29 April, 1995, partly on-site in the township of Ipelegeng and partly in the public library of Schweizer-Reneke. The intention was to give the community of Schweizer-Reneke as wide an exposure as possible to the programme. The workshop included some 20 participants representing the range of community-level organisations and interests, and moderated by a team from Oxford Brookes University, University of Natal and MIT. The workshop was conducted under the auspices of the Interim Development Committee of Schweizer-Reneke and the local RDP Co-ordinator. The workshop included four phases of work (see Figure CF.3), summarised as follows:

(1)   Deciding what was needed (key problems and priorities).
(2)   Sorting out how to achieve what was needed (preparing proposals).
(3)   Assessing what will get in the way of implementation (project viability).
(4)   Building a plan of action (tasks, partners, schedules, organisations, etc.) and getting projects going.

The day-by-day programme is illustrated in Figure CF.4 and a brief report on the workshop in Figure CF.6.

The workshop produced a viable Community Action Plan which has set in motion a development process in Schweizer-Reneke. A planning unit was established to work on community-level RDP projects under the auspices of the RDP Forum. The unit is chaired by the RDP representative. It is composed of four project co-ordinators selected from the community. Project teams formed to pursue the tasks identified in each of the following areas:

- housing
- health
- income generation
- water and sanitation

Following the Community Action Planning workshop, the project was presented to the Member of the Executive Council (MEC) for Local Government and Housing of the North-Western Province and to the Provincial RDP Co-ordinator by the project team and community representatives. They were impressed by the practical nature of the process and the projects identified. The following issues were raised:

- The community should continue to be empowered to sustain what had been started.
- The need to incorporate the planning unit within the RDP Forum should be further considered.
- Experts should include people selected to represent minority and low income sections of the community.

Phases	Tasks	Outputs
SETTING IT UP	Plan Workshop	WORKSHOP CHECKLIST *Time/Goals/Activity/Arrangement*

PHASE I: PROBLEM IDENTIFICATION AND PRIORITISATION

Phases	Tasks	Outputs
WHAT DO YOU NEED	Identify Area Problems and Opportunities	CHART 1 *Problems/Opportunities/Why/To Whom*
	Undertake Community Survey	Survey Information
	Identify Community Problems and Opportunities	CHART 2 *Problems/Opportunities/Why/To Whom*
	Determine Goals and Priorities	(On Chart 2) *Now/Soon/Later*

PHASE II: STRATEGIES, OPTIONS AND TRADEOFFS

Phases	Tasks	Outputs
HOW TO GET WHAT YOU NEED	Allocate Resources	CHART 3 *Proposals/Relative Costs/Targeting Resources*
	Identify Proposals	CHART 4 *Do Ourselves/Need Help/Done by Others*
WHAT GETS IN YOUR WAY	Identify Constraints	CHART 5 *Technical/Organisational/Political/Financial/Human Resources*
	Review Sequence of Proposals	(On Chart 5) *Now/Soon/Later*

PHASE III: PLANNING FOR IMPLEMENTATION

Phases	Tasks	Outputs
BUILDING A PLAN OF ACTION	Identify Proposal/Tasks	CHART 6 *Tasks/Partners/Funding Sources*
	Develop Schedule	CHART 7 *Steps/Time*
	Design Proposals	CHART 8 *Preliminary Sketches* MAP 1
GETTING PROJECTS GOING	Identify Project Teams	CHART 9 *List of Members*
	Decide Immediate Tasks	CHART 10 *Key Steps*

Figure CF.3 Summary of Community Action Planning phases, Schweizer-Reneke, South Africa.

Monday	Tuesday	Wednesday	Thursday	Friday
Opening Introductions	WHAT IS NEEDED: Determine Goals and Priorities (on Chart 2)	*Review What is Needed*: Review Town Problems and Opportunities	BUILDING A PLAN OF ACTION: Develop Schedule CHART 7	GETTING PROJECTS GOING: Decide Immediate Tasks CHART 10
Overview of the Town Situation	HOW TO GET WHAT YOU NEED: Allocate Resources CHART 3	HOW TO GET WHAT YOU NEED: Identify Proposals CHART 4 (2nd round)	BUILDING A PLAN OF ACTION: Design Proposals CHART 8	GETTING PROJECTS GOING: Organise Planning Unit Co-ordinate with Provincial Level
WHAT IS NEEDED: Identify Area Problems and Opportunities CHART 1	HOW TO GET WHAT YOU NEED: Identify Proposals CHART 4	WHAT GETS IN YOUR WAY: Identify Constraints CHART 5 (2nd round)	BUILDING A PLAN OF ACTION: Survey Site Map 1	
Lunch	Lunch	Lunch	Lunch	
WHAT IS NEEDED: Undertake Community Survey	WHAT GETS IN YOUR WAY: Identify Constraints CHART 5	BUILDING A PLAN OF ACTION: Identify Proposal/Tasks Chart 6	Presentation to Town Council Representatives	
WHAT IS NEEDED: Identify Com. Problems and Opportunities CHART 2	WHAT GETS IN YOUR WAY: Review Sequence (on Chart 5)		GETTING PROJECTS GOING Identify Project Teams and Immediate Tasks CHART 9	
Summary of Day's Activities	Summary of Day's Activities	Summary of Day's Activities	Closing Barbeque	

Figure CF.4 Overview of workshop programme, Schweizer-Reneke, South Africa.

Time	April 22–May 4	April 28	May–August	Mid-September
Phase	TOWN LEVEL PILOT WORKSHOP	PROVINCIAL LEVEL ROUNDTABLE	POLICY PAPER	NATIONAL LEVEL DISSEMINATION SEMINAR
Location	Schweizer-Reneke	Mmabatho	Durban	Pretoria (tentative)
Aims	**PROJECT PLANS AND ISSUES**	**RDP ISSUES AND NEXT STEPS**	**LESSONS/AGENDA FOR NATIONAL SEMINAR**	**POLICY DISCUSSIONS AND FUTURE DIRECTIONS**
Participants	• S-R Interim Development Committee • S-R Community Representatives • S-R Town Council Representatives • University of Natal • CSIR Representative • Oxford Brookes • Ridge Development • MIT (See Note A)	• MEC (Local Govt. and Housing) • RDP Provincial Co-ordinator • RDP Local Co-ordinator • Community Representatives • Oxford Brookes • Ridge Development • University of Natal • MIT	• University of Natal	• University of Natal • Project Team • RDP representatives as necessary • RDP Co-ordinators • Funding Agencies • NGOs • Provincial MECs • Oxford Brookes • National RDP Co-ordinator • Minister of Housing
Objectives	"Jump-start" the development process Produce a Community Action Plan Expose strengths and weaknesses of method	Presentation of S-R findings Expose provincial-level issues Links to RDP objectives	Review other projects Document S-R experience Prepare agenda for national seminar	Assess applicability of S-R experience at national level Review likely constraints to broader implementation To define further projects and decide next steps
Responsibility	*RDP Officer*: invitations, venue *Brooks University*: workshop timetable, methods, documentation *University of Natal*: technical assistance	*RDP Officer*: set up meeting	*University of Natal* with other project teams *Ridge Development* (Re: Dept. of National Housing)	*RDP Office/Ministry of Housing*: invitations, venue *University of Natal*: background paper, agenda, logistics, etc.
Outputs	Community Action Plan Methodology issues	Issues to consider Next steps	Background paper Seminar agenda	Further pilot projects Policy recommendations

Note A: Also included are the following: Local government co-ordinating committee, Civil Association, PAC Representative, ANC Representative, Women's League, BESG–NGO Representative, and the S-R Hospital

Acronyms: MEC: Member of Executive Chamber; BESG: Built Environment Support Group; ANC: African National Congress; RDP: Reconstruction and Development Programme; S-R: Schweizer-Reneke; CSIR: Centre for Scientific and Industrial Research; PAC: Pan African Council

Figure CF.5 Phases of work, Schweizer-Reneke, South Africa.

- The workshop identified the desirability for community RDP projects to run in parallel with local authority RDP projects.
- The need was expressed to keep the provincial level fully informed of the progress.
- The next steps should enable the programme to operate not only locally but also at provincial and national levels.
- The Schweizer-Reneke Project Teams, assisted by the University of Natal, will run a presentation for RDP District Officers to inform them about the Schweizer-Reneke process.

References

Parnell, S.M. & Pirie, G.H. 1991. Johannesburg. In Lemon, A. (ed.), *Homes Apart: South Africa's Segregated Cities*.

Switting, M. 1996. Negotiating change: building local democracy in South Africa. *The Urban Age* 3 (4).

THE INDABA IMPERATIVE
A Small Town Application of Community Action Planning
Mark Napier on Community Involvement

With current housing policy requiring that development projects include consultation with interest groups in a social compact, a new component has been added to project management with which the architect, planner or other project partner might be relatively unfamiliar. This commentary describes an occasion where a well defined approach to community participation was employed in articulating and formalising a range of residentially-based needs. This kind of approach must form an essential building block to the consultation process necessary for any intervention aimed at improving the built environment.

Three days before the second Freedom Day, in a quiet little dorp in the North-Western Province, an unassuming handful of foreign academics and local RDP committee members initiated a small exercise in community participation. Wandering around the sand-swept township and shack settlement of Ipelegeng, peri-Schweizer-Reneke, newcomers and residents noted with respective amazement and familiarity the bewildering mixture of evidence before them: the hope in the small squares of carefully cultivated grass redeemed from the wasteland, the hopelessness of the locked, dripping standpipes; the ingenuity of home-builders' creations from home-cast concrete blocks, the feebleness of flimsy corrugated iron roofs against the extremities of the oscillating North-Western weather; the exuberance of the soccer and basketball games on the open lands, and the contrast between the plenteous shebeen venues (taverns) and the single, doctorless clinic.

Returning to the central town library, the group sits down together around a table and begins to articulate its thoughts and feelings. The "experts" from Britain and America quickly lose their aura and become cheerful, almost humble, facilitators asking questions which at first are not too difficult to answer: "So what are the main problems here in Ipelegeng?" "Why are these problems?" "To whom are they problematic?" Participants are urged to see the host of issues which spring to mind as opportunities rather than problems. Large sheets of newsprint and fat felt tip pens obligingly record long lists of apparently insurmountable hurdles as groups cluster around tables, heads bent in communal concentration. Emerging at last from their huddles after an hour, the newsprint is put up against the wall and one spokesperson is democratically press-ganged into presenting the findings: "Well, it's the water supply, as you all know. There is hardly any water for a start, the pipes are leaking, we can only draw water twice a day, and then the water has little things floating in it. What everyone would really like is a water connection to each house but we know this isn't going to be possible until the main supply from the Vaal is sorted out. The new pipeline will cost billions and all our lobbying so far has come to nothing. Until then the people in the middle of town keep on watering their gardens and the lush town lawns while even the water we need for drinking is limited and inferior." The representatives of the other groups follow with similar tales of inadequate health care, lack of opportunities to work, poor housing, and a desperately depressed living environment.

"Right! Get back into your groups and let's have some solutions", comes the slightly shocking response. "Divide your next sheet into four columns and describe a series of projects which will deal with these problems. What can we do ourselves in these projects, what tasks will we need help with, and what do we need an outside expert to do? Use this to identify the projects which you are mostly able to initiate and drive yourselves."

Figure CF.6 An article on the Schweizer-Reneke workshop, published in "asc" magazine by the South African Advisory Bureau for Development.

And so the process carries on for the four days – huddle, present, huddle, agonise, rethink, present, rework, re-present – until gradually the action plans take shape. The partners who will be needed in the projects are identified, tasks are isolated, funders are discussed, hurdles and ways around them are confronted, and bar charts are drawn which begin tomorrow and stretch into the year ahead. Gradually over the days of the workshop expectations are transformed into feasible, community-driven projects. Without losing sight of the larger needs, like enough water of acceptable quality for greater Schweizer-Reneke, ways are devised of chipping away at the huge block of initial hopelessness: schemes in which community plumbers form teams that fix leaking water pipes, plans for longer opening hours and better staffing at the clinic, better sanitation practices through education programmes, job-creation projects, improvements to building materials supplies, and better access to building skills training are just some of the ideas which are fleshed out in detail.

As individuals present the group ideas, and present again in front of the gathered assembly, confidence grows. The assembly also expands as news of the exercise in participative affirmation spreads. New groupings entering mid-way are welcomed, and the whole process takes a step backwards to orient and include them. On the morning of the final day of the workshop, a few brief speeches sum up the meaning of the 27th of April 1995 (First Anniversary of the first democratic election in South Africa) and it seems oddly appropriate to be working on this public holiday. Just before lunch, a small group of town councillors arrives to see what these people have been doing in their library for the last four days. They are treated to a formidable presentation of what the community intends to do, and how the Town Council, the local politicians, and even a handful of professionals, might be able to participate in their plans for the improvement of their own living environment. As a final step of the workshop, the authors of the action plans are invited to add their names to working groups who will begin to implement what has been discussed. The foreigners, observers and academics promise to return in the next few months to see how the needs expressed here have been translated into action.

Without fanfare and almost unnoticed, a small group of community leaders and representatives have been given a vision of what their neighbourhood could be like, and have been empowered to begin realising some parts of that dream. Only time will tell whether the authorities, professionals and investors will also come to the party. They have certainly been invited, but this time it is the people who are handing out the invitations.

Mark Napier – Building Technology Division of the Centre for Scientific and Industrial Research (CSIR), Pretoria, South Africa.

Case Files **233**

SCHWEIZER-RENEKE
SOUTH AFRICA

URBAN UPGRADING

234 Action Planning for Cities

PHASE I: PROBLEM IDENTIFICATION AND PRIORITISATION

> Problems can be quickly identified, based on direct experience. The range of participants enables problems to reflect on a wide variety of issues.

WHAT DO YOU NEED?

IDENTIFY AREA PROBLEMS AND OPPORTUNITIES ON CHART 1

■ *Procedure:*

  ✔ Consider the area as a whole, and identify the key problems and the opportunities on a chart [Chart 1].

  ✔ Consider <u>why</u> it is a problem [and how it is an opportunity] as well as <u>who</u> does it directly affect, and <u>where</u> is the problem or opportunity found in the area.

■ *Things to keep in mind:*

  ✔ You may consider writing the problems and opportunities on a piece of paper (one per paper) instead of on a Chart, and placing them on a table or on the floor. The group then selects the key problems by turning over the ones considered not so important. The group then jointly decides <u>why</u>, <u>who</u> and <u>where</u> about each problem and opportunity.

❐ *Example of chart to be filled:*

Chart 1

Problems Opportunities	Why? How?	To Whom?	Where?

> Urban area information is used to give context to the local issues in the community: some area-wide problems will directly affect the community.

Case Files **235**

WHAT DO YOU NEED?

UNDERTAKE COMMUNITY SURVEY

■ *Procedure:*

✓ Divide into groups to survey the different sectors of the community. If the community is small, it is still useful to breakup into teams, and then compare what different teams saw.

✓ Each group should have "<u>lookers</u>" – those who identity the problems and opportunities of the area by observation, and "<u>listeners</u>" – those who talk with people to understand the concerns from their point of view.

■ *Things to keep in mind:*

✓ It may be useful to identify a "writer" – a person to keep notes – in each group. It is difficult to remember what you see and hear unless you make sure that someone takes things down.

> "Lookers" are metaphors for outsider expert evaluations. "Listeners" solicit insider, or non-expert points of view.

> Surveys are conducted using techniques from the action planning menu described in Chapter 2.

> Maps can be prepared separately by focus groups (women, elderly, children) and then compared.

> It is imperative to have a <u>plan</u> on which to take notes and locate problems and opportunities.

> A camera may be useful for documentation. A Polaroid is best, but film is expensive (and all the children will want their picture taken!).

PHASE I: PROBLEM IDENTIFICATION AND PRIORITISATION

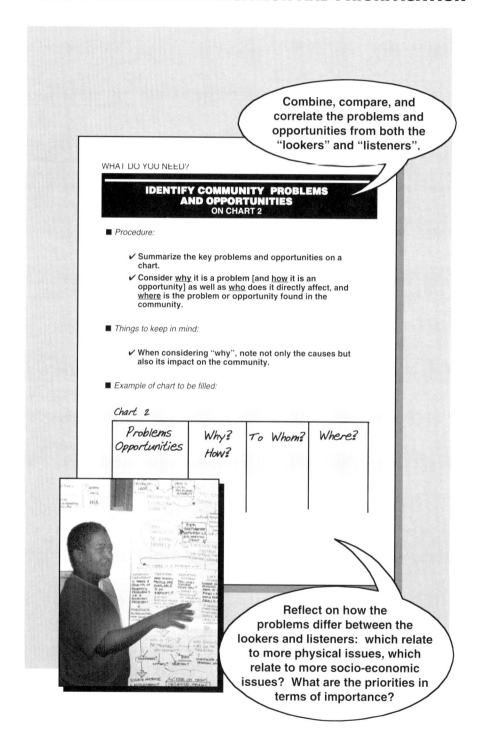

Case Files **237**

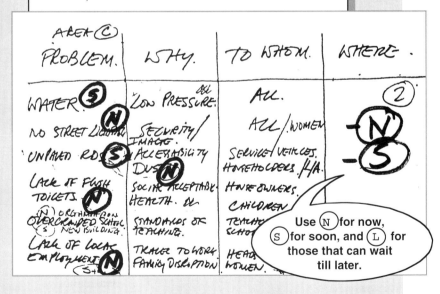

238 Action Planning for Cities

PHASE II: STRATEGIES, OPTIONS AND TRADEOFFS

> This chart starts the process of focusing down to a few key, manageable projects.

HOW TO GET WHAT YOU NEED

ALLOCATE RESOURCES
ON CHART 3

■ *Procedure:*

   ✔ Collect all of the "NOW" items from Chart 2 and determine their relative cost.
   ✔ Each group should then decide how to allocate their limited resources in selecting which project to do.

■ *Things to keep in mind:*

   ✔ It is easier if only a few relative costs are used; inexpensive as "1" [For example: poster announcement], more expensive as "5" [For example: small school building], and very expensive as "10" [For example: a water network]. In this example, each group would get 10 "resources" to allocate.
   ✔ The groups should be encouraged to negotiate with the other groups to get what they need. For example, "Our leftover 5 with your leftover 5 can be joined for a 'very expensive' item of 10."

■ *Example of chart to be filled:*

NOW NEEDS	COST/ RESOURCE	A	B	C	TOTAL
LOW PRESSURE WATER	8			3	3
STREET LIGHTS	3			3	3
DUST ON ROADS	2		2		
FLUSH TOILETS	10				
CROWDED SCHOOLS	4				
EMPLOYMENT	5				
IMPROVED PICK UP TO BUDGETS	2	2			
SECURITY FOR WOMEN	2		2		
FIX/MAINTAIN BROKEN WATER PIPES	4		4		2
IMPROVED POLICE RESPONSE	1	1	1		2
ACCESS TO SPORTS FACILITIES	1	1	1		2

> Costs are indicative of a wide range of resources including time, people, equipment, etc.

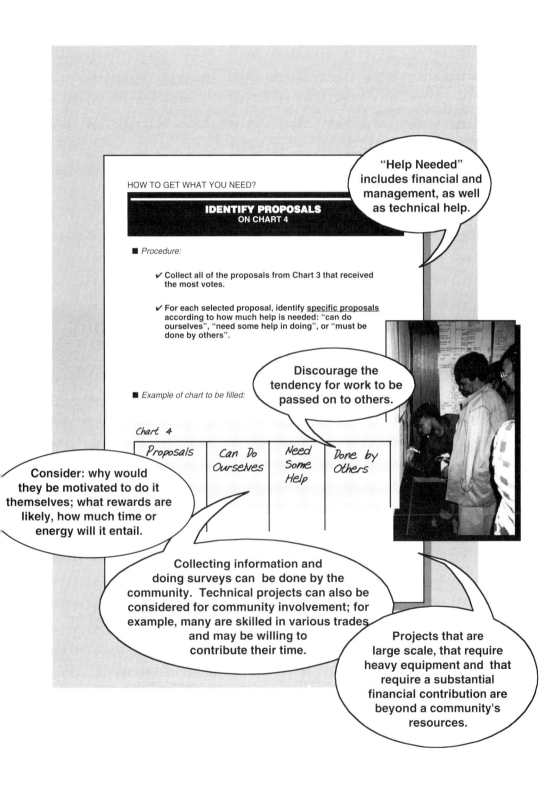

240 Action Planning for Cities

PHASE II: STRATEGIES, OPTIONS AND TRADEOFFS

> This chart provides an assessment of the feasibility of a project. It can also be used to identify needed skills training in a community.

WHAT GETS IN YOUR WAY?

IDENTIFY CONSTRAINTS
ON CHART 5

■ *Procedure:*

✔ Collect all of the "CAN DO OURSELVES" items from Chart 4 and identify the specific constraints that need to be overcome. Ask <u>"What will get in my way?"</u>

✔ Consider "technical, organizational, political, financial, and human resources" as well as any other that you feel important.

■ *Things to keep in mind:*

✔ The most important thing is to identify the specific things that cause difficulties and which are liable to threaten the success of the project.

✔ It is useful to further identify the few really critical things that stand out among all of the constraints. Reflecting on all of the things, ask yourself: "which 1 or 2 things are really serious bottlenecks and may be impossible to overcome."

■ *Example of chart to be filled:*

Chart 5

"Can Do Ourselves" items	Technical	Organizational	Political	Resources (Financial, Human)	Other

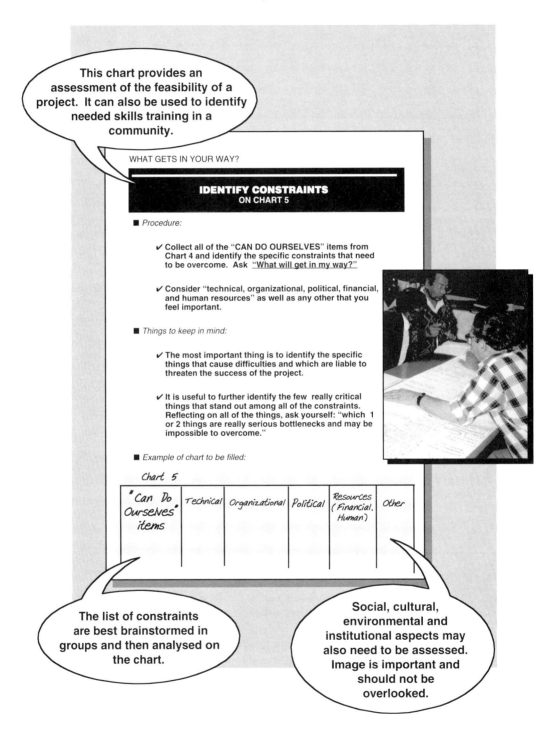

> The list of constraints are best brainstormed in groups and then analysed on the chart.

> Social, cultural, environmental and institutional aspects may also need to be assessed. Image is important and should not be overlooked.

WHAT GETS IN YOUR WAY?

REVIEW SEQUENCE
ON CHART 5

■ *Procedure:*

  ✓ Go back and look over the proposals and the constraints you identified, and reflect on how this influences their feasibility.

  ✓ Determine if the proposals can be done "now", "soon", or "later", by placing an (N) (S) or (L) on Chart 5.

■ *Things to keep in mind:*

  ✓ The key in deciding is the feasibility of the proposals when considering their potential constraints.

■ *Example*

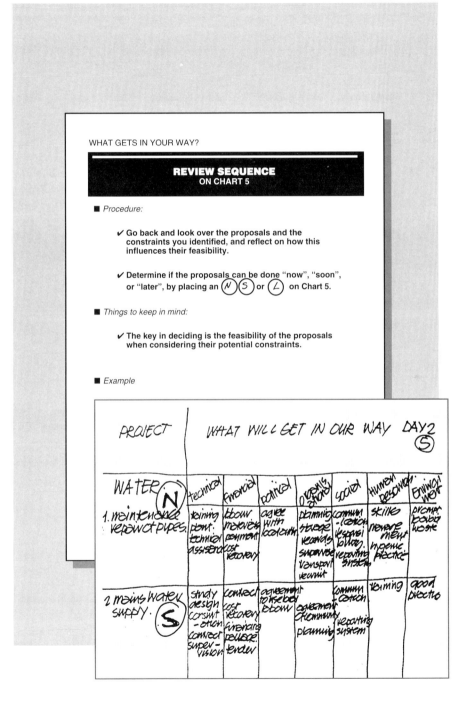

242 Action Planning for Cities

PHASE III: PLANNING FOR IMPLEMENTATION

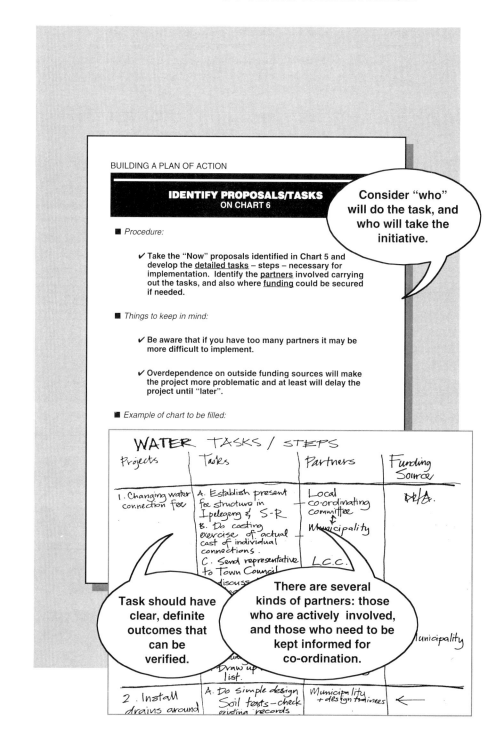

Case Files **243**

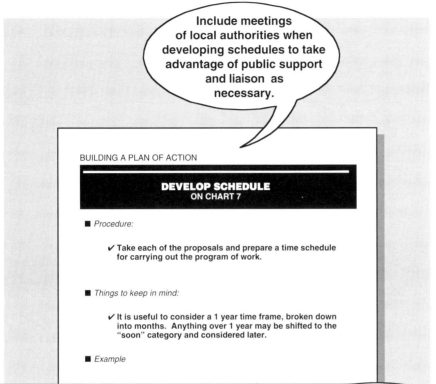

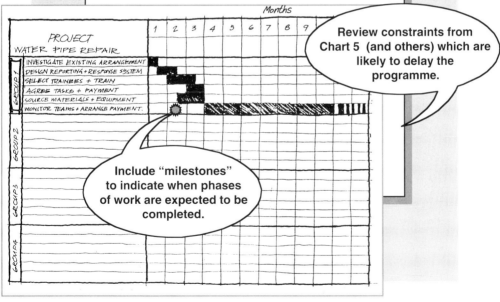

PHASE III: PLANNING FOR IMPLEMENTATION

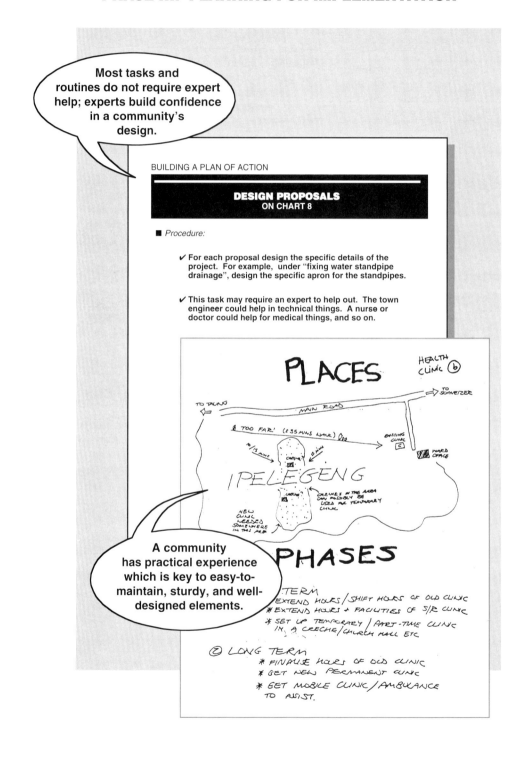

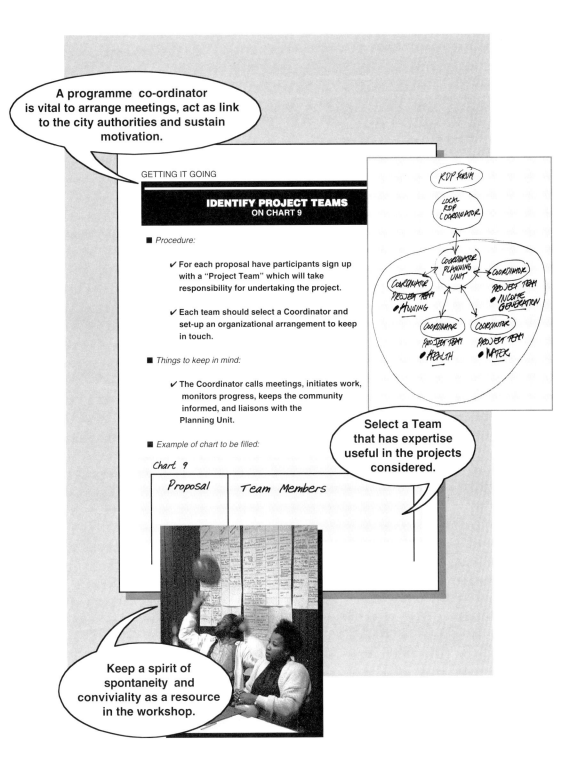

246 Action Planning for Cities

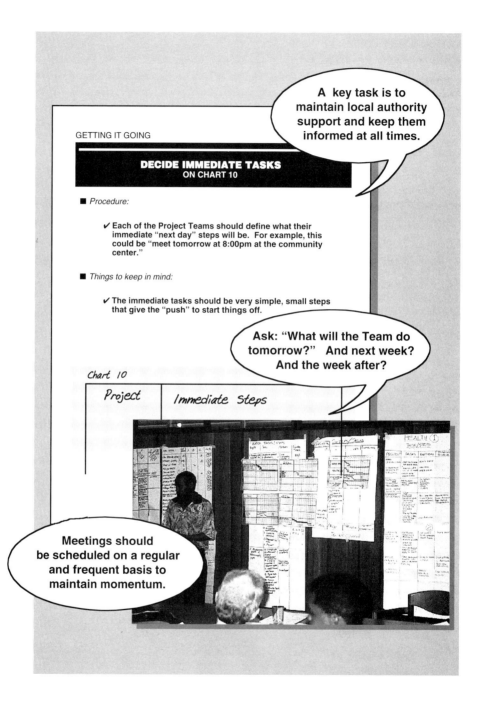

Index

academic enquiry 10
action planning 23
　characteristics of 29–34
　definitions 24
　phases 48, 187, 188
　process and 42–51
action planning menu 34–43
administrative boundaries, mapping of 110
advocate role of outsider 68
aid
　benefits 7
　development 3, 4
　tied 5
alternatives analysis 95
American Institute of Architects 95
analysis phase 45–6, 92
apartheid 224
Appraisal ZOPP 92
appropriate technologies (ATs) 27–8, 29
attitudes 193

Bangladesh 9, 84, 85, 86
Belfast: "The Bird Can't Fly" project 147, 164–73
　Ahlund Commission 166
　alignment 172
　Beechmount 166
　Clonard Area 166
　Community Development Bank 166
　community redevelopment 166
　cul-de-sac housing 167
　housing of Catholic areas 170
　military security 167, 170
　Peace Lines 167–8, 169
　projects 166
　Sports 166
　the "Troubles" 167–8
　workshop phases 165
　Youth Relations 166
　Youth Speak 169
BID 179

bottom-up approach 65
brainstorming 37, 215
Brasilia 16
Britain 24, 95, 96
British Council 146
building community 100, 101

Cambodia, Battambang 39, 54, 55, 56–7
Canada 91
CAP 195, 226
capacity building 12, 14, 187
catalyst, planning as 12, 162
CENDEP 145
Central America 84
Chandigar 16
charettes 95, 139
charts 84, 88, 187, 200
cheap labour myth 78
Chile 40, 87
CIDAP 176
city agencies 113
city authorities 106
city plans 106
clearing-house role 113
co-ordination 106
coalition-building 99
cognitive mapping 46
commercial centres, mapping of 110
communities
　definition 13
　spatial relation 111
community action 26
Community Action Planning *see* Microplanning
community-based organisations (CBOs) 20, 26, 121
community-based programmes 31
community demarcations 110
community development corporations (CDCs) 187, 194, 207
community groups 52

community participation 29
community standards 194
community upgrading 84
complementary linkage 50
conflict linkage 50, 51
confrontational settings 76
consequential linkage 50
construction standards 193
Construcuni 179
consultants 18, 43
continuity 65
costs of running events 99

DAC 7
DANIDA 91
data-intensive methods 106
decentralisation 29, 193–4
decision making, shared 70, 77
dependency 8, 11, 101, 102
design stage 72, 78
developing country, characteristics of 4
developing strategies 100, 101
development, endogenous 5
Dhaka 84
diagramming 37
diffuse settlements 32
direct observation 35–6
domination 71
downtown communities, characteristics of 151

Eastern Europe 96
economic indicators for monitoring 53–4
education 8, 10, 127–8
Education for Neighbourhood Change 90
Egypt 36, 54
empowerment 6, 29, 71
enablement 11, 26, 29, 125
enabler paradigm 30
enterprise development 54
environmental indicators for monitoring 54
event 96
expanding participatory programmes 65, 104, 105

facilitator role 52, 83
field-based action planning 49
field-based evaluation 140
field-based research 130
field-based secondments 130, 141
field-based workshops 130–9, 145–6
   characteristics 145
   learning outcomes 146

flexibility 24, 63
follow-up phase 97
FONAVI 179
FONCODES 179
formal systems of production 31
Fourier, Charles 16
framework
   for tools and techniques 63, 66
   planning 24
funding 104

games 40–2
garden cities 16
getting started phase 96
good practice 20
GOPP (Goal Oriented Project Planning) *see* ZOPP
Grameen Bank 54
group work 42
guidebooks 133, 135–6, 139
guiding concepts 23

Hammerschold, Dag 28
handbooks 187, 194
highjacking by professionals 64
historical origins of planning 17
homeowner's file 194
Honolulu 16
Housing Options and Loan Package 193
housing programmes 15

ideal participation 109
ideal participatory community 67
ideal participatory partners 110
identifying problems 100, 101
implementation 43–4, 72, 77, 78, 100, 101, 103, 105, 137
income 78
incrementalism 26, 30, 31
India
   Bhogal 43
   "Reach out to the Moon" project 146–7, 159–63
   sterilisation camps 9
infant mortality 7
informal settlements 11, 18
informal systems of production 31
information flows 114, 116
initiation stage 72, 78
innovation 77
Institute of Physical Planning and Municipal Economy 184
institutional framework 146

institutional learning 20
instrumental problem solving 125
interest group 68, 69
international funding agencies 20
International Monetary Fund (IMF) 8
International Union of Local Authorities (ILUA) 84
interventions 26, 31
INVERMET 179
Ipelegeng 223–4
issues stage 97

Jamaica
  McIntrye Lands 152
  Portmore 152
  "Something is Happening in Southside" project 42, 146, 150–8
    areas of concern 153
    community development organisation 155
    community facilities 156
    economic development 157
    microenterprises 155
    projects 155–8
    recreation 156
    Southside neighbourhood 153
    strengths, opportunities and problems 154
    upgrading of houses 156
    vacant lots 155, 158
Japanese aid 18

Kenya 93
Kingston Restoration Company 157
knowing-in-action 125
Koenigsberger 23, 24–5, 28

La Asesoria 179
land invasions 25
land reforms 192
Latin America 84
leadership 65
learning 24, 123, 139–41
learning by doing 225
learning from practice 128
learning in practice 128, 130
life expectancy 7
linkage analysis 31, 49–51
loan schemes 54
local government 194
location for project 83, 88
logical project framework 91
low cost labour 74

maintenance stage 72, 77, 78
mapping 39, 110
market enablement 26, 122
Massachusetts Housing Partnership (MHP) Challenge Grant Program 207
master plans 3, 106
materials 83, 88, 101
measurement of plans 37, 39
mega-agency role 113
Microplanning 64, 65, 70, 81, 83–7, 105–6, 134
Milton Keynes 16
MIT 184
modelling 39, 47
moderators 83, 88, 104
monitoring outcomes 101
monitoring, project 51–7
Municipal Corporation of Delhi 162

negotiation 126
neighbourhood 40
neighbourhood-based organisations 52, 208
Neighbourhood Initiatives Foundation 64, 81, 87, 91, 184
new towns 16
Nixon, Richard 9
non-governmental organisations (NGOs) 9, 122, 161, 162
non-neighbourhood 32
Nordic countries 91
now, soon, later chart 88

objectives analysis 95
OECD 7
  Development Assistance Committee (DAC) 91
on-site training 194
one-off projects 65
options stage 97
oral testimonies 36
organisational indicators for monitoring 54
orthodox development theory of 4–7, 13
  challenges to 7–11, 16–19
  definitions 5–6
  Truman design 5
outsiders 67–8, 106
over-arching concept 140
overlay maps 110
Overseas Development Agency (ODA) 91, 146
Owen, Robert 16
ownership of project programmes 101

participants 88–90, 191
participation
  low cost labour 74
  imposition 74
  stakeholder 31, 225
  types of 68
participation levels 66–7, 69–71, 76
  consultative 69
  full control 70–1
  indirect 69
  none 69
  shared 70
  use of matrix to consider 72
participation phase 66, 92
participatory partners
  ideal 112
  spatial relation of 111
participatory planning 32
Participatory Rapid Appraisal (PRA) 29, 70
Partner ZOPP 92
partners in development 74
partners in research 130, 140
partnerships 12, 31, 111, 112
performance standards 23
Peru: "With/In Formal Development"
    project 147, 174–9
  El Trébol 177
  erosion 179
  formal co-operative housing 176
  information 175
  market 176, 178
  method 175
  presentations 175
  shared tenement housing 176
  squatters 175
  strategies 175
  street vendors 176
phases of action planning 48, 187, 188
picture analysis 41
pilot projects 65, 225
Planning for Real 40, 64, 70, 81, 87–91,
    105–6
  kit 88, 89, 91
  stages 88
planning framework 24
planning stage 72, 78
Planning Weekends 95, 139
PNUD 179
Poland 84
  "Housing in Transition" project 148,
    180–4
    choices 183
    learning settings 184
    presentations 182
policy 20
political boundaries, mapping of 110

poverty 8
practice 127
practitioner 68
Pre-ZOPP 92
preparation phase 96
presentation formats 146
presentation skills 146
PREVI 176
Prince of Wales's Institute of Architecture
    95
prioritising 37
pro forma deference to participation 75
problem solving 46–7, 125, 192
problems 111–15
  analysis 92
  definition 83–4
  identifying 100, 101
  stage 97
production stage 97
professionals 68
programme design 129
project planning matrix (PPM) 94, 95
project planning phase 95
project scale 194
projects 77
provision 26
public meetings 88
public/private partnerships 26

quiz cards 210

Rebuilding Communities 145, 149–84
reconnaissance 54, 55
Reconstruction and Development
    Programme (RDP) 224, 225
reflection-in-action 126
reflective practice 126
Regional/Urban Assistance Team (R/
    UCAT) 95
reluctant communities 67, 110, 112
Replanning ZOPP 92
resource surveying 37, 40
Riverside Cambridgeport Community
    Corporation 207
Rochdale Canalside planning weekend 96
role playing 40–2, 139

Schumacher 28
self-help 25, 223
semi-structured interviews 36
service contractor 74
setting in motion 101
settlements 36

shacks 223
shadow programmes 130, 140
shared relationship 83
SIGUS 145
site planning 187, 191–5
skills 122–6
slums 11, 18, 25, 33
social boundaries 110
social indicators for monitoring 54
social maps 39
solutions stage 97
South Africa 53–4, 84, 85
   Reconstruction and Development
      Programme 106
   Schweizer-Reneke Pilot Project
      Programme 41, 84, 115, 187
      constraints 240
      design proposals 244
      development schedule 243
      goals and priorities 237
      identification of proposals 239
      identifying area problems and
         opportunities 234
      identifying community problems and
         opportunities 236
      identifying proposals/tasks 242
      immediate tasks 246
      overview 228
      phases of work 227, 229
      project feasibility 240
      project teams 245
      resource allocation 238
      sequence 241
      survey 235
      urban upgrading 223–46
speed of response 76, 78
squatter settlements 25, 110
squatters 29, 163, 175, 223
Sri Lanka 65, 83, 84
   Colombo 187, 191–5
      designs 195
      dwelling considerations 204–5
      government policies 195
      objectives and issues 201
      physical programming 195, 199
      procedure 203
      site information 198
      socio-economic programming 195, 200
      utility infrastructure 203
   Gramadoya 193
   Mahawelli development area 192
   Million Houses Programme 65, 83, 191
   National Housing Development Authority
      (NHDA) 84, 191
   Pradashya 193

stakeholders 30, 146
   participation 31, 225
   relationship 79
   role 68
standards 17, 46
stepping-stone communities 32
story-telling 200
strategic planning 30, 53, 56–7
Sudan 35
support 194
support policies 20
support programmes 192, 193
surrogate role of outsider 68
survey 235
synthesis stage 97

Take-off ZOPP 92
taking a position 140
talent surveys 37
Task Force 95, 96
teaching 123
technical assistance 121
technical indicators for monitoring 53
techniques 63–4, 65
technology 8, 189
technology transfer 9, 18
tools 63–4, 66–71, 76
   assessing 71
   characteristics 81
   choice of 105, 111
   community types and 108–11
   comparative matrix of project goals
      100–1, 107
   comparison of dependency,
      implementation and expansion of
      programmes 101–5
   framework 66–72
   model for participation 77–8
top-down government 26
tradeoffs 187, 204
training 12, 65, 104, 127–8, 191
   on-site 194
   underlying principles 141–3
training materials 132, 133
training needs 130
training of moderators 83
training-of-trainers 65, 84, 194
transect walks 35
transitory communities 67, 109, 110, 112
transitory neighbourhoods 32
triangulation 126
trust walks 41
typography maps 40
typologies 54, 55, 137, 138

U/DAT 81
United Nations 91
  Global Strategy 121
United Nations Development Programme
    (UNDP) 14, 121
United States 95
upgrading 193
urban area information 234
Urban Community Assistance Team
    (UCAT) 81, 95, 105–6
urban institutions 113
urban management 26, 95, 122
Urban Management Programme for Asia
    and the Pacific 195
urban upgrading 121, 187
US Agency for International Development
    (USAID) 91, 146, 184
USA
  Boston 84, 184, 187
    building capacity 212–221
    GAMEPAK 210, 211
    INFOPAK 210
    PAK-I 210
    PAK-II 210
    PAKMAN 210
    Planning Assistance Kit (PAK) 207–11
    Public Facilities Department 207
  Cambridgeport 90
  Raleigh, North Carolina 16
  Topeka, Kansas 45

Villa El Salvador, Peru 176
Voluntary Service Overseas (VSO) 141

Wales 96
wisdom 126
working parties 88
workshop particpiatory monitoring 52
World Bank 4, 6, 121, 179, 184
  Economic Development Unit 84

ZOPP 70, 81, 91, 105–6

Project Planner – WALLCHARTS

A companion to the book: *Action Planning for Cities*,
Nabeel Hamdi and Reinhard Goethert, John Wiley & Sons, Ltd. 1997.

■ Run a successful *Action Planning* workshop with a 22 inch × 28 inch wallchart. The chart provides an overview of the process and all the steps in an easy-to-follow format.
The chart can assist you in three ways:

— as a guide for running workshops.
— as a management tool in organising, evaluating and arranging logistics for workshops.
— as a training tool for practitioners.

■ All the essential stages are included:
(Example from CAP Wallchart No. 1 follows)

— "Statement of Problems and Opportunities"
— "Documentation of Key Information"
— "Making Community Map"
— "Setting Actions and Tasks"
— "Planning for Implementation"

Each state includes Tasks with detailed steps, illustrated with examples. "Hints for Getting Started" are provided with a sample schedule and logistic requirements.

■ Four Community Action Planning wallcharts are in preparation. No. 1 is available now.

— CAP Wallchart No. 1: **Linking Community with City**, developed and field-tested in Bangladesh.
  (Available now – soon available in Handbook format: US$25 for single copies)
— CAP Wallchart No. 2: **Urban Upgrading**, developed and field-tested in South Africa.
  (Reformatted from example in the book)
— CAP Wallchart No. 3: **Site Planning for New Communities**, developed and field-tested in Sri Lanka.
  (Reformatted from example in the book)
— CAP Wallchart No. 4: **Building Neighbourhood Capacity**, developed and field-tested in Massachusetts, USA.
  (Reformatted from The Pakman example in the book)

☐ YES, I want to order CAP Wallchart No. 1
Linking Community with City
US$12.50 plus $3.50 postage and handling.

Name: _____

Institution: _____

Address: _____

City/State/Postal Code: _____   Country: _____

Fax or E-mail: _____

Form of payment: _____

☐ Please send me information on
CAP Wallcharts Nos 2, 3, and 4

SIGUS: Fax (617) 253-8221   E-mail: sigus@mit.edu

Affix stamp here

SIGUS Wallcharts
School of Architecture and Planning
Room N52-357A
Massachusetts Institute of Technology
Cambridge, MA 02139
USA